*Representative
Americans*

Representative Americans

Americans

THE REVOLUTIONARY GENERATION

Norman K. Risjord

University of Wisconsin–Madison

D. C. HEATH AND COMPANY

Lexington, Massachusetts   Toronto

ILLUSTRATION CREDITS

Cover: *Abigail Adams*, Courtesy of the Massachusetts Historical Society; *Benjamin Franklin*, Courtesy of the Fogg Art Museum, Harvard University. Bequest, Francis Calley Gray Collection; *Thomas Jefferson*, Bowdoin College Museum of Art, Brunswick, Maine; *Charles Willson Peale*, Courtesy of the Pennsylvania Academy of the Fine Arts; *Noah Webster*, National Portrait Gallery, Smithsonian Institution, Washington, D.C.

Revolutionary Symbol: The Pennsylvania Journal and Weekly Advertiser; *State House of Boston:* Library of Congress; *Battle Scene:* Courtesy of the American Antiquarian Society; *Old Building:* The I. N. Phelps Stokes Collection of American Historical Prints, New York Public Library.

p. 3	Courtesy of the Fogg Art Museum, Harvard. Bequest, Francis Calley Gray Collection.
p. 19	Courtesy of the Museum of Fine Arts, Boston.
p. 37	The Bettmann Archive, Inc.
p. 57	Courtesy of the Mount Vernon Ladies Association.
p. 73	Courtesy of the Massachusetts Historical Society.
p. 87	Courtesy of the American Jewish Historical Society, Waltham, Mass.
p. 99	National Portrait Gallery, Smithsonian Institution, Washington, D.C.
p. 109	Courtesy of the Pennsylvania Academy of the Fine Arts.
p. 118	The Peale Museum, Baltimore.
p. 121	Courtesy of the Harvard University Portrait Collection.
p. 124	Courtesy of The Bostonian Society.
p. 126	Courtesy of The Society for the Preservation of New England Antiquities.
p. 127	Mrs. Samuel Chamberlain, Marblehead, Mass.
p. 139	Courtesy of the Pennsylvania Hospital, Philadelphia.
p. 161	Yale University Art Gallery. Gift of George Hadley, B.A. 1801.
p. 167	Courtesy of the Frick Art Reference Library.
p. 175	National Portrait Gallery, Smithsonian Institution, Washington, D.C.
p. 193	National Portrait Gallery, Smithsonian Institution, Washington, D.C.
p. 213	Smithsonian Institution, National Anthropological Archives.
p. 231	Bowdoin College Museum of Art, Brunswick, Maine.
p. 251	Lithograph from *Lewis Mountain*. Published by C. Bohn, 1856. Courtesy, University of Virginia Library.

Copyright © 1980 by D. C. Heath and Company.

Published simultaneously in Canada.

Printed in the United States of America.

International Standard Book Number: 0–669–02710–3

Library of Congress Catalog Card Number: 79–88134

To BERNARD MAYO

*who taught me that
biography is the human heart of history*

Preface

The purpose of this book is to make history human, to put some tissue on the skeletal framework of names and dates. By using a biographical approach, I hope to make the past more concrete and vivid and to reveal a heritage that the present-day reader can feel and experience. *Representative Americans* is directed at the interested but inexpert student of history, whose memory is taxed and whose attention is exhausted by lengthy textbooks and ponderously researched tomes. Individual life stories are morsels to be tasted and sampled without overfilling. They hint of greater delights beyond, when knowledge beckons and leisure time permits.

I became interested in the biographical approach to history through a course in "Representative Americans" taught by the late Bernard Mayo at the University of Virginia. A few years ago, at the University of Wisconsin, I began teaching a course by the same title, one that had been offered for more than twenty years by William B. Hesseltine and before him by Carl Russell Fish. I suspect that the original inspiration for this course was Ralph Waldo Emerson's oft-given Lyceum lecture, "Representative Men," which stemmed, in turn, from Thomas Carlyle's heroic view of history.

My selections are not "representative" in the sense of "average" or "common"; neither do they present heroes of the sort chosen by Emerson and Carlyle. Instead, I have searched for human beings with whom the reader can identify, without attempting to emulate. Among heroes, I prefer those with lives made poignant by tragedy, such as George Rogers Clark or Chief Joseph. I have also chosen people who illustrate ideas that are important to historians and that are elusive for students. Benjamin Franklin, for example, represents the American in process of becoming, and Thomas Jefferson illuminates, through his varied efforts at revolutionary reform, the concept of Liberalism.

For pedagogical purposes the antithesis of the Napoleonic hero admired by Emerson and Carlyle may be the most useful. The biographical approach does present a convenient avenue to what some have called the "underside" of history — the poor, racial and ethnic minorities, and women. Political / diplomatic history, which is the focus of most surveys, is essentially the story of white males. Conscientious teachers who seek to rescue women and minorities from the obscurity of the biased past find themselves hampered by the paucity of literary records. As a result, such groups commonly enter the historical narrative in one of two ways: either as statistics or through a heavy emphasis on "rights" movements. The first approach is dull and the second risks stereotypical distortion. The biographical approach allows the instructor to delve into the contributions of an Abigail Adams, a Margaret Fuller, or an Amelia Earhart; of a Sequoya, an Osceola, or a Jackie Robinson. Such people, though justly concerned with their "rights," enriched the American past in other ways as well.

The focus of this volume is on the Revolutionary generation, the men and women who founded the American republic. They were understandably preoccupied with the fundamentals of society and government. I have tried to reflect this concern by choosing politically minded individuals; but I have also sought individuals whose contributions were in science and the arts. The result, I trust, is a composite portrait of an age.

Norman K. Risjord

University of Wisconsin–Madison

Contents

PART I
Nation Builders

1. The American Mold: Benjamin Franklin — 3
2. Samuel Adams, Pure Republican — 19
3. George Washington, Gentleman Revolutionary — 37
4. The Swamp Fox: Francis Marion — 57
5. Abigail Adams: Partner in Home Rule — 73
6. Aaron Lopez: An Immigrant's Story — 87

PART II
Character Builders

7. Noah Webster: The Search for National Identity — 99
8. Charles Willson Peale: Patriotism in Color — 109
9. Charles Bulfinch: An American Style in Building — 121
10. Isaac Backus, Crusader — 129
11. Benjamin Rush, Patriot Physician — 139

PART III
Empire Builders

12. Pioneers of Business: Eli Whitney and John Jacob Astor — 161
13. Conqueror of the Northwest: George Rogers Clark — 175
14. James Wilkinson, Imperial Schemer — 193
15. Tecumseh: Indian Statesman — 213
16. Thomas Jefferson: A Summary View — 231

Index — 253

MAPS

Boston and Vicinity ca. 1775	*33*
From Long Island to Valley Forge, 1776–1778	*45*
The Siege of Yorktown	*47*
The Revolution in the Carolinas, 1779–1782	*62*
The Northwest in the Revolution	*180*
The Ohio Campaigns, 1792–1795	*203*
Lands Ceded by the Indians, 1795–1809	*218*
The Tecumseh Alliance, 1809	*223*

Introduction

Each generation of Americans has a special flavor, a character of its own. Some are marked by a dominant personage ("Jacksonian"), others by a prevailing ideal ("Progressive"). Crisis and conflict shaped the generations that endured the Civil War and the Cold War. Sometimes a memorable decade, such as "Gay Nineties" or "Roaring Twenties," imprinted the generation that lived and outlived it. Yet no simple rubric comes easily to mind when one thinks of the Revolutionary generation. Their accomplishments were too grand, their interests too varied to be encompassed in a single phrase.

There were, nevertheless, some dominant themes in the era, patterns of achievement that give it meaning. One such, certainly, is the Revolutionary experience itself, the winning of independence. Thus, the first section of this book examines the careers of people who made and fought the Revolution. The military campaigns, for example, are followed through the careers of George Washington and Francis Marion; life on the home front is seen through the eyes of Abigail Adams. The quotation from Thomas Paine's *Common Sense*, which introduces the section, bespeaks the sense of occasion felt by the participants, the momentous opportunity they had to affect the course of human events.

Once independence was achieved and republican institutions given shape, it was still necessary to create a country, a fatherland. The section headed "Character Builders" examines the lives of people who sought to mold an American national character. Some, like the lexicographer Noah Webster and the painter Charles Willson Peale, searched, quite self-consciously, for an American style in language and the arts. Others, such as Isaac Backus and Benjamin Rush, saw the Revolution as an opportunity to cleanse American society of Old World corruption, an opportunity, as it were, for a national baptism. From this searching self-analysis emerged a national consciousness — a nation became a nationality.

In giving birth to a nation the Revolutionary generation also gave birth to an empire. The portraits in the third section reveal this paradox. The American republic was from its very inception an empire, a self-governing people who ruled — sometimes tyrannically — over others. The vast interior of the continent, empty but for Indians, was there for the taking.

George Rogers Clark was among those who conquered it; John Jacob Astor helped to exploit it. The western epic abounded in tragedy and villainy, as the stories of Tecumseh and James Wilkinson suggest, but it also had its share of glory and gain. For good and ill, the empire builders charter the course of American history.

The book ends with a sketch of Thomas Jefferson, whose purchase of Louisiana, so he thought, ensured that America would ever be "an empire for liberty." But he was of course far more than an empire builder; he was the nerve center of his generation. His political involvement touched the lives of Benjamin Franklin, Samuel Adams, and George Washington. During his diplomatic service he came to know John and Abigail Adams. Through his scientific interests he encountered Benjamin Rush, Eli Whitney, and Charles Willson Peale; and his interest in the West involved him in the lives of George Rogers Clark, Tecumseh, and James Wilkinson. By his pen (as author of the Declaration of Independence) he laid the foundation for the American republic; by his sword (as President) he made that republic a respected member of the international community. The variety of his interests, the grandeur of his accomplishments bespoke an unusual man in a stirring age.

Representative Americans

Part 1

Nation Builders

"The sun never shined on a cause of greater worth. 'Tis not the affair of a city, a county, a province, or a kingdom, but of a continent — of at least one eighth part of the inhabitable globe. 'Tis not the concern of a day, a year, or an age; posterity are virtually involved in the contest, and will be more or less affected, even to the end of time, by the proceedings now. Now is the seed-time of continental union, faith and honor."

— Thomas Paine, Common Sense (1776)

1

The American Mold: Benjamin Franklin

Benjamin Franklin leaned over the side and watched his vessel slash the heaving waters of the Atlantic. The year was 1757. He was on his way to England to present his colony's request for

royal government. Businessman, scientist, and politician, Franklin was embarking on a new career. He would spend the next quarter-century abroad, with only brief visits to his Philadelphia home. From colonial emissary he would become spokesman for a new nation.

A thought came to him. Franklin turned his gaze from the water and went in search of a quill. *Poor Richard's Almanac,* the publishing venture that had started him on the way to wealth, needed a preface for the 1758 edition. With time on his hands, Franklin decided to expand the usual preface, to include the best of Poor Richard's counsels from the almanacs of twenty-five years. The collec-

Benjamin Franklin (1706–1790).   *An engraving by Charles Nicholas Cochin done in 1777, after Franklin arrived in Paris as Revolutionary envoy. The fur cap, donned on shipboard, proved a hit in Paris. Framing a philosopher's face, it must have symbolized Europeans' impression of America — strange, even quaint, yet wise and resolute.*

tion, he informed readers, was put together by an old man, an admirer of Poor Richard's homilies. When Franklin landed in England, he mailed the preface to his nephew, a Boston printer. The nephew decided to publish it separately from the almanac, under the title *Father Abraham's Speech.* Reprinted later as *The Way to Wealth,* the essay spread throughout the colonies and even followed Franklin to Europe, where it was translated into several languages.

The sayings of Father Abraham expressed more than homely advice; they contained a very pointed ethical system. The list of virtues amounted to a New Testament: "A penny saved is a penny earned" (frugality); "Lost time is never found again" (industry); "Tis hard for an empty bag to stand upright" (self-reliance); "Having been poor is no shame, but being ashamed of it is" (self-promotion). Not all the virtues were new-found. Temperance and moderation, so loved by the ancient Greeks, met Franklin's approval: "Anger is never without a reason, but seldom a good one." Christianity, with its emphasis on brotherly love, also found its way into his writings, but with a shopkeeper's twist: "Love your neighbor, yet don't pull down your hedge." The code was not all of Franklin's devising. It flowed from the two great developments of modern times — the Protestant Reformation and the rise of capitalism. But it was Franklin who put it in the language of everyman. It amounted to a new religion for mankind — a Gospel of Work.

In a nation of shopkeepers, where even the poorest farmer raised a "cash crop" for market, the new faith required no evangelist to spread the word. It was accepted as naturally and as eagerly as gold coin. And it proved to be the most potent ethical system ever devised, for it promised its rewards, not in the heavenly Hereafter, but in this life. The reward for virtue was success, and the terms of success could be defined by each individual — wealth, power, fame, or all three. It was the ethos that mastered a continent and produced the most powerful nation in the world, a power that relied not on fleets and armies, pomp or imperial dominion, but on the self-interested pursuits of freeborn individuals. The creed was Americanism. Benjamin Franklin was its first apostle.

The Way to Wealth

Franklin's life was the first American success story, the prototype of the self-made man. His English grandfather was a blacksmith. His father, who had moved across the Atlantic to Boston in 1685, was a candlemaker. Born in 1706, Benjamin was the youngest boy in a family of ten. His father, an intensely religious man, instilled the Protestant virtues of hard work, thrift, and piety in Ben at an early age.

Within a year of his birth appeared one of the first American newspapers, the *Boston News Letter*. It was modeled on the great literary journals of Queen Anne's England but suffered in the comparison. Most of its content consisted of the Sunday sermons of Boston clergy, with an occasional shipping notice or official proclamation. Ben's older brother James, after learning the printing trade, started a rival paper in 1721. It was a livelier sheet, if only because James had a gift for crusades that antagonized royal officials. "Freedom of the press" under English law meant only freedom from prior restraint, such as censorship. A printer was still held responsible for what he said, and if authorities considered it "seditious," the printer might find himself in jail. That was James's lot within a year; and Ben, who had been apprenticed to his brother to learn the printer's art, soon found himself running the paper.

His happiest moments, unfortunately, came when his brother was in jail, for James was as domineering at home as he was quarrelsome abroad. Ben endured the tension for a time after his brother's release, and then made plans to run away. This course of action was risky. Apprenticeship was a legal contract binding the young man to a period of servitude (usually three to five years) in return for learning a trade. The punishment for breaking such a contract was a fine, a whipping, or both. Ben escaped anyway, evading pursuit by taking ship to Philadelphia. The passage cost him nearly all his savings, and when he landed he spent his last penny on a loaf of bread. Here then is the first Franklin portrait — the ragged youth strolling wide-eyed down the streets of an unfamiliar city stuffing hunks of bread into his mouth. The rags were there; riches lay in the future.

Success came slowly. He quickly found work in a printing shop, but efforts to set up his own business led to several failures. Journeying to England in search of financial backing, he suffered the humiliation of having to borrow money to finance the trip home. However, by 1730, seven years after his arrival in the city of brotherly love, he had his own printing shop and a newspaper. In that year the Pennsylvania assembly assured his future by making him public printer. Newspapers subsisted on the public business, because advertising did not yield enough revenue for any paper to survive. The publisher who was privileged to print the acts of assembly, pronouncements of the governor, and proclamations of royal authority had the most lucrative job of all. Within two years Franklin won similar privileges in neighboring Delaware and New Jersey. Before long he had branch partnerships in Boston, New York, and Charleston.

His newspaper, the *Pennsylvania Gazette*, was not the only one in Philadelphia, but it was easily the most entertaining. Besides the customary political discussions and commercial notices, Franklin included humorous stories and social notes. He was the first publisher to solicit advertisements for his paper and the first to devote entire columns to ads when rivals were sparing only a few lines. In 1733 he introduced an almanac. Annual summaries of practical information were immensely popular in Britain, and, besides, the project would keep his printing press humming. To save expenses, he wrote it himself; to give it a corporate appearance, however, he published it under the pseudonym of Richard Saunders. The title was both table of contents and running advertisement:

> Poor Richard, 1733. *An Almanack for the year of Christ 1733, being the first after Leap year, wherein is contained the Lunations, Eclipses, Judgment of the Weather, Spring Tides, Planets' Motions and Mutual Aspects, Sun and Moon's Rising and Setting, Length of Days, Times of High Water, Fairs, Courts, and observable Days. Fitted to the Latitude of forty degrees and a meridian of five hours West from London, but may without sensible error serve all the adjacent places, even from Newfoundland to South Carolina. By Richard Saunders, Philom, Philadelphia (Printed and sold by Benjamin Franklin at the New Printing Office near the Market.)*

Needless to say, the introduction of the first American almanac rated a special notice in the *Pennsylvania Gazette*.

The *Almanac* was a blazing success. Rude, humorous, and informative, it suited exactly the needs of a busy people preoccupied with getting on in the world. Franklin's homely aphorisms brought smiles to his readers and often a nod of agreement:

> *"Men and mellons are hard to know."*
> *"After three days men grow weary of a wench, a guest, and rainy weather."*

He was full of timely advice that conveyed the Protestant ethic without the appearance of a sermon:

> *"Time is money."*
> *"If you know how to spend less than you get, you have the philosopher's stone."*

But it was popular mostly because it reflected the attitudes of many Americans.

> [It was critical of monarchy.] *"Kings and bears often worry their keepers."*
> [It was democratic.] *"An innocent plowman is more worthy than a vicious prince."*
> [It was hostile to professionalism.] *"Lawyers, preachers, and tomtit's eggs, there are more of them hatched than come to perfection."*
> [And it was suspicious of formal education.] *"Read much, but not too many books."*

The *Almanack* spread Franklin's reputation the length of the continent. As a result, his printing business boomed, and he took on partners and established branch offices in other cities. In 1751 the king appointed him postmaster general of the colonies. This office was the only one with inter-colonial authority in America and was quite an honor. Breathing new life into the service, Franklin established official mail routes and regular deliveries from Boston to Charleston. The patronage added to his power (there were twelve postmasters in his employ), and access to mail routes improved the circulation of both newspaper and almanac. He had found the way to wealth.

Scientist and Tinkerer

His famous kite experiment was made the following year in 1752. Franklin became interested in electricity after watching a friend experiment in a home laboratory. He wrote to a London acquaintance for equipment and later reported his findings to him.

Franklin knew nothing of electricity when he began playing with it, and it was just as well. European scientists had discovered the basic properties of electricity, but their search for a comprehensive explanation had temporarily sidetracked the whole inquiry. Unacquainted with European theories, Franklin simply assumed that electric current was a fluid and that it flowed from a place of surplus (the "positive" pole) to a place of shortage (the "negative" pole). Although we now know that the dynamics of energy are more complex than this, Franklin's concept was to serve the scientific world for almost two centuries. When his London friend published his discoveries, Franklin became an international celebrity.

Yet Franklin was no theorist. He made no effort to find a comprehensive explanation for the behavior of electrical particles. The letters describing his experiments read like kitchen recipes. He was concerned with the how of matter, not the why. The kite experiment was a simple extension of his ability to jump electricity in his lab. Because the spark resembled lightning, he tried flying a kite in a thunderstorm. When a key at the end of the kite string became electrically charged, he had his proof that lightning and electricity were one. With that discovery the field of electricity became a legitimate branch of natural science. Its pioneers had been popularly regarded as laboratory faddists, performing amusing tricks. Franklin's experiment was one of his most important scientific contributions.

Even that experiment did not inspire speculation on the nature of electrical energy. He thought instead of the practical uses. In the laboratory sharply pointed poles held close to one another diminished or eliminated the spark. Why wouldn't a grounded metal rod gradually diffuse electricity into the air, and thus prevent the buildup necessary for a lightning bolt? The following year, 1753, *Poor Richard's Almanack* contained an article on "How to Secure Houses, etc. from Lightning." Lightning rods quickly came into general use, though sooner in Europe than in America. American farmers worried that the projecting staff might attract a lightning bolt.

Putting a scientific discovery to immediate practical use was typical of Franklin — and of the society from which he sprang. His other contributions were similarly mechanical and inventive, not philosophical. The most famous of these was the Pennsylvania fireplace (or "Franklin stove"), a self-contained metal furnace that was more efficient and less smoky than the open fireplace. Inventing gadgets to make life easier has always been an American trait. Ours is a society that has gloried in its Franklins, Edisons, and Fords, but has never given birth to a Newton or an Einstein.

Philadelphia "Booster"

Science earned Franklin his international reputation, but it never occupied much of his time. Gradually he turned the printing operation over to employees and engaged himself in public service, a natural outlet for a successful businessman. Indeed, he had mingled public service with private business from the beginning. Even before he established his own printing office, Franklin organized his fellow artisans into a club. Self-improvement was the initial purpose of the "Junto," with members meeting weekly to discuss public issues and books that they had read. Private advancement soon turned to public concern, for it was evident that whatever benefited Philadelphia was of advantage to its shopkeepers. The Junto's first project was a public library, a natural result of its literary interests. Finding the private collections of its members insufficient, the club set up a committee to buy books financed by an annual subscription among the members. Permitting outsiders to subscribe was a logical extension, and so was formed the Library Company of Philadelphia. The subscription library was popular among city merchants, also bent on self-improvement, and gave the Junto some standing in the community.

Franklin's *Pennsylvania Gazette* also lent a hand. Quite often the newspaper would point out the need for some local improvement; the Junto would endorse the idea and then search for support. The Junto's endorsement, in turn, would occasion additional comment in the *Gazette*. After a series of newspaper essays demanded improvements in the city's defenses, a militia company was formed, with Franklin prominent among the officers. Fire protection was another crying need, and in 1736 Franklin formed the Philadelphia Contributionship, a combination insurance company and volunteer fire department. Among the subscribers, naturally, were members of his militia company.

A public hospital was next on the Junto's list. Several colonial cities boasted houses for the sick, but none on a scale that Franklin proposed, with separate facilities for easily communicated diseases. Such an undertaking was more than the city could afford; consequently, Philadelphia went to the legislature for an appropriation, but rural assemblymen balked. Franklin resolved the impasse by suggesting a legislative appropriation of two thousand pounds on condition that Philadelphia produce a like amount. The idea attracted the greedy as well as the frugal, and from this "matching grant" was born the Pennsylvania Hospital.

The year the hospital opened, 1755, also witnessed the start of Franklin's greatest triumph, the College of Philadelphia. It was a natural "booster" enterprise. Philadelphia had already overtaken Boston in population and commerce; a college would help make it the cultural center of the colonies as well. Yet Franklin did not want an institution wedded to the church, like the New England colleges. Something that would suit the needs of Philadelphia's practical, hard-working merchant class would suit the city better. Interested merchants subscribed four thousand pounds as an endowment. Franklin himself drafted the college charter, found a suitable building, appointed the first president, and assisted the search for faculty. The College of Philadelphia (renamed, with the Revolution, the University of Pennsylvania), was a new concept in the educational world. Ignoring theology, slighting Greek and Hebrew, the curriculum instead focused on modern languages, mathematics, and science. Like the self-taught jack-of-all-trades who founded it, the College of Philadelphia offered practical skills to a secular people.

By mid-century Philadelphia was one of the most progressive cities in the world. Equal in size to Edinburgh or Bristol, it was second only to London in the British empire. Its main streets were paved and gas-lit, a force of constables maintained the peace, and a central water system (with hollow logs for pipes) was under construction. And much of this was due to the booster spirit of Benjamin Franklin.

Apologist for Revolution

Civic spirit and personal ambition pushed Franklin onto the political stage early in his career. In 1736 he was named clerk of the assembly, a position that put him at the center of the legislative whirl. Under William Penn's liberal charter, Pennsylvania had a single-house legislature elected on a broad freehold suffrage. With democracy had come machine politics. Well-organized Quakers from Philadelphia and the Delaware River valley dominated assembly deliberations and controlled the principal offices.

Early in the century the Quakers had posed as defenders of colonial freedom against imperial domination. They resisted the claims of the Penn family, especially on questions of taxation, and they regularly opposed the governors sent to rule the colony. In the 1740s, just as Franklin came on the scene, the Quakers' power began to fade. War between France and Britain, which began in 1744 (the War of the Austrian Succession), caused Indian conflict on the colony's western borders. Assembly Quakers, through a combination of parsimony and religious zeal, refused to finance additional defenses, calling instead on the Penns for help. Disgruntled westerners soon formed an opposition party, and because of the preponderance of Scots-Irish in its ranks, the party was labeled Presbyterian.

Franklin remained on good terms with all parties. When a French invasion fleet appeared at the mouth of the Delaware in 1747, he mustered his volunteer militia company and threw up defenses. Westerners were impressed, frightened Quakers were relieved, and Governor Penn was delighted. The war ended the following year in a sort of armed truce. Both sides, however, expected a renewal of fighting. In 1754 Governor William Shirley of Massachusetts, commanding the royal forces in America, summoned an intercolonial conference at Albany, New York, to discuss frontier defense. Pennsylvania sent Franklin as its delegate.

Franklin had already concluded that the key to military unity was political union. He expressed the thought in a famous cartoon depicting a rattlesnake divided into segments, each labeled with the name of a colony. The caption was "Join or Die!" Franklin's plan called for a governor general appointed by the king to rule the colonies. He would be responsible for military defense and imperial relations. Internal affairs, however, would be handled by an intercolonial parliament. His scheme was an interesting blend of royal and popular interests. If effected, it might well have forestalled, or at least delayed, the Revolution; but it was too far in advance of its time. Colonial assemblies, jealous of their local authority, ignored it; and Britain was preoccupied with a new war.

Frontier fighting had already broken out by the time that the Albany conference met; war was officially declared in 1756 (called the Seven Years' War in Europe; the French and Indian War, or simply French War, among Americans). The war opened with the French occupation of the forks of the Ohio, at Pennsylvania's back door. Once again the assembly fell to bickering with the Penn family over taxes and defense appropriations. In 1757 Franklin sailed for London to bargain directly with the Penns. He was also instructed to see if there was any possibility of converting Pennsylvania into a royal colony so that the king would aid in its defense. Though failing in both aims, he did advance his own fortune by making valuable contacts among the Whig elite that governed the empire. When the war ended, he was allowed a brief visit home before the assembly sent him back, this time as agent for the colony. So successful was he that by the end of the 1760s he was asked to represent the interests of Georgia, New Jersey, and Massachusetts as well.

Franklin's success was not entirely deserved, for he spent much of his time representing his own interests. He joined in a number of projects for the development of lands won from the French, including the establishment of a fourteenth colony west of the Appalachian Mountains. He made no objection to the schemes of Prime Minister George Grenville for imperial reorganization and saw nothing wrong with the Stamp Act. Requiring official stamps on legal documents, newspapers, and other items was an ancient method of raising revenue in England. Franklin even tried to secure appointment as stamp distributor for one of his Philadelphia cronies. Yet, agile as a cat, he landed on his feet when the colonies erupted over the tax.

Invited to testify before a committee of the House of Commons in 1766, Franklin explained the colonists' opposition to the Stamp Act. External taxes, such as customs duties, were within the power of Parliament, he said, because they were a means of regulating trade. On the other hand, internal excises, levied for the purpose of raising revenue, were the province of the colonial assemblies. Indeed, such taxes were their only source of income. Even if feeling that it had such power, Parliament would be impolitic to exercise it. The subtle distinction between internal and external taxes provided a color of legitimacy to the colonial protest. Americans, it could be argued, were simply upholding the constitutional rights of Englishmen. Franklin's testimony, published in all the colonial papers, made him a hero. So long as he did nothing to tarnish it, the lustre would remain.

To assume the role of agitator would have wrecked his influence in London, so Franklin moved through official circles with discreet calm. He dutifully presented the inflammatory resolves of the assemblies he represented but avoided any personal involvement.

In 1772 his friendship with British officials paid off. He was offered (probably for a price) a chance to copy a number of letters written during the Stamp Act crisis by Thomas Hutchinson, lieutenant governor of Massachusetts. Though an American himself, Hutchinson was alarmed by the violence in Boston and suggested that the imperial government give its officials more authority. The plea was commonplace enough; nearly every governor in America felt the same. But in self-governing Massachusetts, where even the Governor's Council was elected, the request was dynamite. Properly edited, Hutchinson's statements would seem like an effort to set himself up as dictator. Franklin sent the letters to Samuel Adams, who published them gleefully. It kept the revolutionary agitation going in the quiet months before the Tea Party.

Publication of the Hutchinson letters caused a furor in Parliament and an official investigation. When suspicion centered on the wrong man, Franklin publicly admitted his guilt. A committee of the privy council submitted him to brutal questions for hours, then stripped him of his office of postmaster general. His influence gone, Franklin sailed for home in the spring of 1775. Somewhat to his surprise, he arrived to a hero's welcome.

The Nimble Rebel

Franklin landed in Philadelphia a few weeks after fighting started at Lexington and Concord. Pennsylvania was girding for war, but its party system was in shambles. The Quakers had long since fled the assembly, unable to cope with the chronic need for military action. Franklin's friend Joseph Galloway had taken over their apparatus; his party, however, was riven by the Revolutionary movement. Galloway himself rejected any notion of independence. The old Presbyterian party was likewise divided, with John Dickinson, radical pamphleteer of the 1760s, pleading for reconciliation. In the assembly a new radical party was taking shape, drawing strength both from the vitals of Philadelphia (the "Sons of Liberty") and from the hinterland.

The assembly sent Franklin to the Continental Congress, where he found himself part of an ultraconservative delegation that wanted nothing to do with independence. Throughout the winter of 1775–76 the delegates from the Middle Colonies — New York, New Jersey, Pennsylvania, and Delaware — searched for an imperial compromise. Franklin let the New Englanders and Virginians carry the radical torch. Then, in April 1776, with talk of independence becoming daily more open, he activated his old voluntary military organization. Sidestepping the conservative assembly, the militia called for elections to a provincial convention in order to draft a constitution for an independent state. In May, Richard Henry Lee of Virginia presented Congress with a resolution of independence. Pennsylvania's conservatives resisted at first, but under pressure from the approaching state election, they yielded, and the resolution passed. Together with Thomas Jefferson and John Adams, Franklin was named to a committee to draft a declaration.

Four days after they finished their task, July 8, 1776, Pennsylvania held its election, and the constitutional convention met a week later. Franklin attended that, too, helping to draft the most democratic of all the early state constitutions. At his suggestion the convention retained the unicameral assembly of the colonial regime. Upper houses, it was thought (with the British House of Lords in mind), were the bastion of the wealthy. The convention also eliminated the property qualification for voting, allowing all male taxpayers to vote. To make sure that the assembly reflected the wishes of its constituents, the constitution provided for annual elections and allowed delegates to serve only four years out of every seven. Never before had Franklin showed much interest in democratic reform, but with customary flexibility he helped shape one of the most radical instruments of the time — and that at age sixty-nine.

Diplomat of the Revolution

Richard Henry Lee's resolution, which Congress approved on July 2, 1776, actually had two parts. It suggested that, in addition to independence, Congress seek help abroad. France, still smarting from the loss of its North American empire thirteen years before, was the most likely prospect. In desperate need of guns and powder, Congress had already taken steps to sound French opinion. In April the Secret Committee of Correspondence, of which Franklin was a member, sent Silas Deane to Paris. Deane was a Connecticut merchant with transatlantic connections; moreover, he was a business partner of Robert Morris, who was (or soon would be) the wealthiest merchant in America. Morris, a delegate from Pennsylvania, was also a member of the Secret Committee.

During the summer, word came from Franklin's contacts in Europe that France was disposed to be friendly; in September Congress expanded the Deane mission to include Franklin and Arthur Lee, the latter still serving as Virginia's colonial agent in London. It was Franklin's fourth trip across the Atlantic, and he expected it to be his last. Because his wife had died while he was on his last errand abroad, he gave his American cash to Congress as a loan and turned his personal papers over to friends. Thus, with his affairs in order, he sailed away in a blustery November. On the previous voyage he had dangled a thermometer over the side to pass the time and had discovered the Gulf Stream. This time he took regular soundings and made copious notes with a view to publishing his findings in France. Driven by wintry gales, the ship crossed in the record time of four weeks — still an uncomfortable voyage for an old man. Age had not dulled his sense of theater, however, and he went ashore wearing the fur cap that he had found so useful during the trip. That and his scientific reputation assured him a tumultuous welcome.

Franklin arrived to find Silas Deane emptying the French arsenals of military hardware. It developed that Deane had made the acquaintance of one of the more colorful figures in the French court, Pierre Augustine Caron de Beaumarchais, amateur musician, watchmaker, playwright, and professional spy. Beaumarchais had made himself useful to young Louis XVI by recovering items that invited blackmail, and he had also found time to obtain information for Louis's foreign minister, Comte de Vergennes. It was on one such double venture that he had encountered Arthur Lee in London in 1774. Lee had apparently made an arrangement with Beaumarchais to secure arms for Virginia in exchange for tobacco. Nothing came of this deal, but Beaumarchais revived the scheme after fighting broke out in America, proposing that the French king supply Congress directly with weapons from French arsenals. The French military agreed because they had just developed a new type of musket and were eager to unload their obsolete weapons. To avoid implicating the French government, the arms would be exported under the mercantile cover of Roderigue Hortalez and Company. They would be shipped to Santo Domingo in the West Indies, where they would be transferred to American vessels.

Deane eagerly accepted what he assumed to be a gift from the French government. Within three months he and Beaumarchais collected enough arms and clothing for thirty thousand men, plus two hundred cannons and one hundred tons of powder. Every empty niche on the outgoing vessels Deane crammed full of silks, lace, and French wines, all consigned to Robert Morris of Philadelphia. Men of the eighteenth century did not see a sharp distinction between public and private business; in this regard, however, Silas Deane's vision was more blurred than most.

Franklin, who arrived in the midst of this undertaking, cooperated eagerly. But Arthur Lee, who appeared shortly after, was more suspicious. Until the arrival of Deane and Franklin he was America's chief emissary in Europe, and he disliked the competition. Moreover, he had been the first to contact Beaumarchais, though for some mysterious reason he had not seen fit to communicate his earlier arrangement to Congress. Virginians had never liked Yankee traders, and Arthur Lee was a suspicious man by nature. His suspicions seemed confirmed when Deane told him that the arms were not actually being swapped for Virginia tobacco; they were more on the order of a loan. Lee was certain that when Congress repaid the loan Deane and Beaumarchais, perhaps even Franklin, would each take a cut.

Fortunately for the commission, Arthur Lee was as ornery at court as he was at home. After two visits Vergennes refused to speak to him again. Franklin tactfully suggested that Lee visit Spain and Prussia to see if more friends could be found for the new republic. When Lee obliged, things settled down. Deane shipped supplies; Franklin handled the diplomacy.

Congress knew in advance exactly what it wanted from France. Its terms were incorporated in a Model Treaty, which it sent over with Franklin. Congress wanted neither a formal alliance nor French armies in America. The Revolution was more than a war for independence. It was a contest of republic against monarchy; and the pure republicans, among them Tom Paine and Samuel Adams, did not want a corruptive monarchy in their midst. An informal arrangement, under which France supplied financial aid and military supplies, was the most that they would tolerate.

Franklin realized that the terms of the Model Treaty were unrealistic. On his own responsibility, he offered Vergennes a formal military alliance and the promise of American help in actions against the British West Indies. Vergennes declined, offering only a loan of two million livres (a French coin roughly equivalent to the Spanish dollar). The difficulty was that the French were not sure of their new ally. General Washington was badly defeated at Long Island in the summer of 1776, and that autumn he lost New Jersey. By December, British armies were poised in Trenton and Princeton for a descent on the American capital, Philadelphia. Until the Americans won a battle in the open field (midnight raids, such as Washington's descent on

Trenton at Christmastime did not count), the French remained skeptical. King Louis XVI, moreover, was a cautious man. He would risk a few coins to embarrass the British, but his treasury could not sustain another war. (Ironically, the French aid to the American cause did help bring on the French Revolution in 1789.)

Franklin occupied himself profitably while he waited for good news, moving out to the mineral spa of Passy to be among people of literary and philosophical interests. He had learned French chiefly by lip-reading; but, as his eyes grew older, he found himself at a disadvantage at dinner parties — so he invented bifocals. He also redesigned his stove, attached a lightning rod to his umbrella, and proposed daylight saving time. Hot-air balloon ascensions were the fad in Paris that year, and Franklin never missed one. He predicted that airborne armies would make war obsolete. Since there was no defense against them, he thought, no nation would dare attack another.

The war news continued bad, but he kept up his spirits. While on a tour of the French countryside, he found himself one night at the same inn with Edward Gibbon, and invited the British historian to join him. Gibbon replied that he had a high regard for Franklin's scientific talents, but loyalty to his king prevented him from interviewing a "revolted subject." Franklin replied that he had a high regard for Gibbon as a historian, and that if the decline and fall of the British empire should become his subject, Franklin "would be happy to furnish him with the ample materials in his possession."

Then came news of Burgoyne's surrender at Saratoga, New York. A disaster for the British, it was the first important American victory. Franklin coyly suggested that since the two sides were militarily equal, it was time for peace. Vergennes countered with an offer of a full military alliance and the promise that France would enter the war. Franklin accepted, and the treaty was signed in February 1778. Three months later France declared war on Great Britain. Spain, promised the recovery of Gibraltar and Florida, joined the conflict a year later. Unable to stay neutral, the Netherlands entered in 1780. Due in part to the shrewd diplomacy of Benjamin Franklin, the American Revolution had become a world war.

Peacemaker

Arthur Lee returned home in 1778 to vent his suspicions. Before long his allies in Congress secured the recall of Silas Deane. Massachusetts and Virginia backed Lee; delegates from the middle states sided with Deane. The Deane-Lee affair distracted Congress for a full year, delaying the appointment of new commissioners or any consideration of peace terms. In the end Congress compromised. John Adams, representing the Massachusetts-Virginia axis, went to London with authority to negotiate the peace settlement; John Jay, allied with Robert Morris's middle-state faction, was sent to Spain. All negotiators were told to do nothing without the consent of France.

Left alone in Paris without formal authority, Franklin contented himself with an expanded social life. The technicality of marriage had never much restricted his activities; now that he was a widower, he was free even of the nags of conscience. He fell in love with, and offered marriage to, Madame Helvetius, a wealthy widow who presided over a salon of literary personages. She accepted his poems but declined his offer of marriage. It would inhibit her salon. Before long, Franklin took up with Madame Brillon de Jouy, wife of the treasurer of Paris. She was under forty, he seventy, but they shared an interest in chess and music. In the winter of 1781 she departed for a tour of Italy, and Franklin wrote her disconsolately:

> *I often pass before your house. It appears desolate to me. Formerly I broke the Commandment by coveting it along with my neighbor's wife. Now I do not covet it any more, so I am less a sinner. But as to his wife I always find these Commandments inconvenient and I am sorry that they were ever made. If in your travels you happen to see the Holy Father, ask him to repeal them, as things given only to the Jews and too uncomfortable for good Christians.*

Just at that moment the pace of events quickened. After ravishing Virginia in the summer of 1781, Lord Cornwallis became trapped at Yorktown by a combined American-French army. He surrendered in October, the campaign in the Southern states ground to a halt, and by the end of the year the British possessed nothing but two coastal enclaves, New York and Charleston. The succession of disasters forced a change in ministries. Lord North was replaced by the more conciliatory marquis of Rockingham. The new colonial secretary was the earl of Shelburne, a longtime friend of Franklin's.

While on her tour of Italy, Madame Brillon met an English traveler who offered to carry a letter to Shelburne. Informed of the offer, Franklin promptly wrote his old friend, the letter arriving even before the change in British government. In April 1782 Shelburne sent a secret agent to Passy to talk to Franklin. The move bypassed both the British foreign secretary, who wanted a hand in the negotiations, and John Adams, whom Congress had designated as chief negotiator.

Finding Shelburne's agent agreeable on most issues, Franklin hastily summoned John Jay from Madrid, and the two decided to violate Congress's instructions. Pressed by the British campaign in the South and nearly bankrupt, Congress in 1780 had instructed its three-man commission to conduct peace negotiations in tandem with the French, accepting whatever Vergennes could win.

Franklin considered this unnecessarily meek. Vergennes was a staunch ally, but his first commitment was to France. He had no interest, for instance, in an American republic that sprawled across the North American continent. A weak one, confined to the seaboard and forever dependent on France, was more to his liking. Franklin and Jay decided to open secret talks with the British. When these progressed satisfactorily, they informed John Adams, who hurried over from London to join in.

In October 1782 Jay drafted some preliminary articles. They included independence for the United States with boundaries that extend west to the Mississippi and from the Great Lakes to the 31st parallel (the northern boundary of Florida). The British agreed but then balked on questions of the Loyalists and American debts. Because the states had confiscated the property of Loyalists who had fled, the British felt that their American allies ought to be recompensed. Since this was a question for the states to decide, the American commissioners could agree to nothing more than a prohibition of future confiscations. The debt problem was likewise evaded. Americans, principally Southern planters, owed some four million pounds to British merchants when the war began. Most were willing to pay their debts, but they were understandably reluctant to pay interest for the war years. In the defense of the Southern debtors, Franklin pointed out that British armies had damaged property far in excess of the debts. He even suggested that the British consider ceding Canada in payment for war damages. In the end, the treaty simply declared that debts ought to be repaid; specific arrangements were left for the future.

The secret Anglo-American agreement was signed in November 1782. The Americans then assigned Franklin the task of informing Vergennes that he had been betrayed. Vergennes already knew of the negotiations (his spies were everywhere), but he was surprised at the terms that the Americans had won. "The British buy peace, rather than make it," he grumbled. He then asked Franklin to keep the agreement secret until France and Spain could win concessions for themselves. Franklin declined. Congress, being the chief authority in America, would have to be informed, and no one could rely on that body to keep a secret. Besides, he had a swift packet waiting at Le Havre.

Franklin did admit, however, that the separate signing revealed a split in the Franco-American family that the British might hope to exploit. What better way to repair the rift, he suggested, than by a new loan? Vergennes had to agree. And so the packet vessel that carried the articles of peace ending the Revolution also brought a fresh infusion of gold for a bankrupt Congress. It was Franklin's final triumph. By a rigid adherence to American interests, within the bounds of honor, he had secured as much at the diplomatic table for the young republic as its armies had won in the field. He had also established a basic framework for the conduct of American foreign policy: cordial relations with all nations; temporary alliances where needed, but binding commitments to no one.

Franklin at eighty-three was ready to come home, but Congress did not get around to replacing him until 1784, when Thomas Jefferson was sent to Paris. On the homeward voyage he occupied himself with the problem of air pollution, publishing on his arrival a description of a new coal-burning stove that would consume all of its own smoke.

Second only to Washington in the pantheon of American heroes, he was wooed by all in the hectic politics of the post-Revolutionary years. In 1787 he served in the convention that drafted the Federal Constitution, contributing his own prestige to the new government. His final years were spent supervising the American Philosophical Society, which he had founded a quarter of a century before, and writing essays. His final production, finished just before his death in April 1790, was "An Address to the Public from the Pennsylvania Society for Promoting the Abolition of Slavery."

Franklin was too much a rationalist to be swept by any religious faith, though he prudently contributed to every church in Philadelphia. One religious tenet he did hold, however, was a belief in reincarnation. That formed the basis of his epitaph, which he drafted early in life and always carried with him:

The Body
of
BENJAMIN FRANKLIN
Printer
(Like the cover of an old book,
Its contents worn out,
And stripped of its lettering and gilding),
Lies here, food for worms.
Yet the work itself shall not be lost,
For it will, as he believed, appear once more,
In a new
And more beautiful edition,
Corrected and amended
By
The Author.

SUGGESTIONS FOR FURTHER READING

Carl Van Doren's *Benjamin Franklin* (1938) is a classic that repays reading still today. It is splendidly written, brimming with anecdotal detail, a work as lively and personable as Franklin himself. Esmond Wright, *Benjamin Franklin, A Profile* (1970), is an anthology of historians' viewpoints. Gerald Stourzh, *Benjamin Franklin and American Foreign Policy* (1954), focuses on his diplomatic career. Franklin's family life is the subject of *The Private Franklin* (1975) by Claude-Anne Lopez and Eugenia W. Herbert, and his public career is analyzed by Thomas Wendel, *Benjamin Franklin and the Politics of Liberty* (1974).

2

Samuel Adams, Pure Republican

Consider the great revolutions of modern times—the American of 1776, the French of 1789, the European uprisings of 1848, and the twentieth-century upheavals in Russia and China.

There is great disparity among them. Some were slow, agonizing, and bloody; others swift and sure. Some were middle class in origin; others relied on factory workers and peasants. They led to democracy and dictatorship, aggressive imperialism and xenophobic withdrawal, free enterprise economies and communism. Yet one thing they all had in common was an appeal to the down-and-out. As time went on, as eighteenth century blended into nineteenth and twentieth, the appeal became more conscious; the methods of mobilizing the "lower orders" became more sophisticated. But the appeal itself remained the same — it was a promise of power, of political decision making, of control over one's own destiny.

Samuel Adams (1722–1803). *John Singleton Copley portrayed Adams on the day after the Boston Massacre, gripping one statement of American rights and pointing to another, as he demands of Lieutenant Governor Thomas Hutchinson a "redress of grievances."*

19

True revolutions — not simply changes of the guard (*coups d'état*, in French) — are essentially democratic in means and result. They overthrow an established power elite and, with it, the rationale for its authority. They appeal for support to the "outs" and, to some extent, incorporate them in the new decision-making apparatus. Victorious revolutionaries then formulate a new rationale for power, founded on the concept of broader participation; and they persuade the vast indifferent majority that the change is for the better. The next revolution promises an even wider distribution of decisions and results.

Despite these common threads, revolutions vary with time and circumstance, and the American Revolution was a product of the eighteenth century. America in 1775 was a predominantly rural, middle-class society. The ultra-wealthy were rare; a peasantry bound to the soil was unknown. Urban wages were higher than in Europe, and most craftsmen owned or rented their own shops. A working class that would be disciplined by factory whistles and the momentum of machines still lay in the future. The leather apron, worn by all craftsmen from coopers to tinsmiths, was a badge of distinction. Even the landless poor, perhaps one-fourth of the rural population, lived in expectation of acquiring wealth and status. If they did not, they usually removed to new surroundings. Spacial mobility sometimes substituted for social advance.

The gaps in social rank were nevertheless apparent to all. Commentators habitually spoke of the "middle orders" or the "lower orders" of society. Though not frozen into social classes, people in a preindustrial society with minuscule economic growth did not readily change position either. Social standing depended largely, but not exclusively, on wealth, as occupation, education, speech, dress, and manners were also important. Those at the top assumed the right to govern, and few contested their role. Political authority, so ran the common theory, belonged to those who had a stake in society, for only they would exercise power responsibly. Thus every colony required a certain amount of landed property (or a house in town) as a condition for voting or holding office.

The property qualification was a loose-knit skein that did not exclude many from the political process. Colonial assemblies, in their running battle with imperial authority, relied heavily on the fact that they were popularly based. In most colonies more than half the adult white males could vote, yet every assembly was a gentlemen's club. True decision making was in the hands of a tiny, sometimes self-perpetuating, elite. As a result, many felt excluded from the political process, even if they possessed the technical right to vote. In the agitated years preceding the Revolution, "popular leaders" appeared in nearly every colony seeking to mobilize this mass of discontent. Their appeal was the promise implicit in social upheaval. A running current stirs up mud from the bottom. And of these popular leaders no one was more ingenious or more successful than Samuel Adams. His story illuminates the "internal revolution" that accompanied the War for Independence.

The Making of a Populist

Samuel Adams, born in 1722, was that rare sort of revolutionary who could boast a Harvard education. There was nothing "common" at all about his background. His father, a retired ship captain and master of a brewery, was a leading figure in Boston politics. He suffered a serious financial reversal, however, in 1740, when imperial authorities dismantled a colonial bank in which he had invested heavily. Samuel, who graduated from Harvard that year at the age of eighteen, wrote his senior thesis on the right to resist authorities. He was a foe of empire ever after.

When his father died a few years later, Samuel inherited a share of the brewery, but he soon drove it into insolvency. He never had a head for business. Politics was his life and for the next half-century his principal source of income. He was America's first professional politician. He started slowly, serving first as clerk of the town market (inspecting weights and measures). In 1753 he was elected town scavenger, and three years later he became one of the town's tax collectors. In this role he was an instant success, being reelected annually for the next nine years. The reason for his popularity was simple: he failed to collect the taxes. After nine years in office he was eight thousand pounds in arrears to the town. Enemies accused him of embezzling the money, but he had nothing to show for it. Personally in debt, he was living in a rundown house and was dependent on the income of his second wife for food and clothing. He had been either negligent with his accounts or excessively softhearted with his constituents — or, most likely, a combination of the two. In 1772, after he had achieved fame as a patriot leader, the town excused him from the amount that he still owed.

The one requisite for an aspiring politico was membership in a club. Political clubs were the means by which Boston politics was organized. The town meeting was the heart of the city. It chose the governing selectmen and all officials, down to the lowly town scavenger. Pure democracy in action, the town meeting suffered the ills of democracy. It was an unwieldy body that easily lost direction. The clubs offered the necessary leadership, drafting resolutions for action, nominating candidates for office, and incidentally looking to the interests of their members. Merchants formed one club, artisans another; political radicals had several. Samuel Adams joined every one that he could. It was said that he had the heaviest schedule of lodge nights of anyone in Boston. "Sam the Publican," his critics called him, though being a strict Puritan he seldom drank. (He must have been a trial to tavern keepers.) He was a gregarious individual who enjoyed the company of mechanics and dockworkers. By the time that he attained a station in the town hierarchy, he already had a strong following among the lowly.

By 1760 Sam had become a member of the inner circle of town leaders, most of whom were members of the Boston Caucus, meeting in the attic of Tom Dawes's house on Purchase Street. This venerable club (his father had been a member) had ruled the town meeting for decades. When young John Adams was admitted to the group some years later, he recorded his impression of its meetings:

> *There they smoke tobacco till you cannot see from one end of the garrett to the other. There they drink flip, I suppose, and there they choose a moderator, who puts questions to the vote regularly; and selectmen, assessors, collectors, wardens, fire-wards, and representatives* [to the assembly] *are regularly chosen before they are chosen in the town.*

The Publican and the Lawyer

Massachusetts politics in 1760 was nearing the point of explosion. For two decades the able and popular William Shirley had governed the province, maintaining his authority by the judicious use of patronage. The chief beneficiaries of Shirley's largesse were Thomas Hutchinson and his family allies, the Olivers. Hutchinson himself was president of the Council, lieutenant governor of the province, and a member of the superior court. Besides being a capable leader, he was an accomplished scholar. His *History of the Colony of Massachusetts Bay* (completed in England after the Revolution broke out) stands as some of the best historical writing of the century. The complaint against Hutchinson was that he monopolized all the best offices. His circle was commonly known as the Court party because of its close association with the governor. His opponents were dubbed the Country party, though the name was not entirely accurate. Among its most prominent members were Boston merchants and lawyers who would gladly have served the "court," if given the opportunity. Chief among these was attorney James Otis, Sr.

In 1760 Country leaders saw an opportunity to embarrass Hutchinson, while staking out an elevated moral position for themselves. War with France had been under way for five years, and with the surrender of Canada to British forces in September 1760, victory was in sight. Early in the war the Royal Navy had prohibited trade with the French islands in the West Indies, but the rule proved hard to enforce. The trade in sugar and molasses (which could be purchased more cheaply from the French) was vital to

New England's rum industry and the chief source of hard currency. Expert seamen, blessed with a long and jagged coastline, New Englanders became the world's craftiest smugglers.

Smuggling was hard to stop because the common law limited the authority of customs officials. In ordinary times they had to secure a search warrant from a court in order to board a vessel, and the warrant had to list the illegal items being sought. In a war emergency Parliament had authorized the use of general warrants, or writs of assistance, under which inspectors could pry at will until they found something incriminating. Such writs had been sanctioned by the Massachusetts Superior Court in 1755 and were in use throughout the war.

The death of King George II in 1760 voided all the judicial writs issued in his name and forced Massachusetts officials to return to the superior court for new authority. Deciding to contest the writs, Boston merchants hired as their attorney James Otis, Jr., son of the Country party leader. Otis developed the novel argument that the English constitution (an unwritten collection of precedents accumulated through the centuries) protected the right of privacy. The colonists, as transplanted Englishmen, were protected by that same constitution. Thus, general search warrants, even if authorized by Parliament, were contrary to this higher law. "An act of Parliament against the constitution is void," declared Otis. "An act against natural equity is void."

The argument no doubt came as a surprise to many Britons, whose concern had been to limit the King's powers, not Parliament's, but it was an ingenious extension of the Whig philosophy. And it placed the party contest in Massachusetts on a new level. Instead of a fight for the spoils of office, it was thereafter a contest between imperial authority and local self-government, between a tiny coterie of the rich and the common people. It is not likely that Otis grasped all these implications, but Samuel Adams, who was soon locked with him arm in arm, surely did. When Chief Justice Hutchinson, speaking for the court, rejected Otis's argument and upheld the writs, he made himself into a perfect political target—a colonial elitist defending imperial authority.

The French and Indian War caused tensions between Britain and her colonies; its end, ironically, brought even more. Destruction of the French empire in North America loosened the bonds of the British empire, for no longer were colonies and mother country dependent on one another for defense. The victory, moreover, left Britain with new responsibilities. No longer confined to the seaboard colonies, Britain's North American possessions extended from Hudson's Bay to the Gulf of Mexico. Protecting such a vast territory, against Indians on the one side and jealous European powers on the other, promised to be both difficult and expensive. It was clear that imperial authority had to be strengthened, and some means had to be found to make the colonies contribute to their own defense.

The task fell to George Grenville, the latest in a succession of ministers given royal favor by King George III. Grenville's Revenue Act of 1764 struck at both problems at once. To improve the crown's revenue from the colonies, the act reduced the duties on imported sugar and molasses. Previous duties, prohibitively high, had been designed to exclude sugar from French or Dutch islands and to force the colonists to purchase British-made sugar, from Jamaica or Barbados. Under the new system the mainland colonists would be allowed to purchase the cheaper French and Dutch sugars, provided they paid for the privilege. What is more, collection procedures were tightened to ensure the new taxes were actually paid. To end smuggling, the Revenue Act authorized the establishment of vice admiralty courts in key American ports. Functioning without juries and under maritime law, these courts, Grenville hoped, would more easily secure convictions.

When Samuel Adams read the new statute (colonists quickly dubbed it the Sugar Act), he reached for his quill. His blast, circulated by friendly newspapers, was the first written assault on the powers of Parliament. Adams's argument sprouted from the Otis seed. Never before, he pointed out, had Parliament taxed the colonies for the purpose of obtaining revenue. Previous duties, such as those on sugar and molasses, had been for the purpose of directing colonial trade. Trade regulation was within Parliament's powers; collection of revenue was not. Only the colonial assemblies could levy revenue assessments against Americans.

The argument was both ingenious and appealing. In the past century Parliament had sustained its own position against the king by a judicious use of the power of the purse. For years the colonial assemblies had done the same in their chronic fights with royal governors. It was an axiom of Anglo-American history that power over money bills was the root of every other legislative power. Especially was this true in Massachusetts, where the assembly commonly extracted political concessions from the governor before paying him his personal salary.

When Adams put down his quill, the Boston Caucus went to work. The town meeting passed a caucus-drafted resolution asking Boston's representatives to introduce a petition for the act's repeal. Catching the Court party by surprise, the petition slipped through the House of Representatives. The appeal won attention in other colonies, and before long there was a general protest. From Adams's quill to caucus to town meeting to assembly to intercolonial uproar—the pattern would become a familiar one in the next few years.

Mobilizing the Mob

The Stamp Act, approved by Parliament in 1765, was an even more serious threat to colonial self-government. It had nothing to do with foreign trade and was simply a revenue tax: an excise on goods produced or exchanged within the colonies. Selected items were required to carry stamps, to be purchased from specially designated collectors. The revenue was to be devoted to imperial defense, but this satisfied Americans not a bit. The Virginia House of Burgesses showed the way by publishing a series of fiery resolves drafted by Patrick Henry.

The Virginia resolves were a heavenly gift to Samuel Adams, whose own ranks were in sad disarray. The cause was James Otis, Jr., already demonstrating the mental imbalance that would destroy him. After a brilliant summary of the "Rights of the British Colonies" in 1764, Otis began to backpedal. A new essay in early 1765 upheld the powers of Parliament, and in the spring elections Otis won reelection to the House of Representatives by the narrowest of margins. Adams needed an issue that would obscure the organizational and philosophical difficulties created by Otis.

On August 14, 1765, a mob raided the house of Andrew Oliver, city stamp distributor and a brother-in-law of Lieutenant Governor Hutchinson. Oliver resigned the following day, and the Stamp Act was a dead letter in Massachusetts. Two weeks later a mob tore up Hutchinson's house, scattering in the street the manuscript for Volume II of his *History*. Boston's outburst caused renewed violence elsewhere. At Virginia's suggestion a Stamp Act Congress met in Philadelphia to draft a joint protest against the tax. By the end of the year radical organizations, styling themselves Sons of Liberty, had sprung up in every major city. The maelstrom of violence had brought the lower elements of American society to the surface. Nowhere was this more apparent than in Samuel Adams's Boston.

Mob violence was not new to Boston or to any other colonial city. Boston even had a regularly scheduled brawl. Every Guy Fawkes Day (November 5) mobs that collected at each end of town marched into the city center carrying effigies of the pope. A huge fight ensued, then a celebration of sorts. Sometimes the violence turned against official authority, as when seamen resisted the press gangs of the Royal Navy or shopkeepers harassed customs officials. Rarely did the mob get out of hand, however. The "leather aprons" had acknowledged leaders of their own.

One such was Ebenezer Mackintosh, a shoemaker by trade, leader of the South End mob, and victor in the papal riot of 1764. In the spring of 1765 the Caucus Club took him in, rewarding him with the town post of inspector of leather. It was Mackintosh who led the August attack on the stamp distributor's house, and in November Mackintosh achieved a union of the urban mobs. Instead of the annual brawl, hundreds of "leather aprons" attended a huge feast at a city tavern. The bill, no doubt, was paid by the Boston Caucus.

In all this can be seen the hand of Samuel Adams. Among the first to recognize the potential in politically directed violence, Adams also realized early that the mob action had to be kept under control. Already by the fall of 1765 merchants who had participated in the early riots were becoming frightened. To keep his coalition together, Adams had to still their fears. His opportunity came with the repeal of the Stamp Act in the spring of 1766. Parliament's action was anticipated well in advance, for the House of Commons debated the question for weeks. The Boston Caucus spread the word that reaction to the repeal was to be peaceful. When the news finally arrived in May, the entire city burst forth with lighted candles — a silent demonstration of unity and purpose.

Adams and Hancock

There was a revolution of another sort in the spring of 1766, this one in the assembly. Six months earlier, in the midst of the riots, Samuel Adams won election to the House of Representatives, replacing a member who had recently died. In the 1766 election the Popular party (as the Country party now styled itself) won control of the lower house. When the legislative session opened later that year, the house elected Adams its clerk, thus placing him in charge of drafting petitions and resolutions. Popular leaders also elected one of their own to the Council (Massachusetts was the only colony in which the lower house elected the Governor's Council, which was also the upper house of the legislature, or General Court). Finally the House of Representatives ordered the construction of a visitors' gallery. The Sons of Liberty would ensure that debates were properly attended.

In the meantime Adams consolidated his own power. He organized a secret committee, calling itself the Loyal Nine, which directed the radical movement. Benjamin Edes and Jonathan Gill, publishers of the *Boston Gazette*, were early members. So were James Otis — though his erratic behavior cost him influence—and Joseph Warren, the physician who would lose his life on Breed's Hill. In 1767 Samuel persuaded his country cousin, John Adams, to leave Braintree to open a law practice in Boston. He was soon admitted to the smoke-filled attic on Purchase Street.

The most important addition to this inner circle of revolutionaries was John Hancock, who had recently inherited an international shipping business. A vain man and a dandy who clothed himself in royal purple, Hancock was eager for power and glory. The caucus secured him a post as town marshall, and on muster day he would sit astride his charger, uniform blazoned with gold epaulets, side by side with the governor, as the colony's citizen-soldiers plodded slowly in review. In the political changeover of the spring of 1766, Boston elected him one of its four representatives in the General Court. Strolling past Hancock's house some time later, Samuel Adams observed: "This town has done a wise thing today. . . . They have made that young man's fortune their own." What Boston could not claim of Hancock's purse, the Loyal Nine did.

Within a year Boston's revolutionaries had a new British provocation to exploit. The Townshend Taxes of 1767 were customs duties on goods brought into the colonies from abroad. Among the goods taxed were paper, paint, glass, and tea, none of them vital to colonial life. Under the distinction Benjamin Franklin had made in testimony before the House of Commons, such taxes were external and therefore legitimate. And they might have been endured but for the stinger in the tail. The revenue would be used, declared Chancellor of the Exchequer Charles Townshend, to defray the costs of royal government in America, including the payment of governors' salaries. The remark was tactless at best; in Massachusetts, where the governor's salary had been a political issue for decades, it was considered a dangerous threat.

In February 1768 the House of Representatives sent to other colonies a circular letter denying that Parliament had any sort of tax power in America, internal or external. Americans could not be taxed by a body in which they had no representation. All colonies but one approved the letter and flooded the king with petitions for redress. New York and Philadelphia merchants organized a nonimportation association, refusing to purchase British goods until the obnoxious acts were repealed. Boston merchants were more reluctant, but the Sons of Liberty announced — and enforced — a ban of their own.

The heavy-handed tactics of the Sons of Liberty (Adams had only limited control over the tough-minded "leather aprons") alienated the merchants, as in the days of the Stamp Act riots. The Popular party might have disintegrated but for further British provocations. Outraged by the circular letter, the colonial secretary told Governor Bernard to "require" the assembly to revoke it. Under the Massachusetts charter the governor could not "require" the assembly to do anything, though he could dissolve it and send it home. Bernard, knowing this, should have softened the language, but instead he used the secretary's tactless term. By a vote of 92 to 17 the representatives refused to back down. The governor thereupon dissolved the assembly. The assembly barred the door against his proclamation while it drafted a petition to the king for the governor's removal.

During the summer the Sons of Liberty ruled the streets of Boston, blacklisting merchants who carried British goods and intimidating customs officials. Fearing for their safety, the collectors retired to Castle William in the Boston harbor. The illicit trade with the West Indies boomed. In September 1768 British authorities sent General Thomas Gage and a regiment of regulars to Boston to restore order. Gage's troops had been in New York since the end of the French War, ostensibly to protect the frontier, though in fact they never left the city. The army presence had caused considerable tension in New York, whose assembly refused to contribute to the costs. In unruly Boston it was an invitation to disaster.

Samuel Adams, some reported, threatened to raise an army from the country that would "destroy every soldier that dare put his foot on shore," but that was rhetorical bombast. In a more calculating moment he took advantage of the colony's outrage to place more radicals on the Governor's Council, giving him, for a time, a majority.

The soldiers restored the customs officials to duty, but there was constant friction. Townspeople accused them of crimes and hauled them into court on the slightest pretext. Poorly paid soldiers made themselves even more unpopular by accepting part-time jobs in the city. The city's commerce had floundered since the end of the war, and the nonimportation agreements stifled it further. Unemployed sailors and dockworkers watched with dismay, as "lobsterbacks" took jobs at below-normal wages. Soldiers were taunted on the streets and assaulted in the alleys. Both sides felt themselves the victims of aggression.

The blowup came in early March of 1770. For days anonymous leaflets peppered the citizenry with predictions that the troops were planning a massacre. The atmosphere grew tense. On the evening of March 5 a group of boys started throwing snowballs at a sentry. As a crowd gathered and bells began to ring, the sentry called out the guard. John Adams later described the scene:

> *The multitude was shouting and huzzaing, and threatening life, the bells ringing, the mob whistling, screaming and rending like an Indian yell, the people from all quarters throwing every species of rubbish they could pick up in the streets.*

The soldiers took the abuse until one was knocked down by a fragment of brick. He fired his musket, whether by design or accident, and the rest also opened fire. When the smoke cleared, five townsmen lay dead or mortally wounded. They were Samuel Gray, ropemaker; Crispus Attucks, a Black who frequently brawled with soldiers; James Caldwell, sailor; and Patrick Carr, Irishman, whose mob activities went back to the Guy Fawkes Day riots. The fifth victim was Samuel Maverick, a young apprentice and apparently an innocent bystander.

In town meeting at Fanueil Hall the next day Samuel Adams made the most of the "bloody work in King's Street," as he termed it, demanding withdrawal of the army altogether from Boston. For weeks the *Boston Gazette* produced eyewitness descriptions, and the Sons of Liberty kept up the harassment of soldiers. Even so, tensions subsided. Like a crack of lightning the shooting seemed to clear the air. Thomas Hutchinson, assuming the governorship on the departure of Bernard, handled the crisis adroitly. He quickly ordered the arrest and trial of the eight soldiers. The soldiers, in turn, hired John Adams as their defense counsel. Accepting from a sense of duty Adams then did so well that only two were found guilty. Both received the comparatively mild sentence of branding by hot iron.

Parliament also helped defuse the tension. At the time of the massacre it already had under consideration a repeal of the Townshend Taxes. Behind the move lay the demands of merchants hurt by the American refusal to buy British goods. Parliament ultimately decided to retain the tax on tea, as a face-saving gesture, but for the moment it mattered not. By the time that news of the repeal reached Boston, the nonimportation movement had collapsed. City merchants simply rebelled against the petty tyranny of the Sons of Liberty.

In the spring election of 1771 the Popular party barely managed to retain control of the House of Representatives. James Otis, who had suffered periodic fits of insanity since 1769, managed to win a seat; but when the session opened, he broke down completely. Amidst the taunts of the Court party, he was carried out of the hall, a jabbering idiot. The governor's partisans recovered control of the upper house that winter, and by the end of the year even John Hancock was having doubts that the resistance was worthwhile. He ran against Adams in the election of 1772.

The months after the Boston Massacre were lonely ones for Samuel Adams, who was facing the dilemma of every revolutionary. To demonstrate his position he had to use force, yet the resort to violence alienated the people he needed most — the uncommitted majority. Adams waited, pouncing upon every rare bit of good fortune that came his way. The Hutchinson letters, sent him by Benjamin Franklin, helped some. They embarrassed the governor and put him on the defensive. For weeks the *Boston Gazette* printed bits and pieces, fanning the public interest. After explaining and expanding, the governor then fell into guilt-oozing silence. Such tactics enabled Adams to pass the time, but they were not the stuff of which revolutions are made. The public, always eager for "normalcy," would eventually have found him tiresome. He was saved by another British blunder.

In the summer of 1773 Parliament undertook to reorganize the East India Company, the joint stock venture that had monopolized British trade in the Far East since the days of Elizabeth. To improve the company's profits, Parliament conferred on it an additional monopoly — that of distributing tea to American colonists. Because tea was taxed under the Townshend system, Americans had taken to smuggling Dutch tea. The competition had contributed to the difficulties of the British East India Company. By giving it a monopoly, Parliament hoped to enable the British company to compete with the Dutch. What it forgot, apparently, was that tea was a political symbol in America, a symbol of resistance to parliamentary taxation. Were Americans now to be bribed of their rights by the offer of cheap English tea?

That, at least, was the question raised by radicals in New York and Philadelphia, who first recognized the political potential in the act. Adams, made cautious by a succession of defeats, was slower to react. By mid-October, however, the *Gazette* was unleashing editorial salvos, and the town meeting sent a delegation headed by Adams to demand the resignation of the company's tea agents. Governor Hutchinson, determined to stop the slow erosion of royal authority, commanded them to stay. When a tea ship, the *Dartmouth*, entered Boston harbor on November 27, Adams set up a guard to prevent it from landing its cargo. The captain agreed to return to England, but Governor Hutchinson refused to let him go.

Under the law, if a vessel failed to discharge its cargo within twenty days, customs officials would board and unload it. The governor waited for the December 16 deadline, knowing that the officials would be protected by General Gage's soldiers. On the night that the deadline expired, a mass meeting was held at Fanueil Hall. In the midst of the discussion, Adams rose to declare, "This meeting can do no more to save the country." It was evidently a signal, for the meeting promptly adjourned to the harbor. There the crowd watched a dozen "Indians" unload the *Dartmouth*, dumping 342 chests of tea into the water.

The Tea Party was a calculated gamble by Boston's radical leaders. They had to restore the revolutionary ardor of their followers and to regain their standing among popular leaders in other colonies. It was a bold gamble, for it was an act of petty vandalism that might have alienated property-conscious Americans. And it was widely denounced. Only Parliament's reaction made the Tea Party a success.

Parliament was furious. For almost a decade it had retreated in the face of American violence, repealing first the Stamp Act, then the Townshend Taxes. This time it would meet force with force. In the spring of 1774 the king's chief minister, Lord North, introduced a series of punitive measures. One closed the port of Boston until the city paid for the tea. Another suspended the charter of Massachusetts, conferring dictatorial powers on the governor. The appointment of General Gage as governor placed the province under military rule. Other laws added to the powers of customs officials and forced citizens to quarter soldiers in private homes.

The Coercive Acts, as the colonists called them, united Americans as never before. If Parliament, by the flick of a quill, could destroy civil government in Massachusetts, no colony was safe. Food and fuel flowed into locked-up Boston. When Virginia suggested an intercolonial conference to discuss joint action, other colonies quickly agreed. The Massachusetts assembly, meeting in mid-June, promptly took up the Virginia proposal. Fearful that Governor Gage might dissolve it, Adams locked the door of the House, but one member, pleading a "call of nature," ran to alert the governor. Behind locked doors, with the governor's proclamation dissolving the assembly thundering in the streets, the House elected five delegates, including Samuel and John Adams, to attend the Continental Congress, scheduled for September 1, 1774, in Philadelphia.

That "Brace of Adamses"

"We have had numberless prejudices to remove here," John Adams wrote home from Philadelphia. "We have been obliged to act with great delicacy and caution. We have been obliged to keep ourselves out of sight, and to feel pulses, and to sound the depths; to insinuate our sentiments, designs, and desires by means of other persons, sometimes of one province, and sometimes of another." New Englanders were never a popular breed. Other colonists considered them nasal-voiced hypocrites who covered sharp trading practices with a cloak of Puritan piety. The "brace of Adamses," as George III scornfully referred to them, had to tread with special caution. Moderates to the south suspected them of being republicans, or worse, "levelers" (an eighteenth-century form of communist) bent on independence.

At the outset only the Virginians seemed to share their views. Led by Patrick Henry and Richard Henry Lee, the Virginians had come to the conclusion that Parliament had no legislative power at all in America. Domestic legislation was exclusively the province of the colonial assemblies, and Parliament could act only in the fields of defense and foreign affairs. This position, stated by Thomas Jefferson in "A Summary View of the Rights of British America," seemed radical, but it still fell short of independence.

Congressional conservatives, led by Franklin's friend Joseph Galloway, drew most of their strength from the middle states. Galloway agreed that Americans had certain rights that Parliament could not transgress. But he also felt a need for central authority, lest society dissolve into chaos. Parliament was the only such authority available; it must be allowed to govern, even to the point of levying taxes.

The most important thing, all recognized, was to maintain a united front. Differences had to be resolved or papered over. Thus the "brace of Adamses" concealed their true views and worked through others. Samuel scored a point on the second day when a delegate suggested opening the sessions with prayer. Responding to a protest that no prayer could be satisfactory to delegates of such religious diversity, Adams announced that "he was no bigot, and could hear a prayer from any gentleman of piety and virtue." Strict Congregationalist though he was, he suggested that one of the Anglican ministers of Philadelphia might be a proper chaplain. It was only prudence, he explained at home, since "some of our warmest friends are members of the Church of England." He had in mind the Virginians, of course. The only question mark in the Virginian delegation was the wealthy and conservative squire of Mount Vernon, George Washington. He came in for special treatment. After an evening with the Adamses, Washington wrote home to assure his countrymen that nowhere in New England was there any notion of independence.

Before long, Congress was moving with the slick efficiency of a Boston town meeting. Joseph Galloway suggested that it meet in the Pennsylvania assembly house, but Congress chose instead Carpenters' Hall, meeting-house of a radical city guild. On the suggestion of a Virginian, Congress selected as its secretary a nonmember, Charles Thomson, head of the local Sons of Liberty. John Adams, writing home, described Thomson as "the Sam Adams of Philadelphia."

On September 16, after Congress had wrangled for a week over the nature of American grievances, Paul Revere rode into town with a set of resolutions in his saddlebags. A silversmith of good repute and member of the inner circle of Boston radicals, Revere carried resolutions that had been adopted by a popular meeting in Suffolk County, Massachusetts. The author was Sam Adams's close friend, Dr. Joseph Warren. Adams himself may have had a hand in them; certainly he knew of them before he left for Philadelphia. The Suffolk Resolves declared that the Coercive Acts had violated the governmental compact between crown and people; they suggested that the colonists arm for self-defense.

The timing was perfect, for the Suffolk Resolves presented Congress with an agenda and put conservatives in a quandary. To reject them implied approval of Parliament's policies, to accept them implied approval of the radicals' stand. While conservatives fumbled in confusion, Congress approved the Suffolk Resolves. It then instituted a continental embargo on trade with Britain in retaliation for the acts of Parliament. A final Declaration of Rights and Grievances reflected the radical view that Parliament could act only with colonial consent. Congress then adjourned until the following May.

The First Continental Congress was a triumph for Samuel Adams, who managed it with the finesse learned from years in the Boston Caucus. It approved all his suggestions; it endorsed his view of imperial power. The outbreak of war, and after that true independence, was only a matter of time. The revolution, for which he had worked so long, had dawned.

Bitter Victory

Massachusetts was an armed camp by the fall of 1774. Militia drilled on every village green. Especially prepared units, or Minutemen, turned out at every alarm. On September 1, the day that Congress assembled, General Gage ordered a raid on a colonial arms cache across the river from Boston in Cambridge. When word of the order leaked out, a crowd gathered. Rather than risk an incident, Gage countered the order; but by then thousands of Minutemen had started for Boston prepared for a fight. Similar incidents occurred throughout the winter, as the British searched for arms depots from Cape Ann to Narragansett Bay.

The inevitable clash came on April 19, 1775, when Gage sent an expedition to seize the arms cache at Concord. A secondary objective was to arrest Samuel Adams and John Hancock, who were rumored to be in the vicinity of Lexington. Alerted by Paul Revere, Adams and Hancock slipped out of town just ahead of the British. From the safety of a marsh they listened to the bloody encounter on Lexington green. The outbreak of war left Adams ecstatic. "O What a glorious morning is this!" he exclaimed to Hancock. Sad to say, it was probably his last sense of glory.

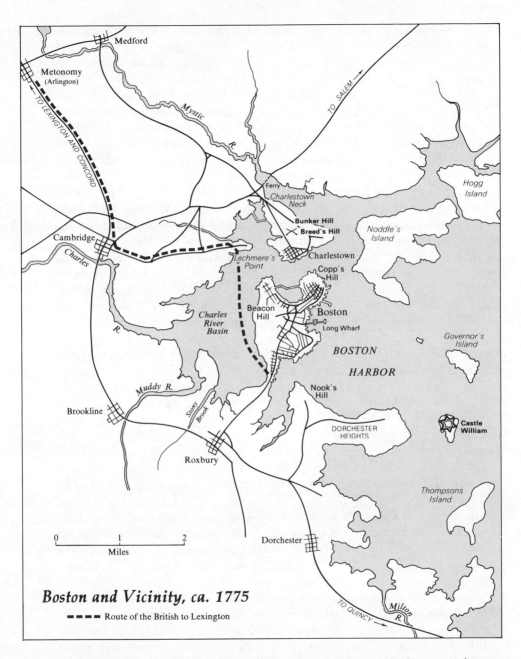

Boston and Vicinity, ca. 1775

▪▪▪▪ Route of the British to Lexington

A few days after the battles of Lexington and Concord, the two Adamses and Hancock departed for Philadelphia to attend the Second Continental Congress, leaving Dr. Warren and the Committee of Safety to lead the army of volunteers gathering around Boston. The previous year they had gone by carriage, but this time John Adams decided that Samuel ought to learn to ride a horse. Horsemanship, he felt, was essential to the "character of a statesman." Left unsaid was the obvious fact that a man on horse was a more fleetfooted rebel. Sam the city boy required two servants to load and unload him at first, but by the time they reached Philadelphia he was an accomplished cavalier.

After the Battle of Breed's Hill (popularly but mistakenly called Bunker Hill) on June 17, Massachusetts asked Congress to assume direction of the army. Congress agreed, authorizing several regiments of Maryland and Virginia riflemen. It was John Adams who suggested Washington for commander. His purpose was to make the war truly continental. Samuel went along, but reluctantly; he still suspected Washington for his conservatism, nor could he accept the idea of a regular army. He wanted the war fought with citizen-soldiers, with each colony maintaining its own.

From that point on, John Adams was the dominant figure in the Massachusetts delegation. It was he who took the floor to reply to the hesitant pleas of the moderates from the middle states. He chaired the committees that organized the army and founded the American navy. Samuel was ineffective in debate, too shrill in tone, too willing to assume that all who disagreed with him were traitors to the cause. A doctrinaire revolutionary, he lacked the gift for compromise. Only the Virginia Lees could tolerate him, and they had a wide circle of enemies of their own. The Adams-Lee alliance drew a great deal of attention because of its radical stance, but it never controlled Congress.

The war itself drew Congress into ever more radical steps, and masked for a time the declining influence of Samuel Adams. Ignited by Tom Paine's pamphlet *Common Sense*, a movement for independence grew steadily through the spring of 1776. Richard Henry Lee's resolution declaring the American governments "free and independent states" induced Congress to appoint a committee to draft a declaration, but Samuel Adams was not on it. Others had moved to the forefront of the movement that he had started.

His service in Congress became a constant trial. Philadelphia, for him, was a sewer of corruption. Lest congressional delegates become distracted by its ballrooms and theaters, he secured passage of a rule forbidding members of Congress from attending public entertainments. Outraged Southerners simply ignored the regulation.

A political Puritan, Samuel Adams felt that unless the new nation adhered to the pristine simplicity of its revolutionary ideals, it would go the route of ancient Rome. He disliked the French alliance and fumed throughout the war about the corrupting influence of French aristocrats in America. He sided with the truculent diplomat Arthur Lee for the same reason. Silas Deane and Deane's partner, Robert Morris, Adams felt, were corrupt speculators, men without conscience or country, bending the misfortunes of others to their own profit.

In 1779 Adams retired from Congress, returning to Massachusetts to aid in the drafting of the state constitution. Cousin John drafted most of the document; but Samuel was responsible for the religious article, which left the Congregational church established by law and supported by the state. Other faiths were simply tolerated. A tax for the support of religion was levied on all heads of families. Dissenters, who were excused from such taxes in colonial days, had to contribute to their own churches as well. Nonchurchgoers were taxed for the benefit of the established church. It was the most repressive religious code in America. But in Adams's mind the logic was simple: the future of the republic depended on the morals of its citizenry; morals, in turn, relied on formal religion, and the church needed the support of the state.

After the war he battled sin in Boston with the same gusto that he had battled corruption in Philadelphia. A nightclub that featured dancing and card playing, and permitted ladies with escorts, was his chief target. Adams predicted that it would lead to Roman orgies and the downfall of the republic. The newspaper tempest went on for months and eventually became an election issue. Thus occupied, politicians ignored a brewing storm in Massachusetts' western counties.

The state constitution drafted by John Adams was only a slight modification of the colonial charter. It retained property qualifications for voting and holding office and left sizable powers in the hands of the governor. Other states (though not all) adopted similar frames of government. In most places (Pennsylvania was the chief exception) a tightly knit group of seaboard merchants and planters controlled the new governmental machinery. Popular leaders, who had played such an important role in provoking the British, were shunted aside, their expectations shattered. And Samuel Adams was too concerned with the Sans Souci Night Club to see the point. He did not even show concern when the embattled farmers of Massachusetts rose up against state authority in 1786 under the informal direction of Daniel Shays. Adams cheered the suppression of the rebellion as a victory for law and order.

In the 1790s Samuel Adams became a supporter of Thomas Jefferson — to the embarrassment of the mercantile oligarchy that dominated his own state — yet he never shared Jefferson's ideals. He was a democrat in taste and manners, but not in philosophy. He had long outlived his time when he died in 1803. Yet the promise he held out to the common people in those heady days preceding the Revolution outlived him. He had helped to found a republic based on the consent of the governed. The people would be back to redeem the promise he had made and then abandoned.

SUGGESTIONS FOR FURTHER READING

The standard biography is John C. Miller's *Sam Adams, Pioneer in Propaganda* (1936), but the style is plodding. Far more entertaining and informative are

Esther Forbes, *Paul Revere and the World He Lived In* (1942) and Catherine Bowen, *John Adams and the American Revolution* (1949). The most recent studies of popular politics in pre-Revolutionary Boston are Merrill Jensen, *The Founding of a Nation, A History of the American Revolution, 1763–1776* (1968), and Pauline Maier, *From Resistance to Revolution* (1972).

3

George Washington, Gentleman Revolutionary

In contrast to unruly Boston, George Washington's Virginia was a placid land where change came slowly. Virginians were a proud people who revered tradition. No tradition was stronger (nor less factual) than the *ancien dominion*, the notion that Virginia was the land of the Cavaliers, royalist refugees who fled England during the Puritan revolution of the 1640s. The upper crust of Virginia society was not descended from English artistocracy, it was as self-made as Benjamin Franklin. Byrds, Carters, Nicholases, Burwells, Pages — nearly all originated among ship captains and shopkeepers. They edged to the top merely by appropriating more of the virgin continent than others did.

Virginians came from much the same segment of English society as New Englanders, but they buried their background in myth. Instead of the bourgeois ethics of

George Washington (1732–1799). *This portrait, done in early 1781, was one of five of Washington painted by Charles Willson Peale. It was a dark moment for the Revolutionary cause — the British were storming across the South and the treasury was empty. Nevertheless, Washington stands leaning on a cannon in jaunty pose, a confident smile on his face.*

the Gospel of Work, they revered the English Cavalier, the code of the gentleman. Their prescription was not for achieving success but for utilizing it.

Gentlemen were not made; they were born. Wealth was essential but was not sufficient, for it took more than one generation to make a gentleman. Education, dress, manners, speech — signs of established wealth — were the requisites. The Virginians' ethical system was as fine-tuned as Franklin's, but the emphasis was different. Protestant virtues such as thrift and hard work were honored more in word than in deed. Virginians lived instead by the Greek ideals of temperance and moderation. They excused sins of the flesh so long as transgressions were modest. Truth, honesty, duty, justice — those were the virtues honored by Virginians.

The code of the gentleman was both rigorous and flexible. It was concerned with social behavior rather than with moral judgment. Acquisitiveness was not a listed virtue, nor was it a fault. Individuals could pursue happiness defined in almost any way that they wished. To most of them it meant landholding, for land defined the individual's place in society. Restrained by neither government nor religion, they became free-wheeling landeaters. While New Englanders of 1750 explored the eternal mysteries of sin and redemption, Virginians were exploring Kentucky.

Established by law in Virginia (as in all the Southern colonies), the Church of England was more a social institution than a religious one, inspiring neither intellectual nor emotional commitment. Sunday was a festive occasion when, after a perfunctory service, the gentry gathered to swap horses and land. The clergy were uninfluential, ill paid, and often absent. When the Revolution came, there were only sixty or seventy Anglican ministers in the entire colony; most parishes were simply vacant. Dissenting churches had largely filled the void: Presbyterians were the most numerous; Baptists and Methodists were winning converts in the backwoods. Most dissenters, however, came from the lower economic orders. The gentry adhered to the establishment because it was one of the pillars of their authority.

The parish was both religious congregation and subdivision of a county. It was ruled by the vestry, a self-appointed group of gentlemen who appointed and paid the minister, prescribed rules for the church, and provided such social services as the care of widows and orphans. The county court handled all other local government. Made up of justices of the peace appointed by the governor, the court met four times a year. In addition to judicial functions it maintained roads, appropriated funds for the poor, and licensed taverns. Staffed by the more prominent planters in each locality, the vestries and the county courts were the base on which the gentry dominated the social and political life of Virginia.

Washington's Virginia was a rural society with few opportunities for getting ahead. By the time of his birth in 1732, the best lands east of the mountains were taken. Those who would improve their lot had to move west. Towns were few and tiny. Williamsburg, the seat of an empire that extended as far as the Great Lakes, had no more than fifty houses. Norfolk was a busy seaport, but Alexandria and Richmond were just getting started when the Revolution began. Virginia's magnificent river system discouraged the growth of cities. Nearly every planter had access to water and maintained his own contacts with agents in London or Glasgow. Few required the services of city merchants.

Tobacco had been the principal staple of Virginia since the beginning of the colony, though planters were abandoning its culture by the time of the Revolution. Declining price was the principal reason. Many planters, especially in the northern part of the colony, found wheat more profitable. But that changeover was still in the future when Washington was born. Tobacco was king in 1732, and times were good. Law, order, stability — that was the social atmosphere in which the young Washington grew.

The Making of a Gentleman

The Washingtons could trace their English lineage back several hundred years, but they were not among the inner core of Virginia elite. Augustine Washington was a man of modest fortune, built largely by himself. He possessed two plantations in Virginia's Northern Neck and a share in Lord Fairfax's iron furnace. He was a member of the vestry, a justice of the peace, and sheriff of Westmoreland County. His second wife, Mary Ball, whom he married in 1730, came of very prominent family. He had three children by his first wife; George, born in 1732, was the first of six more.

We know little of George Washington's early life. He received some schooling, probably in Fredericksburg, his mother's home. His surviving notebooks indicate some elementary Latin and mathematics, with a sprinkling of English literature. The training was not intense — he had difficulty with words all his life — but it was characteristic of his society. He also learned how to survey lands, probably an apprenticeship for a career. As a younger son, he would not expect to inherit much of his father's estate.

His father died when George was eleven, leaving an estate of ten thousand acres and fifty slaves. Most went to George's older half-brothers, Lawrence and Augustine. Lawrence had been schooled in England and served for a time as a captain in the British army. During the War of the Austrian Succession he participated in a famous raid on the Spanish Main and named his plantation Mount Vernon, after his commander. He married the daughter of Colonel William Fairfax. Young George, too, became part of the Fairfax circle when he went to live with his brother.

Lord Fairfax (the only English aristocrat who made a home in Virginia) had inherited title to the Northern Neck, the stretch of fertile land between the Potomac River and the Rappahannock. He sold off most of this imperial domain, with his sales agents (Carters, Lees, and Fitzhughs) taking sizable portions for themselves. Augustine Washington shared a business venture or two with Lord Fairfax, Lawrence married into the family, and young George became best friends with the peer's grandson, George William Fairfax. In Virginia such contacts were the way to wealth.

Washington prospered as a surveyor and sank every spare penny into land. By 1750 he possessed two thousand acres of fertile bottom lands in the Shenandoah Valley. When Lawrence died of tuberculosis in 1752, his widow leased Mount Vernon to George (he inherited it when she died). His brother's death also left vacant the post of militia adjutant for the Northern Neck. Applying for the job, George secured it with the rank of major. Valuable contacts and good fortune had come his way; Washington had the good sense to make use of both. By the time that he was twenty-one, he had power, wealth, and office. The imperial contest between Britain and France opened the way to immortality.

The Making of a Soldier

The peace that came to Europe in 1748 brought little more than an armed truce to North America. Both British and French expected the contest to resume. Anyone looking at the map could see the most likely point of conflict — the forks of the Ohio. France had a firm hold on the St. Lawrence Valley and the Great Lakes; Britain owned the Atlantic seaboard. Both had vague claims to the interior of the continent south of the lakes, though the Indians were the true possessors. The French had outposts along the Mississippi River, but the Ohio was a diplomatic no man's land. Whoever held the great meeting place, where the Allegheny River joined the Monongahela, controlled the Northwest.

Virginians felt that the territory in dispute belonged to them under the grant that had established their colony. Their boundaries extended to the South Sea [Pacific Ocean], one Virginian told London authorities in 1750, and even included "the island of California." The swords of Virginians were the cutting edge of the British empire.

In 1749 a consortium of North Neck planters (Lawrence Washington among them) formed the Ohio Company and applied to the king for a grant of land in the West. The company offered to transport settlers into the Ohio Valley at its own expense, reaping its return from the sale of lands. Seeing the strategic value of such settlements, the king granted the company a tract of 200,000 acres along the Ohio River below the forks. A year later the company hired Christopher Gist, an Indian trader, to cut a path from Cumberland, Maryland, on the upper Potomac, to the Monongahela River.

The French, too, could read a map; by 1752 they had a chain of forts from Presque Isle on Lake Erie to the Allegheny River. Indians alerted Virginians to the French advance, and in the fall of 1753 Governor Dinwiddie sent Washington to investigate. In company with Gist, several Indian scouts, and interpreters, Washington journeyed north to the French forts. The French commander was openly aggressive. Louisiana (meaning the entire Mississippi watershed), he told Washington, was French. "It was their absolute design to take possession of the Ohio," Washington quoted him, "and by God they would do it." Realizing the threat to Virginia's interests, Washington and Gist hurried home overland across Pennsylvania. Winter snows closed in, Indians chased them, and starvation threatened until they were rescued by a wilderness pioneer, who furnished them with horses. They were in Williamsburg by January 1754, reporting their story to the governor.

Governor Dinwiddie saw the propaganda value in Washington's report and ordered it printed at public expense. It brought his name to the public eye. Even King George read it with interest. The governor ordered the construction of a fort at the forks of the Ohio and sent a detachment of 150 militia to protect the builders. Washington, promoted to lieutenant colonel, was second in command. By the time that the expedition got under way, the colonel died; Washington, at age twenty-two, found himself in command.

Before he had proceeded far along the trail, Washington learned that the French had occupied the forks of the Ohio. They had constructed a fort of their own, naming it after the governor of Canada, Duquesne. He continued anyway, though he had no orders to do so, pausing only to construct a wilderness palisade, which he named Fort Necessity, along the Monongahela. He proceeded only a few miles further when Gist's Indian scouts informed him that the French had sent out a raiding party. Never doubting that he had come to fight, Washington surrounded them at night, killed ten, and captured twenty. A few escaped to sound the alarm. Outnumbered, Washington retired to Fort Necessity, pursued by the French, who forced him to surrender. When Washington signed a confession that he had "assassinated" the French patrol, the French allowed his tiny army to return to Virginia. The encounter was the beginning of a new imperial conflict. The young soldier clearly had courage; time would bring him prudence.

Washington's defeat convinced Virginians that they could not carry the imperial conflict alone. They begged for help, and in 1755 Britain sent over General Edward Braddock with two regiments of regulars. When the governor placed the Virginia militia under British officers, Washington resigned his commission. But he did agree to accompany Braddock as an unranked aide-de-camp. The army, numbering about two thousand, started up hill from Fort Cumberland in May 1755. After weeks of struggling along the crude Ohio Company road, they realized that the pace was too slow; the French at Fort Duquesne were certain to be alerted and prepared. At Washington's suggestion Braddock divided his army when he came into the valley of the Monongahela. Infantry proceeded ahead with light gear, leaving the supply wagons and artillery to proceed as best they could.

Thereafter the pace quickened. By July the army was eighteen miles from Fort Duquesne, with no sign of the French. Then disaster struck. Alerted by Indians, the French sent out a reconnaissance force. Running headlong into Braddock's army, it quickly scattered into the woods, occupying a succession of ravines along the trail. From this cover the French poured a deadly fire into Braddock's column, killing the British commander in the first volley. Leaderless, the British fled in disorder, while Washington and the Virginians held the rear. The commander of the baggage train, instead of rallying the army, also panicked. Abandoning guns and wagons, the British raced for Cumberland; within a month they were in Philadelphia. Only Washington emerged from the debacle with enhanced reputation. His Virginians had fought valiantly. He himself had two horses shot from under him and took eight bullet holes in his clothing. Governor Dinwiddie offered him the rank of colonel and command of all Virginia forces. He returned to active duty in August 1755 at the age of twenty-three.

The next two years were frustrating ones for the young commander. French victories from Lake Champlain to the Ohio had encouraged the Indians, and the entire frontier blazed into war. The assembly, against Washington's better judgment, insisted on maintaining a string of frontier forts to protect the colony. The outposts immobilized his army and prevented him from taking the offensive. Bored by garrison duty, the militia simply deserted. Washington spent most of his time begging for arms and supplies.

He managed, however, to find time for politics. He stood for a seat in the House of Burgesses in 1757 but failed when he declined to treat the voters as custom demanded. The following year he tried again, with friends managing the campaign while he remained on military duty. The 391 voters of Frederick County managed to consume 28 gallons of rum, 50 gallons of rum punch, 34 gallons of wine, 46 gallons of beer, and 2 gallons of hard cider. The victory cost Washington forty pounds.

He also found time for courtship. His choice of a bride was a shrewd one, as much the result of calculation, one suspects, as emotion. Martha Dandridge Custis was a young widow of twenty-seven who had inherited, through family and marriage, an estate of twenty-three thousand pounds. Her home was on the main route from Williamsburg to the north. Washington stopped there for the night on a visit to the capital in the spring of 1758. Stopping again on his return, he emerged with a promise to marry. For the young widow it was an equally good bargain. He was a military hero with advancing fortune. She also had two children in need of a father. They were the only children the pair ever had.

That autumn Washington embarked on a new military expedition. The British at last had regained the offensive. A new army, under the command of General John Forbes, gathered in Philadelphia for the recovery of the Ohio. Washington's regiment was assigned to help. Forbes decided to carve a new road across Pennsylvania to the Ohio, building supply bases as he went. Philadelphians, envious of Virginia's role in the West, were delighted; and Benjamin Franklin himself contracted to supply Forbes with wagons. Washington was dismayed, arguing that road construction would cause unnecessary delays and give the French time to prepare.

He was right. The task consumed the entire summer and fall of 1758. Washington grumbled and complained every inch of the way. In mid-November, with yet another ridge to cross, Forbes sent ahead a detachment of light infantry under Colonel Henry Bouquet, with Washington as second in command. Overcoming a French ambush, they reached the fort on November 25. The French blew up their works and fled. Bouquet restored the palisade, renaming it Fort Pitt. The war in the West was over; the frontier was pacified. Washington resigned from the army.

He learned a good deal from Forbes — how to move and supply a large body of men, to prevent disease, and to keep up morale. But he was also dismayed with army life. Regular officers, of whatever rank, considered themselves superior to the militia. Washington never forgave the snubs he received. Nor was there much future in becoming a regular, for promotion in the British army was by purchase or favor. Washington would not sacrifice honor for preferment; returning to Mount Vernon, he married Martha and took up the routine of a Virginia planter.

The Making of a Rebel

After a brief tour in the House of Burgesses during the French and Indian War, Washington did not serve in the assembly again for some years. He concentrated on managing his vast estate and learning the art of farming; but, as the Revolution approached, he returned to politics. He lacked Patrick Henry's gift for public speaking and Jefferson's flair with a pen. He was conservative by nature, but that was also part of his appeal. The assembly included him on the delegation to the First Continental Congress in part to balance the flamboyant Henry.

That a man with so much to lose would join a rebellion at all is a marvel. Some imperial regulations, it must be said, cost him money. The royal proclamation of 1763, prohibiting settlement west of the Appalachians, hurt the value of his western lands. British navigation acts restricted the market for tobacco and contributed to its price decline. And Washington, like other Virginians, felt trapped in the web of credit woven by British merchants. Yet none of these things was grievous enough to risk his life and fortune. His motives were strictly political. The Virginia squirarchy was accustomed to running its own affairs, from plantation to county court to colonial assembly. Governors survived only by the judicious use of patronage and by catering to Virginians' land hunger. Parliament's interference upset this cozy relationship. If Parliament could destroy the government of Massachusetts (Virginians reasoned in 1774), no colony was safe: it was time to stand together. Besides, no Virginian could bear to see others carrying the torch.

The Second Continental Congress opened after the battles of Lexington and Concord. Washington pointedly wore his militia uniform, the buff and blue of the Fairfax County Volunteers. It was a sufficient hint for John Adams, who wanted someone from outside New England to take command of the army. Besides, Washington's immense wealth would silence British talk of a "rabble in arms." On June 17, 1775, Washington accepted the post of commander in chief. He refused any pay for his services but agreed to accept reimbursement for his expenses. Except for two brief visits to Mount Vernon, he would spend the next eight years in the field.

Commander in Chief

Washington had not seen military service for fifteen years, nor had he ever commanded in battle. When he took over the army outside Boston, he had much to learn — his soldiers even more so. They were less an army than a mob of untrained farmers. Most regiments elected their own officers and seldom obeyed orders. Unaccustomed to seeing an army function like a town meeting, Washington was aghast. Through the winter he begged Congress to authorize more regulars, but with little success. He encircled Boston with siege fortifications, but it was dull work. His army slowly disintegrated, as militia, signed up for six months' duty, simply went home when their enlistment expired. By midwinter his army of twenty thousand had dwindled to five thousand. At times the besieged outnumbered the siegers. Powder was so low that he had to prohibit shooting.

In February 1776 General Henry Knox arrived with cannon taken from Fort Ticonderoga on Lake Champlain. Washington placed the pieces on Dorchester Heights, where they could menace both city and harbor. Finding their position untenable, the British decided to leave Boston; they sailed on March 17. Washington had his first victory without risking battle. The siege had been tedious, but he had learned much about the art of command. Whether it was enough to meet the British in the open field remained to be seen.

There was no doubt where the British were headed. New York had the

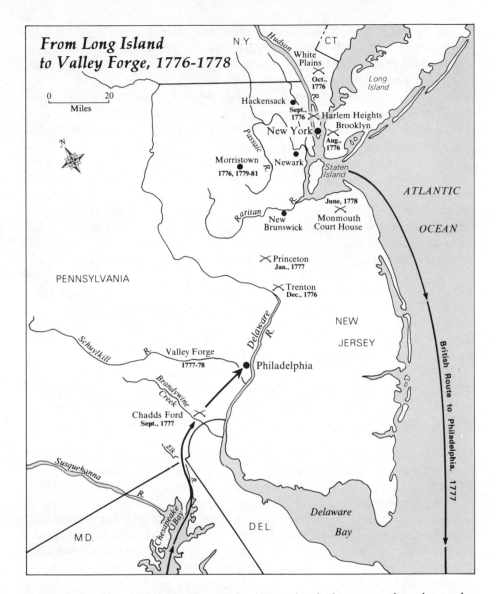

From Long Island to Valley Forge, 1776-1778

finest harbor on the seacoast and a hinterland that was thought to be pro-British. Washington sent his regiments south the day that the British left Boston, and a few days later he moved on himself.

Sir William Howe, who had replaced General Gage during the winter, paused in Halifax, Nova Scotia, to receive reinforcements and then sailed for New York. In late August 1776 he severely whipped Washington's army in the Battle of Long Island, and then chased it out of Manhattan. When Washington crossed to the New Jersey side of the Hudson River, Lord Cornwallis, Howe's chief lieutenant, set out after him. Unwilling to risk another battle, Washington fled for the Delaware River and the security of Pennsylvania. He made it but with little save honor. Cornwallis had New Jersey, and from Trenton, where he posted a garrison, he could descend on Philadelphia the following year. All fronts secure, the British went into winter quarters. It was Christmas 1776.

Washington was in trouble. In a succession of disasters he had lost New York and New Jersey; he had seen the new republic nearly split in two. His army had dwindled to a few thousand, and most of those were due to go home at the end of the year.

With Christmas came hope. Pennsylvania militia, alarmed by the sudden threat to their homes, drifted into camp. The village of Trenton, guarded by a thousand German mercenaries, was isolated and vulnerable. Deciding to attack, Washington crossed the river under cover of night and pounced on Trenton at dawn on Christmas Day. After a brief skirmish the Germans surrendered, though a few escaped to sound the alarm. When Cornwallis came thundering out of New York, Washington slipped around him and burned the British supply base at Princeton. He then went into winter quarters in the hills of northern New Jersey. The British abandoned their advance bases and retired to New York. In a brilliant campaign of two weeks, Washington had recovered nearly all that he had lost in the autumn. His army was not yet able to meet the British in the open, but he had learned to use it in other ways.

Avoiding treacherous New Jersey, the British went by ship to Philadelphia in the summer of 1777. Finding the Delaware River blocked by sunken vessels, they sailed into Chesapeake Bay, coming upon the city from the south. Washington met them at the Brandywine River, but Cornwallis outflanked him and rolled his army backward. Howe occupied Philadelphia, Congress fled to York, Pennsylvania, and Washington took up quarters at Valley Forge. In October he raided the outpost at Germantown, in an effort to duplicate his Trenton escapade, but his troops panicked in the morning fog and fled from a near victory.

That winter at Valley Forge was the worst yet. While his troops suffered in the cold, Washington battled a political assault from Congress. Pure republicans like Samuel Adams never really trusted Washington; too often in the past had republics succumbed to the rule of warriors. Thus, on the eve of the New York campaign, Congress created a civilian Board of War to oversee the army. In the fall of 1777 it made General Horatio Gates, hero of Saratoga, chairman of the board. Congressmen who complained that Washington had yet to win a major battle looked to Gates for hope. As chairman, he was technically Washington's superior.

The complaints of foreign officers, given commissions by Franklin and Silas Deane, added to Washington's troubles. He could not give them the commands that they desired without alienating American officers. Disappointed in their expectations, the foreigners complained to Congress, affording new ammunition to Washington's critics.

Not all of the European volunteers caused trouble, however. The French

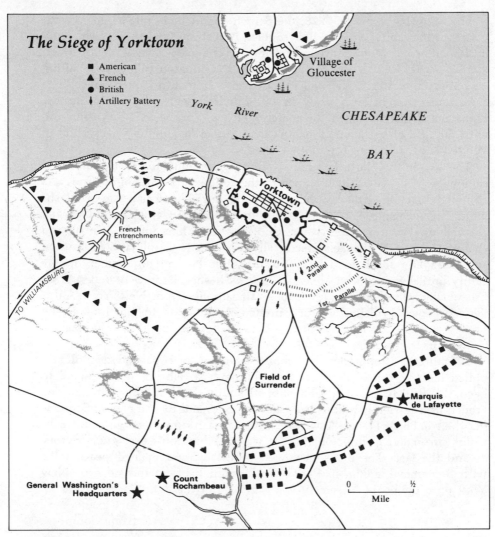

The Siege of Yorktown

- ■ American
- ▲ French
- ● British
- ↓ Artillery Battery

Village of Gloucester

York River

CHESAPEAKE

BAY

Yorktown

French Entrenchments

2nd Parallel

1st Parallel

TO WILLIAMSBURG

Field of Surrender

Marquis de Lafayette

General Washington's Headquarters

Count Rochambeau

0   ½

Mile

Washington conducted the siege in the European fashion. He had his men dig trenches, called parallels, angling obliquely toward the British positions until they were close enough to mount an infantry attack.

aristocrat Lafayette, age twenty-two, arrived early in the war and was a trusted lieutenant. The Pole Kosciusko was a superb engineer; the German De Kalb a fine field commander. During the winter of 1777 Baron von Steuben appeared at Valley Forge to offer his services. Washington put him in charge of training. He taught the army marching orders, how to deploy from column to line of battle, the musket drill, and the use of the bayonet. Never again would Washington's army meet defeat in the open field.

The following summer, 1778, the British abandoned Philadelphia. Occupation of the capital city had not troubled Americans, and the British found it difficult to defend. Sir Henry Clinton, the new British commander, started across New Jersey for New York. Washington followed, awaiting an opportunity for attack, and found it at Monmouth Court House. The two armies fought to a draw in one-hundred-degree heat. During the night the British resumed the march to New York, leaving Washington with the field of battle and a technical victory. Washington set up shop in White Plains, preparing for another siege.

The war in the North became a waiting game, punctuated by raids and espionage, while the British turned to the conquest of the South. Congress assumed direction of the Southern campaign, an oblique criticism of Washington's generalship. Lord Cornwallis subdued South Carolina and Georgia, chewed up Horatio Gates when Congress sent him into the area, and chased General Nathanael Greene all over North Carolina. Washington sent Lafayette south to defend Virginia, but he had no further opportunity until a French fleet appeared in the Chesapeake in September 1781. Cornwallis retired to Yorktown to await supplies from New York. Lafayette occupied Williamsburg and invited Washington to join him. If the French could gain naval control of the Chesapeake, they might have Cornwallis trapped.

Washington's long apprenticeship at war began to pay off. He silently pulled his men out of their battlements, made a feint at Staten Island to keep the British guessing, and slipped south through Philadelphia. The French fleet ferried him down Chesapeake Bay, and by the end of September the combined Franco-American force had Yorktown surrounded. Cornwallis surrendered on October 19. It was Washington's first great victory — and the last. The British changed ministries and opened peace talks with Benjamin Franklin in Paris. Washington kept up the siege of New York until the peace agreement was signed, but the fighting was over.

Cincinnatus

Dismantling Washington's army was more of a trial than creating it. After the fighting died down, the army encircling New York had ample time to contemplate its troubles. And its grievances were real enough. Pay was meager; clothing, blankets, tents, and shoes were chronically in short supply. By 1780 the paper money issued by Congress was nearly worthless, good only for plugging holes in tents. That winter mutinies erupted here and there; batallions deserted en masse. Then on New Year's Day the entire Pennsylvania line packed up its baggage and marched on Philadelphia to present its grievances to the state assembly. The assembly surrendered to all demands, including back pay and special clothing allotments.

A few weeks later New Jersey troops mutinied and presented a shopping list of their own. Washington realized that unless the movement was quelled, the entire army would become uncontrollable. Surrounding the mutinous soldiers with Continental regulars, he forced them to surrender. He then rounded up twelve ringleaders and forced them to execute two of their number. That ended the mutinies.

Attention thereafter centered on the demands of officers, who wanted lifetime pensions of half-pay. Bankrupt itself, Congress could offer only land grants. The generals rejected that, and some began meeting secretly to discuss the possibility of using force. In the early weeks of 1783, as rumors of the Anglo-American peace agreement filtered across the Atlantic, a series of anonymous papers circulated through army headquarters at Newburgh, New York. Washington suspected Horatio Gates of being the author, but that was only a guess. The addresses summarized the army's grievances and suggested the possibility of replacing Congress with more effective government.

The threat forced Washington to act. Though he sympathized with the officers' demands, he could not bear the thought of military rule. Summoning all commissioned officers to a meeting, which he addressed himself, he offered to present their demands to Congress in person. Then, as he read a letter from several congressmen expressing sympathy for the army, he put on glasses, saying: "Gentlemen, you will permit me to put on my spectacles, for I have not only grown gray, but almost blind, in the service of my country." Perhaps overdone, the gesture was nevertheless effective: the officers voted to leave their problems in his hands. Congress ultimately granted officers full-pay pensions for five years; enlisted men got half-pay for four months. By then the army had disbanded, or rather disintegrated, as everyone simply went home.

To remain in contact, a number of officers formed the Society of the Cincinnati in May 1783. Washington agreed to serve as president, though he doubtless would have declined had he anticipated the public furor. The purpose of the society was social, to keep up wartime friendships; but purist republicans suspected it of political designs, and several state legislatures passed resolutions denouncing it. The society met annually for several years and then faded from view.

Presidency of the Cincinnati was Washington's only public commitment after the war. He sincerely wished to lay aside his sword and pick up the plowshare, like his Roman model Cincinnatus. He wished only to rest, he told a friend with a rare quote from the Bible, "under my own Vine and my own Fig-Tree, free from the bustle of a camp and the intrigues of a court."

There were no fig trees at Mount Vernon, nor much of anything else after eight years of neglect. The house was in disrepair; fields were worn out. Restoration of the house was complicated by a constant stream of visitors. Every traveler in the area stopped there for the night, taking advantage of the traditional hospitality of Virginia planters. One night after Washington and several guests had gone to bed, they were aroused by the French sculptor Houdon, who, with an entourage of assistants, had come to do a bust of him. The sitting lasted several weeks during which carpenters put new shingles on the roof, window blinds were installed, and his nephew got married.

Restoring his farmland, on the other hand, was pure joy. He had always been a progressive farmer; he now began to experiment in earnest. Tobacco, he knew, was the curse of Virginia; by 1785 he abandoned it altogether. Wheat and other cereal grains, along with livestock, graced the fields of Mount Vernon. Jefferson sent him seeds from Europe to try in the Virginia clime, and he experimented with cabbages and buckwheat, meticulously recording the results in his diary.

Foreign admirers intruded even on his farming. The king of Spain sent him a prize jackass for breeding, which Washington appropriately named Royal Gift. The donkey was welcome but caused Washington no end of trouble. It arrived in Philadelphia (possibly the only port with which the king was acquainted), and a special messenger had to be sent to pick it up. A cascade of difficulties attended the overseer's slow march home. Yet the earthy humor of the situation appealed to Washington, especially when the donkey proved a rather sluggish stud. Washington told a friend: "At present, tho' young, he follows what one may suppose to be the example of his late Royal Master, who cannot . . . perform seldomer or with more majestic solemnity than he does. However, I have hopes that when he becomes a little better acquainted with republican enjoyments, he will amend his manners and fall into our republican custom of doing business."

With Mount Vernon once again tidy and productive, Washington took up other interests. He owned vast tracts of land in the Ohio Valley, partly the result of prewar purchases but most of it the reward for military service. In 1784 he journeyed to the Ohio Valley to expel squatters and to investigate the possibility of a water route across the mountains. The headwaters of the Potomac were only a few miles from the Monongahela River system, and Virginia was constructing a road between the two valleys. A canal through the mountains, Washington felt, would be a useful tie between East and West. Greater East-West trade would also undermine separatist movements in Kentucky and Tennessee and further strengthen the Union. To clear that river and build canals around the falls, Virginia chartered the Potomac Company in 1785. Agreeing to serve as the company's president, Washington used his prestige to secure private subscriptions and public grants from Virginia and Maryland. His dream of a western waterway, however, did not become reality until a quarter of century after his death.

The Potomac Company dragged him back into politics. Young James Madison, whose goal in life was to strengthen the powers of the central government, saw in the Potomac enterprise a means of opening an inter-state discussion of trade and commerce. Aware of Washington's mutual interest in the Potomac and the Union, he kept the retired hero informed of all political currents in the assembly. Among his projects were amendments to the Articles of Confederation that would give Congress power to regulate trade and impose taxes.

In 1785, while the Potomac Company was under discussion, the assemblies of Virginia and Maryland named commissioners to discuss mutual interests in trade and navigation. Governor Patrick Henry, who was opposed to Madison's schemes, failed to inform the Virginia delegates of the meeting, leaving the Marylanders sitting expectantly in Alexandria. Madison's friends learned of the trick, however, and Washington saved the day by inviting both the disgruntled Marylanders and the embarrassed Virginians out to Mount Vernon. From that meeting came the suggestion of a broader commercial convention, including all the states, at Annapolis in 1786. The Annapolis meeting, in turn, proposed the Philadelphia convention that drafted a new Federal Constitution in the summer of 1787.

At Madison's urging, Washington came out of retirement to attend the Philadelphia convention, served as its presiding officer, and lent his personal prestige to the document that it created. He was the natural choice for president of the new government that assembled in New York in the spring of 1789. Duty and honor obliged him to accept.

The Making of the Presidency

A revolution naturally begets heroes. It is a time when critical decisions are made, when power changes hands, when opportunity beckons. Washington's life spanned some most exciting years — years of imperial struggle, of revolution, of nation building — and at every crucial moment he seemed to be present. Yet he was not simply the accidental product of his times; he was an ambitious man who consciously pursued fame and fortune. When only twenty-one he barraged the colonial governor with letters asking for a military appointment, a post that placed him center stage in the imperial drama. Ambition directed him to wear his military uniform to the Second Continental Congress as a pointed reminder of his earlier service. Nor was his ambition misplaced, for whatever he did, he did well.

Yet there do seem to be two phases to Washington's public career. Ambition vanished after the Revolution. No longer was there any need to push himself to the fore. His public role was more passive, more a response to the needs of others. He filled the new nation's need for a symbol, the people's need for an idol. And for some he filled a political need. Madison used him in promoting the movement for federal reform. Federalists used him for securing ratification of the Constitution, for winning respect for the new government and, later, for keeping themselves in office. That, unhappily, was Washington's downfall, for when he became the creature of party, he also fell subject to the first public criticism of his life. And he proved thin-skinned, as well he might, after all the years of adulation.

As president, Washington relied heavily on the advice of others. James Madison was his closest confidant in the early years, Alexander Hamilton thereafter. Yet his administration is not simply the story of an aged hero manipulated by men younger, more clever, and more ambitious than he. Nor was his administration simply the story of the birth of parties, emerging from the clash of interests and ideas between Jefferson and Madison, on the one hand, and Hamilton on the other. Washington was his own man; he made all the key decisions. The administration, moreover, reflected his character and personality despite the smoke of party battle. And his contributions to the developing governmental system were substantial.

At the beginning he was principally concerned that the new government be respected. The Confederation Congress, insolvent, homeless, and powerless, had been the object of national ridicule. Seldom in its late years could it even raise a quorum. Aspiring politicians avoided it, preferring instead service in the state assemblies. The Constitution gave the new government adequate powers; it was up to Washington to turn the blueprint into a working model.

His character and personality were well suited to the task. Tall and well proportioned, a superb horseman, he commanded instant respect. He was reserved by nature (a trait accentuated by deafness) and moved with grace and dignity. He was a gentleman in taste and manners; there was nothing "common" in anything he did. Yet native sense governed his actions. On the eve of his inauguration the Senate engaged itself in a lengthy and ludicrous debate on what title to address him, finally suggesting "His Elective Highness." Washington, who was quite content with the title of president of the United States, was embarrassed by the whole affair.

His inaugural costume symbolized his determination to blend dignity with republican simplicity. He wore a plain suit of American manufacture but adorned it with a European-style dress sword. Unwilling and unable to return all social calls, he established a system of twice-weekly levees, formal parties to which congressmen and government officials were invited in alphabetical rotation. Purist republicans, from Sam Adams to Jefferson, objected to the pomp, but the government earned popular respect. Prominent men in every state, many of whom had shunned national office, accepted Washington's pleas for service. Though occasionally divided in opinion, the president's cabinet boasted two of the best minds of the day, Jefferson and Hamilton. The Federal Supreme Court was a galaxy of legal talent, from New York's John Jay to North Carolina's James Iredell. By the end of Washington's first term the federal machine was running smoothly. Above all, the first president had wanted a dignified, orderly, stable government, managed by the ablest men available, and respected both at home and abroad — and he achieved it.

Another contribution, of similar vein, was the establishment of governmental precedents. The Constitution was but a scant outline of government. The decision-making machinery had to be fashioned day by day. Washington had the wit to surround himself with able men and the wisdom to seek their advice, a practice that led to the concept of a president's cabinet. The Constitution did not authorize a cabinet; indeed, it seemed to envision the Senate as an advisory body, like the colonial Governor's Council. On foreign policy it specifically empowered the Senate to "advise and consent," a phrase that implied more than the mere acceptance or rejection of treaties. Washington tried to live up to this obligation, but he quickly found that the Senate was too unwieldly a body for intimate advice.

Congress created the three executive departments of State, Treasury, and War, but it was Washington who first thought of using the department heads as a body of advisers. The first occasion, apparently, was in the spring of 1791 when Congress chartered the Bank of the United States to aid the treasury in managing the national debt. Troubled by Madison's argument in the House of Representatives that Congress lacked the power to establish such an institution, Washington considered vetoing the bill. Before he did so, however, he asked the department heads, as well as Attorney General Edmund Randolph, to give their opinions on the matter in writing. Jefferson and Randolph sided with Madison, but Washington accepted Hamilton's argument that the bank was within the "implied powers" of Congress and signed it into law.

Problems of neutrality, posed by the outbreak of war in Europe, forced Washington to refine the process of decision making. Toward the end of 1792 the department heads began meeting as a group to pool ideas. There were early differences of opinion. Jefferson felt that American neutrality was in fact a favor to Britain, who might well expect the United States to side with its old ally, France. He wanted to extract concessions from the British, a trade agreement, for instance, in exchange for American neutrality. Hamilton replied that the treaty of alliance with France, negotiated by Franklin in 1778, was no longer in effect. The overthrow of the French monarchy, said he, negated all previous agreements. Thus, the United States was free to pursue its own interests, including an understanding with the British. Washington blended the two views, and the proclamation that he issued in April 1793 was the product of collective decision making. It pledged the nation to impartial conduct (while recognizing the validity of Franklin's treaty), and it prohibited Americans from warlike actions against either European power. Cabinet meetings became less frequent thereafter, probably because of the increasing enmity between Jefferson and Hamilton, but the precedent was well established.

In putting the republic on a stable course and establishing administrative precedents that would last into the twentieth century, Washington had considerable help. Among the group of men who created the federal government was a wealth of talent. Reordering the government's finances and establishing its credit, for instance, was the achievement of Treasury Secretary Alexander Hamilton. But the maintenance of neutrality in a divided world was Washington's contribution, and it was the more a personal triumph because his best advisers were bitterly divided. No one wished to join the European war, but Hamiltonian Federalists sympathized with the British while Jeffersonian Republicans sided with the French. For some time the president was the only true neutral in government. The French eventually alienated him with their heavy-handed diplomacy, and he feared the import of their subversive ideas. But to the end of his term in office he avoided a fight with either European power — and that was more than any of his successors could boast until the European war ended in 1815.

Neutrality, moreover, brought enormous benefits. Jay's Treaty, negotiated with Britain in 1794, was much criticized by Jeffersonians for not spelling out America's neutral rights. But it ushered in a decade of Anglo-American friendship, during which the West Indies were unofficially opened to American vessels. The resulting boom in trade brought domestic prosperity and a treasury surplus.

Despite its substantial achievements, Washington's presidency was not all profit and glory. Washington lacked the common touch that might have endeared him to the middle American. Urban mechanics and hinterland farmers flocked to the opposition Republican party. In western Pennsylvania the administration's tax policies even provoked open rebellion. The president himself aged rapidly in office. He narrowed the circle of his advisers and grew increasingly intolerant of criticism. Even though his use of federal patronage helped create the Federalist party, he never understood the function of political parties. Confusing criticism with disloyalty, he suspected his opponents of being agents of foreign subversion.

In his Farewell Address of September 1796, announcing to the nation his decision to retire, the president was chiefly concerned with the threat to national unity posed by political divisions. He warned people against forming parties that supported one European nation or another. It was sound advice, even if he did not see that he himself had become a party president. Even then, Federalists were scheming ways of using his name to keep themselves in power another four years.

Such flaws, however, were not obvious to all. The party press criticized him openly, but the vast majority of Americans retained their respect. He was not a loved man, but he was venerated. And his death in 1799 was a signal for national mourning. "First in war, first in peace, and first in the hearts of his countrymen," eulogized his old cavalry commander, Light Horse Harry Lee, and few could disagree.

Even in death, sad to say, he was subject to the use of others. Gilbert Stuart began the process when he returned from England late in Washington's presidency to paint his portrait. Having outspent himself in Europe, Stuart hoped to recoup his fortune by selling copies of the portrait. So many copies were made by himself and his students that it is impossible, even today, to tell which is the original. The famous bust, which has adorned grade-school classrooms for almost two centuries, converted the man into a monument — stern, fatherly, benign, but scarcely human.

There was profit also to be made in Washington's biography. The first to spot this opportunity was a Virginia-born peddler of medical nostrums, Mason Locke Weems. Parson Weems (he was also a one-time minister) collected anecdotes concerning Washington in his travels through Virginia, trying them out on rural audiences. A collection of such stories, he informed a Philadelphia publisher, would "sell like flax seed at a quarter of a dollar." Washington's death enhanced the market, and Weems's eighty-page volume, entitled *The Life of George Washington the Great*, appeared a year later. In this and subsequent editions Weems fabricated all the familiar Washington stories, beginning with the hatchet and the cherry tree. Weems converted the monument into a myth, a national saint, charged with virtue, distilled of humanity.

Yet, Washington has survived the misuses of posterity, just as he survived the abuses of parties in his lifetime. Recent scholars have stabbed through the crust of mythology and recovered the inner man. We may know more about Washington today than his contemporaries did. And what we know begets only admiration. His flaws were human ones — a chilly reserve broken by flashes of temper, a rashness in youth, a narrow insensitivity in old age — but he was a man who lived by his code of honor and duty. In placing him first among their national heroes Americans have chosen well. No nation on earth can boast a better one.

SUGGESTIONS FOR FURTHER READING

Douglas Southall Freeman's *George Washington, A Biography* (7 vols., 1948–1957) is a modern classic. A detailed chronology of the era, it places the reader at Washington's side, seeing events as he saw them. James T. Flexner's biography (4 vols., 1965–1972) maintains the same leisurely pace, and the writing style is a bit more sprightly. For readers short of time, Flexner has condensed his study to a single volume, *Washington, the Indispensable Man* (1969). Many historians have tried to shake Washington off the pedestal on which American folklore (and Parson Weems) has placed him. The most recent of these is Forrest McDonald, *The Presidency of George Washington* (1974). McDonald argues that Washington as president was important only as a symbol; he had little impact on policy, either domestic or foreign.

4

The Swamp Fox: Francis Marion

Was the American Revolution a guerrilla war? Had that question been asked of George Washington, it would have drawn only a blank stare. The word had not even been coined in

Washington's day. *Guerrilla*, Spanish for "little war," described the civilian fighters who harassed Napoleon's armies in Spain a quarter of a century after the American Revolution. Guerrillas are irregulars, without training, uniforms, or insignia, who fight behind enemy lines or on the flanks of regular armies. Lacking professional training and often serving without pay, guerrillas are motivated chiefly by ideology or rage, or both.

Hit-and-run tactics are as old as warfare itself, but the guerrilla concept did not appear until ideological commitment became a part of war. In the dynastic conflicts of the eighteenth century, mercenaries engaged mercenaries, with each soldier committed to nothing more

Francis Marion (1732–1795). *The Swamp Fox was a master of irregular warfare, of secret marches and lightning raids. Yet, with a duality so characteristic of the American Revolution, this woodland chieftain conceived of himself, as this portrait reveals, as a regular and a gentleman.*

than a few grains of gold. The American Revolution, and more particularly the French Revolution, introduced the notion of fighting for a cause: independence and republican government. A committed citizenry, actively engaged in the outcome, is the prime requisite for guerrilla war. It provides manpower pool, supply base, and cover.

As guerrillas normally cannot match regular soldiers in discipline or firepower, they rely chiefly upon isolation and surprise. They avoid open or prolonged combat, preferring sudden assaults, sabotage, and terrorism. Knowing the landscape and its people intimately, they use both to conceal their activities and to achieve surprise.

To return to our question: the American Revolution was in some respects a guerrilla war. The much-maligned militia were essentially irregulars, farmers one day and soldiers the next. Though ill-trained and unreliable, the militia by sheer weight of numbers could shift the odds of battle, as they did in the Saratoga campaign of 1777. George Washington does not fit the common image of a guerrilla chieftain, but his methods were sometimes irregular. His most brilliant campaign — the Trenton-Princeton affair — was essentially a guerrilla-style hit-and-run raid. Such tactics, however, were unusual for him. Washington's constant aim was a skilled professional army, capable of meeting British mercenaries on their own terms. He engaged in open battle even when he lacked clear superiority of numbers (as at Long Island and the Brandywine); and wherever terrain permitted, as at Monmouth and Yorktown, he deployed his army in the European style.

At the same time Washington encouraged the use of guerrilla tactics by others, especially in the South where social conditions and terrain made such a war a necessity. The war in the Carolinas was from the beginning a war among partisan bands, Whigs versus Tories. Partisan leaders, ordinary farmers and shopkeepers before the war, acquired military skill as they fought. The deeds of Andrew Pickens, Thomas Sumter, Isaac Shelby, and John Sevier were the stuff of fireside tales for many years after the war. The best of them all may have been Francis Marion, whose fertile imagination and expert use of the South Carolina landscape earned him the nickname Swamp Fox.

The Making of a Soldier

Francis Marion was the same age as Washington, a prime forty-three when the Revolution broke out. He was descended from Huguenots, French Protestants who had fled the religious persecution of Louis XIV. In 1685 Marion's grandparents settled in the fertile, marshy valley of the Cooper River above Charleston. Some time around 1700 valley planters discovered that their lands were ideal for rice culture, and those who had the capital to build dams and levees prospered well. In the 1730s Eliza Pinckney, an enterprising young woman with West Indies connections, introduced indigo culture into the colony. An upland crop that matured in late autumn, indigo was the ideal complement for rice. By cultivating both, a planter could keep his labor force employed the year around. Indigo, moreover, was subsidized by the British government because the blue dye extracted from it was highly prized on the European continent. For the British it was an important source of foreign gold.

Profits bred capital; capital permitted expansion. By the time that the squabble between Britain and the colonies began, the South Carolina low country possessed a more highly capitalized agricultural system and higher concentration of slaveholding than any other mainland colony did. Wealth also made for conservative rebels. South Carolina was never in the forefront of the revolutionary agitation, although Charleston had an active chapter of the Sons of Liberty. Rutledges and Pinckneys, the political leaders of the low country, reluctantly drifted with the movement for independence, but many a lesser name sided openly or secretly with the mother country. Recent émigrés from the West Indies and some ethnic minorities, such as the Scots, also tended to be Loyalist. As a result, South Carolina's percentage of Loyalists and neutrals was higher than any other state's, except perhaps New York. The Revolution there had the makings of civil war.

The Huguenots, with strong memories of religious and political persecution, supported the revolutionary movement. In Charleston they were the backbone of Christopher Gadsden's Sons of Liberty. Francis Marion, too, was ready for revolution, though he lived the quieter life of country planter. He had bought a plantation of his own on the lower Santee River in 1773 and was a man of some note in his parish. When the South Carolina Provincial Congress met in early 1775, he was among the elected delegates.

In June 1775 the Continental Congress asked South Carolina to raise two regiments of infantry and one of cavalry. To command the regiments, the Provincial Congress chose Christopher Gadsden and William Moultrie. It then elected half a dozen captains, among them Marion, giving each of them authority to raise a company of men. Marion's only military experience was a brief stint in the militia during the Cherokee uprising of 1759; he had never witnessed the excitement and horror of battle. With commission in hand, Marion returned to his parish and within a few weeks had sixty volunteers ready to fight. His was the first organized rebel force in the state.

The management of such a band required a peculiar quality of leadership. American militia had little tolerance for discipline, little patience for training. Military regimen and unnecessary regulations only increased the rate of desertion. An officer led such men by example rather than through intimidation. He inspired respect and obedience by a combination of magnetism and simple psychology. Such traits are difficult to acquire; Marion came by them naturally.

With no enemy to fight in South Carolina, army life was dull during the winter of 1775–76. Marion's company was put to work repairing the forts that protected Charleston harbor. Bored by the inglorious work, his men deserted by the dozen. Even among officers discipline was lax. Around Christmastime one young lieutenant obtained leave to visit his sick father. Instead he went to a cockfight and lingered in the locality for two weeks. When Marion learned of his deception, his response was classic. On returning, the lieutenant entered a room in which Marion sat with other officers. Marion turned his back on the young man who began to stammer an apology for having been away so long. Wheeling, Marion took in the young officer with an indifferent gaze. "Aye, lieutenant, is that you?" he said. "Well never mind; there is no harm done. I never missed you."

The dreary labor paid off, however. In June 1776 a British squadron appeared off the Carolina coast. Aboard was an army fresh from Britain, commanded by Sir Henry Clinton. Arriving simultaneously to take command of the American forces in the South was General Charles Lee. The principal outpost defending the harbor was a fort that Colonel Moultrie's regiment was building on Sullivan's Island. Though they had been at work on the structure throughout the spring, it was only half finished when the British appeared. After viewing the flimsy structure, built of soft palmetto logs, General Lee advised that it be abandoned. The South Carolinians insisted on defending it, and Lee relented.

It took the British several weeks to disembark Clinton's army on an undefended island and to prepare for a naval bombardment of Sullivan's. On the morning of June 28 Commodore Peter Parker at last hoisted the signal to attack, and five British frigates moved into position. The bombardment continued all day with no noticeable effect on the American position. The palmetto logs absorbed the British shot like sponges, while the American fire, directed by Marion, was devastating. Two frigates were heavily damaged; one ran aground and was burned by its crew. The British hovered off the coast indecisively for three weeks; then Clinton's army reembarked on its transports and sailed to join Howe in New York. It would be almost three years before the war returned to South Carolina.

The Making of a Partisan

In September 1776 South Carolina turned her regiments over to the Continental army. Massachusetts-born Benjamin Lincoln replaced Lee as commander in the state. Marion, who fought at Sullivan's Island with the rank of major, was promoted to lieutenant colonel, and before long he was given a regiment of his own. The British retained a foothold in the South with a base at Savannah, Georgia, but they were too weak to pose a threat. Nor was Lincoln much stronger. For the next two years the armies maneuvered about in the watery lowlands between Charleston and Savannah without ever coming to blows.

In December 1779 Sir Henry Clinton, now overall British commander in America, returned to the South. He had become discouraged with the prospect of recovering the northern colonies. Those provinces had never fit well into the British imperial scheme anyway. Repossessing the South would enable the British to salvage something from the war, and rich, Loyalist-minded South Carolina was an inviting prospect.

Clinton landed at Savannah, and Georgia meekly succumbed to British rule. He then marched into South Carolina, and by April 1 the British stood at the gates of Charleston. Though well prepared for an attack by sea, Charleston had few landward defenses. Lincoln garrisoned it anyway, concentrating his entire army there. He took the precaution only of sending out the governor and council and the disabled. Among the latter was Marion, who had suffered a broken ankle leaping from a second-story window. A guest at dinner, Marion had found himself locked in by an overzealous host. Rather than spend the night carousing when there was work to be done, he decamped through a window. The injury reflected a commendable sense of duty, and it saved him from British capture.

On May 12, 1780, General Lincoln surrendered Charleston and with it his entire army. The loss of more than five thousand men was the largest American defeat of the war. It also eliminated virtually all organized resistance in South Carolina. General Clinton issued a proclamation demanding an oath of allegiance of all South Carolinians and making them liable for service in the British army. He then departed for New York, leaving General Cornwallis in charge of the mop-up. Encouraged by the British success, Loyalists eagerly took the oath, and Cornwallis organized them into fighting units. Others, hitherto neutral, discovered a new love for the crown.

In parts of South Carolina, however, Clinton's proclamation aroused antagonism. Discouraged Whigs might be willing to quit the war and return peacefully to their farms, but they resented being pressed into British service. One center of discontent was the Williamsburg district in the low country along the Peedee River above Georgetown. Williamsburg was populated by independent farmers, Scots-Irish for the most part, people with no love for the English. On learning of Clinton's proclamation, they organized militia companies of their own, elected officers, and waited for a summons to fight.

After the fall of Charleston, Congress named a new commander in the South, the hero of Saratoga and rival of Washington's, General Horatio Gates. Gates hurried south, gathering a force of Virginia and North Carolina militia as he went. In August he appeared outside the British outpost at Camden on the Wateree River. Marion, leading a band of refugees from

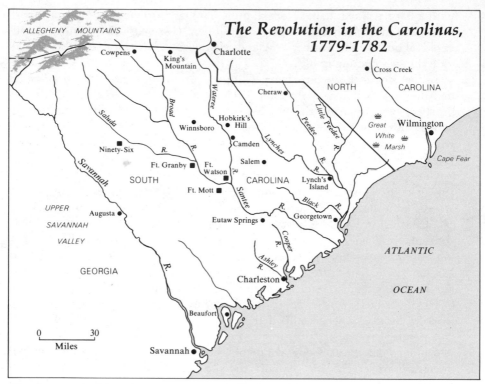

The Revolution in the Carolinas, 1779-1782

Charleston, rode to Gates's camp to offer his services. The general was not impressed. Marion's followers, wrote Gates's adjutant (a wealthy Maryland merchant), were chiefly

> *distinguished by small leather caps and the wretchedness of their attire. Their number did not exceed twenty men and boys, some white, some black, and all mounted, but most of them miserably equipped; their appearance was in fact so burlesque, that it was with much difficulty the diversion of the regular soldiery was restrained by the officers, and the General himself was glad of an opportunity of detaching Col. Marion, at his own instance, towards the interior of South Carolina, with orders to watch the motions of the enemy and furnish intelligence.*

Having learned of the militia units being formed in the Williamsburg district, Marion asked Gates's permission to take command of them for harassing British supply lines. Gates, with apparent relief, agreed. In Williamsburg Marion was greeted with shouts of joy. Many of the partisans had served under him earlier in the war; all knew his reputation as a fighter. Although he was a Continental officer with no legal authority over the militia, Marion promptly took command. With a force of about eighty mounted men he began burning boats along the Santee River, the lifeline of the British army. Given time, Marion might have distracted the British and hampered their operations, but Gates had no patience for guerrilla tactics. On August 16 he met Cornwallis in the open field at Camden and suffered disaster. His militia deserted him, his Continentals were decimated, and Gates himself fled for Hillsboro, North Carolina, 120 miles away.

The previous day Colonel Banastre Tarleton, at the head of a green-coated Tory legion, destroyed the militia of Thomas Sumter ("the Gamecock"), sending him racing for the security of North Carolina. Marion's tiny band of Williamsburgers was the only organized patriot force in the state.

An opportunity to strike back soon presented itself. From a Loyalist deserter Marion's scouts learned that a small British escort was conducting a batch of American prisoners down the Santee road toward Charleston. Laying an ambush, Marion rescued the prisoners, most of whom were Continental regulars from Maryland. To his dismay only a couple of the Marylanders agreed to join him or even to rejoin their unit. Even so, the escapade caught the attention of the press in the North. A legend was born.

The ambush also caught the attention of Lord Cornwallis. The British commander could not afford a victorious band of guerrillas astride his long supply line from Camden to Charleston. He sent a regiment of regulars after Marion and ordered the armed bands of Tories to cooperate in the pursuit. Outnumbered by ten to one, Marion fled across the Peedee, taking refuge in the Great White Marsh, just below Wilmington, North Carolina. The British razed the Williamsburg district, burning the house of every man who had served with Marion. Such tactics failed, as they often do; for every guerrilla intimidated, a dozen more were born. Learning of the devastation, Marion was philosophical. "Tis a harsh medicine," he said, "but it is necessary."

To hold Williamsburg under control, the British deposited Tory companies of thirty to sixty men at strategic points in the district. It was the same mistake that Cornwallis had made in the New Jersey campaign some years earlier, and Marion, like Washington, saw his opportunity. He led his band of sixty men out of the White Marsh. In a day and an evening they rode forty-six miles and crossed three rivers. At midnight they fell upon a Tory band camped at Black Mingo Creek, killed about one-third of them, and sent the rest fleeing. They also captured the Tories' guns, ammunition, and food stocks, as well as all their horses. These supplies were enough to keep Marion for the rest of the autumn.

After Marion struck another Tory encampment, General Cornwallis summoned the first team. Tarleton himself with his regiment of mounted dragoons was sent after Marion. Victory had swollen Marion's force to four hundred, but it was still no match for Tarleton's legion. Tarleton picked up the trail at the Santee, where Marion was engaged in his usual pastime of destroying boats and interrupting British supplies. On the British approach Marion turned and fled eastward across the pine barrens between the Santee and Black rivers. For seven hours Tarleton trailed him through piney woods and dark swamps. But Marion made it across the Black River and disappeared in a roadless bog. He was back in the familiar Williamsburg district where his men knew every deerpath. Tarleton abandoned the chase, suggesting to his weary men that they go find instead the once-defeated Thomas Sumter. "Come my boys!" he cried cheerfully. "Let us go back, and we will find the Gamecock. But as for this damned old fox, the devil himself could not catch him." The phrase was apt enough and quickly caught on. Whigs in the Williamsburg district turned it into a eulogy. The legend now had a name—Swamp Fox.

The Fox of Snow's Island

As the year 1780 came to an end, both armies began looking for secure winter quarters. After Camden, Cornwallis had contemplated the possibility of pursuing Gates into North Carolina. That dream ended early in October when a force of Western volunteers, led by Isaac Shelby and John Sevier, defeated a Loyalist army at King's Mountain. With a victorious army of Tennessee riflemen on one flank and Marion on the other, Cornwallis could not risk a foray into North Carolina. Instead, he placed his army in winter quarters at Winnsboro, just west of Camden. He would move into North Carolina in the spring.

Marion, too, looked for a winter home. He found it on Snow's Island, a heavily wooded ridge of land at the junction of Lynches River and the Peedee. To the east and south lay the friendly Williamsburg district; to the west, separating him from the British at Camden, were the trackless sloughs of Sockee Swamp. In the densest part of the woods his men built wood lean-tos for themselves and elevated bins for their food stocks. To prevent surprise, Marion took possession of all the boats on the river, destroyed every bridge in the area, and felled trees across the fords. The men he did not need he sent home.

Writing long after the war, a young recruit recalled vividly the Swamp Fox in his lair. He was a short man, only a bit over five feet tall, well-built in the shoulders but frail and ill-formed in the legs. The poorly healed ankle left him with a limp. His face, far from handsome, was a collection of angles — long aquiline nose, projecting chin, and long forehead. Yet the eyes, black and piercing, betrayed the strength inside. He had the stamina of men half his age and the ability to endure every privation. There was, in all, a magnetism that commanded instant and enduring loyalty.

There was also a generosity of spirit uncommon in a guerrilla chieftain. After they safely eluded Tarleton, some of his men set to burning Tory houses in retaliation for the damage they had suffered. Marion instantly put a stop to it; he also forbade the mistreatment of Tory prisoners. Both sides used a parole system in the Carolina campaign, letting their prisoners go free on the promise that they would not fight again. If a man violated his parole and returned to action, he was liable for hanging if caught again. Marion, however, was inclined to pardon Tory violators. He understood the easy confusion of simple farmers; sometimes he was even able to enlist them in his own cause. Indeed, such was the conflict of loyalties in the Carolina campaign (along with the rate of military desertion) that, as General Nathanael Greene himself observed, "At the close of the war, we fought the enemy with British soldiers; and they fought us with those of America."

Nor did Marion ever forget that he was a Continental officer acting under orders. He kept General Gates fully informed of his activities, and he was prepared to rejoin the regular army whenever it returned to South Carolina. Gates, however, would not be the one to lead it. After Camden, when Congress asked Washington to name a new commander in the South, Washington sent his best lieutenant, Nathanael Greene.

Taking command in December 1780, Greene made the unorthodox move of dividing his army. He sent General Dan Morgan moving southward along the edge of the mountains, while he kept the main force in the vicinity of Cheraw in the east. It was risky because the British force was superior, and Cornwallis might descend upon either of the American wings. The British commander could not do so, however, without leaving his rear exposed, and therein lay the brilliance of Greene's strategy. Cornwallis, too, divided his army, thus losing some of his numerical advantage. He sent Tarleton in pursuit of Morgan, while he sat warily eyeing Greene.

To distract the British further, Greene sent Colonel Henry Lee with his regiment to join Marion. Simultaneously, South Carolina Governor John Rutledge promoted Marion to brigadier general and gave him command of all militia east of the Santee. By early 1781 Marion's camp at Snow's Island was a hive of activity. Militia were responding to the call for arms for the spring campaign, patrols scoured the Santee road for British supply wagons, and scouts came and went, reporting on the activities of the British garrisons in Charleston and Georgetown.

Light Horse Harry Lee and the Swamp Fox were a brilliant match. A Northern Neck Virginian, Lee was a blend of courtly composure and bristling energy. His regiment was a mixture of cavalry and infantry, well seasoned in Northern fighting. On the march he had found a way to double his speed by having the infantry and cavalry alternate horse and foot. His regiment brought Marion's force up to brigade strength. Although the two officers held equal rank in the Continental army, Lee generously let Marion take command.

Their opportunity came when Morgan defeated Tarleton at the Cowpens in mid-January 1781. Cornwallis promptly set off after Morgan, hoping to trap him against one of North Carolina's many swift rivers.

When Greene joined Morgan to aid in the escape, once again Marion was alone in South Carolina. He and Lee decided to attack Georgetown, the port on Winyah Bay that was the lone British stronghold in the northeastern part of the state. The surprise raid came near to success. Entering the city under cover of night, they captured the British outposts. A redoubt in the middle of town, however, stopped them dead. They lacked cannon and scaling ladders, and neither commander was willing to risk his men in a direct assault. Thus they withdrew, having given the British nothing more than a bad fright.

Pursued by Lord Francis Rawdon, new commander of the king's forces in South Carolina, and weakened by the loss of Lee, who had been recalled to the North, Marion retreated to his Williamsburg homeland. At the Black River crossing he ambushed Rawdon and sent him scurrying back to Georgetown. Marion's respite was brief, however. No sooner had his victorious troops settled into camp than a messenger arrived with news of disaster. A separate British force had marched down Lynches River and occupied Snow's Island. The Swamp Fox had been outsmarted. Concentrating on the Black River gateway to his homeland, he had neglected to cover his rear. He had not even sent scouts to keep an eye on the Camden road.

To avoid being trapped in the British pincers, Marion fled east across Williamsburg. His men, dispirited and anxious to see their families, slipped into the woods. By the time he crossed the Peedee to safety, his brigade was down to eighty men. It was a black moment and time to take stock. He had been in the field for seven months since the disaster at Camden, and what was the result? He had captured some British supplies, burned a few boats, and seen houses go up in flames. That seemed meager enough, yet he had also tied up a regiment of British regulars and innumerable Loyalists. Perhaps most important, he and his compatriots in the hill country, Sumter and Pickens, had demonstrated that South Carolina was far from conquered. To Cornwallis and Greene, facing each other to the north, that was the most important fact of the war.

The Recovery of South Carolina

A few days after the raid on Snow's Island, Marion received news that was more puzzling than disturbing. Instead of coming in search of his debilitated force, the raiders had turned suddenly and dashed for Camden. Nor had the British detachment in Georgetown made any move to close the pincers. Puzzlement turned to joy when a scout rode in with further news — Henry Lee and his legion had returned to South Carolina; Greene himself was not far behind.

In March 1781 Greene and Cornwallis fought a bloody but indecisive engagement near Guilford, North Carolina. The Americans were driven from the field, but Cornwallis was too bloodied to follow up his victory. Instead he retired to Wilmington for rest and supplies. Greene then made the most daring decision of the war. Expecting help from Marion, Sumter, and Pickens, he headed for South Carolina for a concerted attack on the British forts that controlled the state. If Cornwallis followed him, North Carolina and Virginia would be free of danger and the military situation would be essentially what it had been after the fall of Charleston. The clock would be turned back a year, emphasizing to the politicians in London the futility of further war. If Cornwallis failed to pursue, South Carolina belonged to Greene.

Cornwallis refused the bait. Instead, he started north toward Virginia, hoping to expand the sphere of British conquests and perhaps improve British bargaining leverage at the peace table. The road led him, though, to Yorktown.

When he learned that the American army was turning south, Light Horse Harry Lee asked Greene for permission to rejoin his old comrade Marion. The North Carolina campaign had interrupted plans that he and Marion had made for capturing British strongholds on the Santee. Greene, moving his own force toward Camden, the center of the British line of forts, agreed to let Lee and Marion sweep out the low country.

Lee joined Marion on the Black River on April 14. Their first target was Fort Watson at the strategic river forks where the Congaree and the Wateree joined to form the Santee. The outpost, a stout wooden stockade sitting on the flat river plain, was defended by eighty regulars and forty Tory militiamen. Lee and Marion greatly outnumbered the defenders, but without artillery there was little that they could do. General Greene agreed to send a field piece, but there was some doubt that it could arrive in time. The British force that had earlier chased Marion into Williamsburg was still in the field and might appear at any time. Nor did Marion's men have the patience for a siege; they began drifting home to see their families and to weed the corn. As a guerrilla chieftain, Marion had tolerated such behavior; as a regular officer in command of a siege, he found it intolerable.

While Marion fumed at his casual army, one of his officers, Colonel Hezekiah Maham, came up with an idea. With a detachment of woodcutters he built a tower taller than the walls of the fort. On the top was a rough platform with a parapet of logs. During the night soldiers dragged the structure within rifle shot of the fort, and at dawn Marion's sharpshooters began probing every corner of the palisade. The British promptly surrendered.

The fall of Fort Watson was the first American victory over a British strongpoint in the Southern campaign. It was also the first breach in the line of forts that held South Carolina in subjection. The log device, given the name Maham Tower, came into frequent use in the war on British strongholds. His spirits revived, Marion set out to join Greene, who was closing in on Lord Rawdon in Camden.

Before Marion and Lee could join forces with Greene, Lord Rawdon attacked Greene's army on Hobkirk's Hill. The battle, on April 25, 1781, was indecisive, though Greene (who never won a battle in his life) was again forced to withdraw from the field. And, as usual, the British paid too high a price for victory. When the battle was over, Lord Rawdon was too weak to hold Camden. General Greene expressed it well to the French envoy, Chevalier de La Luzerne: "We fight, get beat, rise and fight again."

Rawdon evacuated Camden in early May, putting the city to the torch as he went, and started down the road to Charleston. Americans increased the pressure on the river forts. Thomas Sumter invested Fort Granby at the confluence of the Broad and Saluda, while Lee and Marion attacked Fort Motte, a few miles below on the Congaree.

In prewar days Fort Motte had been a handsome plantation house, owned by a staunchly patriot widow, Rebecca Motte. Because of its strategic location on the supply route from Charleston to Camden, the British had taken possession of the house, forcing Mrs. Motte to move into a nearby farmhouse. The British fortified the place with a wooden palisade fronting on a deep ditch, and jammed a garrison of 150 men into it. On May 8 Marion and Lee began digging siege parallels with a view to storming the palisade. After two days this work was interrupted by signal fires from their scouts, indicating that a British relief column was on the way. Realizing that they lacked time for a textbook siege, Lee and Marion decided to set fire to the house. With chivalric tact they secured Mrs. Motte's consent; she even provided the bow and fire-arrows. A few well-placed arrows set the roof ablaze, while marksmen prevented the British from tearing off the burning shingles. The British commander threw up the white flag; Americans hurried in and put out the fire. Mrs. Motte then treated the entire assemblage, victors and vanquished, to a "sumptuous dinner." In this, as in so many other ways, the civility of the eighteenth century overcame the barbarity of war.

General Greene, hurrying ahead of his own army, arrived at Motte's in time for dinner — and full of new plans. He and Lee would join Sumter in the reduction of Granby, and then the entire army would move to Ninety-Six, the westernmost of the British outposts and the strongest of them all. Marion, meantime, was to return to the eastern part of the state to keep an eye on Lord Rawdon and the main British force. With Ninety-Six in American hands, the British would be left with nothing but Georgetown and Charleston, plus Savannah and Augusta in Georgia.

Marion trailed Lord Rawdon as the British commander retired toward Charleston. On the lower Santee, in the vicinity of his own plantation and in friendly Huguenot environs, he built a new base. Protected by swamps and creeks, his lair was similar to that at Snow's Island but with a different purpose. Instead of being an independent partisan band, striking at the enemy when it chose, Marion's force was one wing of a Continental army, operating under a comprehensive battle plan. That meant constant activity rather than hit-and-run raids. Marion's patrols kept the Loyalists in awe, and his scouts kept careful watch on the British.

Dependence on others was also a source of frustration. With Lord Rawdon quiescent in the Charleston area, Marion could give some thought to Georgetown. Scouts informed him that a mere handful of regulars and Loyalists garrisoned the town. Eagerly he wrote Greene asking permission to attack the port. Along with Ninety-Six, which Greene was already besieging, Georgetown was the last British stronghold. Fast-moving Henry Lee had already taken Augusta and freed the upper Savannah Valley. Preoccupied with his own siege, Greene failed to respond to Marion's request; nor did he answer an urgent follow-up.

Marion, accustomed to being his own master, moved anyway. On May 28 he swept down on Georgetown and put his men to digging trenches. The British garrison, with no stomach to fight, fled to their ships and sailed for Charleston. For almost a year Marion had had his eye on Georgetown; its undramatic collapse was surely an anticlimax. With the British gone, Marion had no use for it. He leveled the fort and returned to the Santee.

Toward the end of the summer came heartening news from the north. Lafayette had managed to box in Lord Cornwallis at Yorktown, Virginia. A French fleet was on its way to blockade the Chesapeake. Washington himself was moving south to take charge. It would be well, wrote the commander in chief, if Greene were to take the offensive in South Carolina to prevent the British from sending reinforcements to Cornwallis.

Greene, having captured Ninety-Six, returned to the low country. His army numbered twenty-four hundred to the enemy's two thousand, but half of Greene's force was militia while the British army was nearly all regulars. The British had changed commanders in the course of the summer. Lord Rawdon, his health broken by the South Carolina climate, returned to England; Colonel Alexander Stuart, a quick-thinking, vigorous Scot, was in charge.

Greene summoned Marion, who moved swiftly up the Santee to join him; together they descended on the British army camped near Eutaw Springs. Stuart, though taken by surprise, quickly deployed his regulars. The American tactics were an extension of the system devised by Morgan at the Cowpens. The militia, commanded by Pickens and Marion, were placed in front, with orders to fire at least once before fleeing. The Continentals would then take over, ready to withstand a British charge made porous by the militia.

Marion's linsey-woolsey farmers astonished the regulars on both sides. Advancing from tree to tree, loading and firing, they smashed into the center of the British line. Then, their ammunition exhausted, they retired in good order, while the Continentals, bayonets in place, passed through. Their conduct, Greene proudly wrote to the German drillmaster Baron von Steuben, "would have graced the veterans of the Great King of Prussia."

For Marion it was a personal triumph. It was the largest number of men he had ever commanded and his first battle fought in the stand-up European style. Yet victory, as usual, eluded Nathanael Greene. The Virginia and North Carolina Continentals broke the British line and entered Stuart's camp. Then their discipline vanished as they fell into the enemy's stock of food and liquor. The delay enabled Stuart to rally his men. Fortifying a brick plantation house, the British held on. At the end of the day both sides collapsed in exhaustion. In the most obstinate fight of the Southern campaign, each side lost about 25 percent in casualties.

To all intents, it was a draw. But Greene, ever on the move, was the first to leave the field, thus allowing the British to claim a technical victory, but it was a Pyrrhic one. Stuart retired to Charleston, never venturing forth again. South Carolina was back in American hands.

The Charitable Partisan

After the battle of Eutaw Springs, Marion dismissed his militia and retired to his own plantation. He was entrusted with keeping order in the eastern district, but the Loyalists were quiet. Everyone seemed to sense that the fighting was over. Governor John Rutledge, who had maintained a floating administration while the armies marched and wheeled, called for the election of a popular assembly. He also issued a proclamation pardoning all Tories who would promise future loyalty and agree to serve in the militia for six months.

Marion was elected to the state senate and reported for his new duties in Jacksonboro, which was as close to Charleston as Governor Rutledge dared to get. Loyalists were the most pressing problem before the legislature. The house-burning tactics of the partisan bands had left lingering rage. Throughout the war the patriot militia, including Marion's followers, had been paid mostly in promises — promises of inheriting Loyalist lands. To redeem the state's credit, the legislature entertained a bill to confiscate the property of certain Loyalists. The state planned to sell the property and to use the proceeds for paying its own army and its other creditors.

To the surprise of all and the dismay of many, Senator Marion openly opposed the confiscation act. He knew how difficult it had been for many to choose between allegiance to a king and adherence to a revolution. He had seen violence beget violence. To bring true peace to South Carolina, Marion felt, the Tories must be forgiven, not punished. He failed to get his way, for South Carolina, together with most of the other states, confiscated Loyalist property until the formal end of the war.

With little patience for legislative routine, Marion fled the assembly as soon as he was able. British forays from Charleston required him to bring his men periodically to arms, but there was no serious fighting. In June

1782 he negotiated the surrender of the last of the Loyalist regiments, requiring the soldiers only to restore the plunder they had taken and to sign a declaration of allegiance to the state. In December of that year the British evacuated Charleston, declaring thereby a formal end to the southern campaign. In Paris, Benjamin Franklin had already signed preliminary articles of a peace treaty.

Like Washington in Virginia, Francis Marion was content to lay down his sword and return to his plantation. There was much to be done, for the British had burned his house, slaughtered his cattle, and confiscated his horses. Some slaves had run away; others, willingly or not, had joined the British and sailed from Charleston with them. The South Carolina assembly voted its thanks for his services and gave him a gold medal, but it was unable to provide back pay. Marion borrowed money to restock his plantation and feed his remaining slaves.

With deceptive ease the guerrilla chieftain slipped into peacetime life, marrying a Huguenot cousin in 1786. She brought a modest fortune to the match, enabling him to rebuild his house and pay his debts. He proved to be a good farmer, and the plantation flourished. Little is known of his later days, perhaps testimony itself of their happy passing. He died in 1795, just as Washington was entering the last year of his presidency. The Swamp Fox was already oral tradition. It is only a modest irony that Parson Weems, newly enriched by his successful portrait of Washington, was the first to give it literary currency. But other, more cautious biographers would follow. Like Washington, Francis Marion was too big a man to need a legend.

SUGGESTIONS FOR FURTHER READING

Christopher Ward's *War of the Revolution* (2 vols., 1952) is the most detailed, technically exact description of the Southern campaigns, and it places the activities of Marion and other generals in the context of the wider war. Robert D. Bass, *Swamp Fox, the Life and Campaigns of General Francis Marion* (1959), is a lively account with numerous vignettes of the man. Hugh F. Rankin, *Francis Marion: The Swamp Fox* (1973), concentrates on the campaigns of 1780–81. The life stories of some other partisan leaders are North Callahan, *Dan Morgan, Ranger of the Revolution* (1961); Alice Noble Waring, *The Fighting Elder: Andrew Pickens, 1739–1817*; and Robert D. Bass, *Gamecock: The Life and Campaigns of General Thomas Sumter* (1961). Those who enjoy contemporary diaries and memoirs might try Henry Lee, *Memoirs of the War in the Southern Department of the United States* (2 vols., 1812, reprinted 1969).

5

Abigail Adams:
Partner in Home Rule

Accompanying the war for independence was an "internal revolution" that altered substantially the structure of American society. New Faces appeared in positions of political power; paper

assets and land changed hands rapidly. To be sure, the "internal revolution" was kept under careful control, and the elite that held power in the new republic was not much different from that which had managed colonial society. Yet important changes were made — in law, in education, in religion, in arts and letters. Even black slaves, the lowest rung of colonial society, won measurably by the Revolution. Northern states either freed their slaves outright or initiated programs of gradual emancipation. Slaves who volunteered for military duty were granted their freedom in all states but South Carolina and Georgia. In New Jersey Blacks even won the vote, for a time.

Such progress was limited, of

Abigail Smith Adams (1744–1818). *Abigail Smith, 21, sat for this portrait just before she became engaged to John Adams. Although the artist's rendering is rather stiff and formal, one can nonetheless detect the quickness, the warmth, and the wit of the woman she would become.*

course. And the persistence of slavery in the South hardly squared with the high-flown rhetoric of the Declaration of Independence. But Jefferson's phrase "all men are created equal" did cause some to worry about the gap between the American dream and the reality. Shortly after the war ended, John Jay and other New Yorkers formed the first secular society for the abolition of slavery. On the other hand, neither Jay nor any other statesman of record thought to apply the principle to women. By "all men" Jefferson doubtless meant "all mankind," but for long years after the Revolution the phrase retained its masculine gender.

Women were not slaves; neither were they free. A variety of legal and social canons constricted their lives. Legally they were treated much like underage children. A married woman could not sue in court, for damages or injury, except in joint suit with her husband. If her husband died without a will and there were children, the wife was entitled to only one-third of the estate. In some cases she was entitled only to the dower, the property that she had brought to the marriage. Unmarried women and widows could hold title to landed property, but custom severely restricted the occupations that they could enter.

Without education, occupational choice was limited anyway. Girls did attend the elementary schools of the North, and most Southern planters provided tutors for their daughters as well as their sons. Beyond the elementary school, however, there was nothing for females prior to the year 1820. As a result, adult women received politeness from menfolk, but rarely intellectual companionship or conversation. Only a rare being could break through this veil of silence to make an imprint on the historical record. One such was Mercy Otis Warren, sister of James Otis and wife of a Massachusetts general. Mercy Warren contributed satirical plays and poems to the patriot cause in the years before the Revolution and later wrote a three-volume history of the war. Another such was Abigail Adams, one of the most fascinating personalities of the time.

Abigail Smith

Abigail Smith was more advantaged than the average woman. Her father, Reverend William Smith, was a Congregational minister whose forebears had amassed a considerable fortune in trade. Her mother was a Quincy, a family that was interlocked by blood and marriage with the elite of the Massachusetts Bay Colony. She grew up in the pristine atmosphere of a parsonage in rural Weymouth. Her religious training was liberal Congregationalist, and she adhered to that faith all her life (except for her sojourn in New York, while her husband served as vice president, when she found the sermons of the Episcopalian minister more congenial).

She was a sickly child; recurrent illness kept her from attending school.

Her father gave her some personal instruction, and she had access to his well-stocked library. Her letters and those of her two sisters indicate an early acquaintance with the English greats — Shakespeare, Milton, Dryden, and Pope — and she knew well the histories, travel diaries, and church literature of her own time. She taught herself French, and her later success with her husband's accounts indicates that she was well versed in arithmetic.

In 1759, at the age of fourteen, she met John Adams, a struggling young lawyer from nearby Braintree. Adams was more interested in her older sister at first, but by 1762 they were in ardent courtship. They married two years later, on the eve of her twentieth birthday. Although both came from pious, rural backgrounds, there was nothing puritanical about either. Their love letters were amazingly open and uninhibited. And their marriage, though broken by long separations while Adams pursued revolutionary politics and diplomacy, was one of the happiest ever recorded.

Seldom has a love been more deeply felt or more exquisitely expressed. But their marriage was more than that: it was a partnership to which each contributed in equal measure. John Adams was a man of extraordinary gifts. His many essays on government were without equal even in that age of spangled brilliance. He was a shrewd and realistic diplomat, an honest and sensible politician. Yet he needed a counterweight. He was a man full of anxieties and hostilities. He wavered continually between a suspicion that others were plotting against him and a fear that he was undoing himself. Though glorying in his reputation as philosopher-statesman, he hungered for the contentment of a rural law practice. John Adams's best biographer states flatly: "Abigail insured his sanity." With her devotion, her intellectual companionship, and her competent management of his affairs, she was "a gyroscope that brought him safely through the stormiest seas."

"Remember the Ladies"

Elizabeth Quincy Smith, Abigail's mother, considered John Adams a small-town attorney of second-rate family and uncertain future. Yet he prospered quickly enough. Before long his casework forced him to divide his time between Braintree and the superior court in Boston. In 1767 Adams moved his family, which by then included daughter Abigail and son John Quincy Adams, to Boston. The prospects there were better, cousin Samuel had pointed out, for a career in the law or in politics. He was soon deeply involved in Samuel Adams's revolutionary machine, attending sessions of the Caucus and serving in the colonial assembly. In 1774 the assembly, barring the doors against General Gage's orders to dissolve, sent him to the First Continental Congress. Abigail returned to Braintree, and, except for brief intervals, the two were apart for the next ten years while Adams served as delegate to Congress and minister in Europe.

They remained in close contact by letter, however. His notes were hastily written, yet intimately descriptive. Hers were splendidly crafted, graced with lines of poetry, and full of suggestion and insight. It was, says the editor of the Adams family papers, "one of the greatest epistolary dialogues between husband and wife in all history."

Abigail Adams shared all her husband's political trials. She favored full independence for the United States at least as early as he did, and she was more open in advocating it. Adams considered it "the choice blessing" of his life that she had "the capacity to comprehend" the great issues of the day. So well formed were her political opinions that Adams raided her letters for apt quotations to use in his own writings. He sent her a copy of Tom Paine's *Common Sense* as soon as it came off the press in early 1776. Abigail was "charmed" with its arguments in favor of independence and wondered how anyone could "hesitate one moment at adopting them." She was, of course, delighted when Congress finally approved the Declaration. "May the foundation of our new constitution be Justice, Truth, Righteousness!" she exclaimed.

That she picked those virtues for the new nation is itself revealing. She was not content simply with self-rule. The creation of new governments, she felt, presented a unique opportunity to repair some of the injustices in American society. The disparities in the educational system particularly bothered her, possibly because of her own lack of formal schooling. In a republic, where the citizenry had an important voice in government, it was essential that education be available to all. The discrimination against women, she suspected, was due to men's "ungenerous jealousy of rivals near the Throne." Equal educational opportunities would ensure future greatness, for women, as mothers, had the greatest effect on the young. "If we mean to have heroes, statesmen and philosophers," she told her husband, "we should have learned women."

She doubtless realized that education would also expand the horizons of women, perhaps even foster a desire for political power; but in the male-dominated world of the eighteenth century such arguments would have been self-defeating. It was first necessary to remove some of the legal chains that fettered women, and that she did try to do. Independence, she reminded her husband, meant the drafting of state constitutions and the revision of legal codes. When Adams and his colleagues set about this task, she begged, "Remember the Ladies, and be more generous and favourable to them than your ancestors. Do not put such unlimited power into the hands of husbands. Remember all Men would be tyrants if they could. If particular care and attention is not paid to the Ladies we are determined to foment a Rebellion, and will not hold ourselves bound by any Laws in which we have no voice, or Representation." The popular slogan "No taxation without representation" had all sorts of revolutionary implications.

Realizing, perhaps, the futility of her crusade, husband John chose to treat her plea as a joke. "I cannot but laugh," he replied. "We have been told that our struggle has loosened the bonds of government everywhere: that children and apprentices were disobedient; that schools and colleges were grown turbulent; that Indians slighted their guardians, and Negroes grew insolent to their masters. But your letter was the first intimation that another tribe, more numerous and powerful than all the rest, were grown discontented." Perhaps, he concluded still with tongue in cheek, the British ministry was responsible. Having without success appealed to "Tories, land jobbers, bigots, Canadians, Indians, Negroes, Hessians, Russians, Irish Roman Catholics, and Scotch renegades, at last they have stimulated the most dangerous group of all to demand new privileges and threaten to rebel."

Abigail's tone had been jocular, but she was deadly serious. Not satisfied with John's reply, she wrote her friend Mercy Warren to ask her "to join me in a petition to Congress." She wanted to rid the country of the ancient "laws of England, which give unlimited power to the husband to use his wife ill," and to institute a new legal code "in our favor upon just and liberal principles." Mercy Warren disappointingly failed to respond. Abigail, not yet through, wrote to John:

I cannot say that I think you are very generous to the ladies, for whilst you are proclaiming peace and good will to men, emancipating all nations, you insist upon retaining an absolute power over wives. But you must remember that arbitrary power is, like most other things which are very hard, very liable to be broken; and, notwithstanding all your wise laws and maxims, we have it in our power, not only to free ourselves, but to subdue our masters, and without violence, throw both your natural and legal authority at our feet —

> "Charm by accepting, by submitting sway,
> Yet have our humor most when we obey."

At least she had the last word. What could John reply to that?

Women's rights were not her only concern. She abhorred slavery and thought that it, too, ought to be abolished in the new order of things. How, she wondered openly, could the Virginians be considered leaders in the cause of liberty when they "have been accustomed to deprive their fellow creatures of theirs"? Some years later — indeed, after her husband had been elected president — she sent a young black servant of hers to night school at the lad's request. When a father of two of the white pupils appeared at her door to protest, she gave him a lecture on "equality of rights. The Boy is a Freeman as much as any of the young Men," she told him, "and merely because his Face is Black, is he to be denied instruction? How is he to be qualified to procure a livelihood? . . . I have not thought it any disgrace to myself to take him into my parlour and teach him both to read and write." For a president's wife it was a becoming posture. And she won. Nothing further was said.

Life on the Home Front

Not least among the treasures in the correspondence of Abigail Adams is the picture it gives of civilian life during the Revolution. Even though Massachusetts saw little fighting after the British evacuated Boston, it suffered the usual wartime problems. Goods were short, labor scarce, and disease rampant.

When John Adams departed for the Continental Congress in 1774, Abigail was left with the care of their Braintree farm. Although she knew little of farming, she proved a capable superintendent of the hired help. When John returned late in the autumn, he found the fields plowed and manured for the spring planting, and the pasture was fertilized with seaweed brought up from the beach. With the outbreak of fighting his absences became more prolonged, her work ever more professional. In the spring of 1776 she wrote to him that "the barley looks charmingly" after good spring rains and that they were about to plant the summer crops. She had let one incompetent hand go and had hired two others at a shilling a day. With the money he had sent her, she had paid yearly taxes, wages to the hired men, and rent on the loan of her father's horse. Impressed, her husband replied playfully that he was beginning "to be jealous that our Neighbors will think Affairs more discreetly conducted in my Absence than at any other Time."

Toward the end of the war she purchased out of her own savings a tract of land that she knew her husband had long wanted. It had once belonged to John's uncle, and he had tromped its woods as a youth. For seven acres she paid two hundred dollars. John doubtless would have bought it anyway for sentimental reasons, but she prudently analyzed the value of the investment. The parcel held, she estimated, forty-five cords of firewood (John had earlier complained that firewood sold for twenty dollars a cord in Philadelphia). He was, of course, delighted with the purchase.

Life in Braintree was exciting while Washington besieged the British in Boston. In February 1776 Mrs. Adams was at her writing table when Washington's newly acquired artillery began booming on Dorchester Heights. The cannon roared all night long, and the next day the town militia marched off to Boston to join the fight. Abigail climbed a nearby hill to watch the artillery duel. The sound, she wrote, "is one of the grandest in nature, and is of the true species of the sublime! 'Tis now an incessant roar; but oh! the fatal ideas which are connected with the sound! How many of our dear countrymen must fall!"

When the militia returned with news that Washington had occupied Dorchester Heights, she was disappointed. "I would not have suffered all I have for two such hills," she wrote with a true appreciation of the ratio between human life and bits of land. Nor was she much comforted when she discovered that the victory enabled Washington to menace the city and harbor. She feared that the cannonade would leave the city a flattened wreckage. From her hilltop perch she watched the British evacuate Boston. Their fleet of 170 ships, the largest ever assembled in America, filled the bay as far as she could see. Afterwards she hastened into Boston to inspect the damage. Their own house had been occupied by a British army physician, and, though it was stripped and dirty, it was intact. The rest of the city was likewise in fair shape. With relief she bade farewell to the war, though she would continue to suffer its privations.

As the fighting shifted to the South, the revolutionary fervor that had gripped Massachusetts began to ebb. Patriotism gave way to profiteering and speculation. A *nouveau riche* of war profiteers came to dominate the social life of Braintree. Abigail ignored them, and they her. "I have not the *honor* to be known to many of them," she wrote with icy disapproval. Wartime disruption also brought a decline in moral standards. "Matrimony is not in vogue here," Abigail reported. "We have ladies but not a gentleman in the whole town. . . . Licentiousness and freedom of manners are predominant."

As the war dragged on, goods became scarce and prices rose. The assembly passed an act regulating prices, but it proved impossible to enforce. Merchants charged what the traffic would bear. Sugar, molasses, rum, and coffee could not be had at any price. Labor, too, was scarce after Braintree's Minutemen went off to war. Without teachers, the schools had ceased to function, and the town children were left to "range the streets." Farmhands were unavailable, and Abigail thought that the women of the town would have to bring in the crops. "I believe I could gather corn and husk it," she wrote John, "but I should make a poor figure at digging potatoes." She was even prepared to fight. If General Howe returned to Massachusetts, she predicted, "an army of women would oppose him." She assured her husband: "We possess a spirit that will not be conquered. If our men are drawn off and we should be attacked, you would find a race of Amazons in America."

In early 1778 John Adams departed for France to replace Silas Deane. Except for a brief reunion in 1780, he and Abigail would be separated for the next six years. In his absence the farm and the family accounts were left completely to her. Ministerial expenses easily ate up the meager pay allotted him by Congress. Abigail and the children had to subsist on the income from the Braintree farm. As prices rose, that became increasingly difficult. To make ends meet, she asked John to send her goods from Paris, which she could sell through friends. John obliged with a trunkful of French cloth and ribbons. Abigail turned the articles over to merchant friends, who sold them on a commission basis. The proceeds enabled her to survive the war in some comfort. Peace brought a collapse in prices and ruin to some of the war speculators. Abigail hastily wrapped up her own "mercantile affairs" and wrung new economies from her family.

American Abroad

Peace did not bring John Adams home. At the request of Congress he and Franklin stayed on in Europe to negotiate commercial treaties for the new republic. Then in 1784 Congress appointed him minister to Great Britain, while simultaneously sending his friend Jefferson to replace Franklin in Paris. Adams was delighted with the honor, but the prospect of further separation was more than he or Abigail could bear. With his encouragement Abigail decided to join him in Europe.

The voyage required extensive preparations. Abigail left the town house in the care of Phoebe, the black maid she had inherited from her father (and her lifetime companion), and found tenants for the farm. She placed the younger boys with her sister and took her daughter, Nabby, with her. The voyage also disentangled Nabby from a suitor of whom Abigail disapproved. (Abigail's judgment of the young man, Royall Tyler, seemed correct at the time, but he later straightened himself out and became a respected chief justice of Vermont. Nabby ultimately married a feckless New Yorker, who was in constant financial difficulties.)

The day before her vessel was to sail, Thomas Jefferson appeared in Boston. Also bound for Europe, the Virginian had made a special trip to persuade her to accompany him on a vessel sailing from New York. Though flattered by his gracious gesture, she refused to change plans at the last minute. The act marked the beginning of a new friendship, however.

After a joyous reunion in London, the Adamses set out for Paris, where John was to join Jefferson in trade negotiations. Abigail's first impressions of France were unfavorable. Farms, she noted, were poorly cultivated, and the villages they passed through seemed "the most wretched habitations of man." Paris, she declared, was "the dirtiest place I ever saw," and, she might have added, the smelliest. Garbage littered the streets; raw sewage trickled down the gutters.

Setting up housekeeping in Paris was a chore. Each servant considered herself a specialist. The upstairs maid would only dust; making beds was the department of a *femme de chambre*. The coachman did nothing but attend to the horses; the cook would not think of washing a dish. With a staff of eight Abigail could find no one willing to do the family wash. Had she not persuaded the two American servants she had brought with her to do double duty, Abigail complained, she would have had to hire eight more "lazy wretches." Nor did she like the constant handouts. At New Year's every servant expected a special gift, as did the clerk of the parish and the newspaper boy. Foreign ministers were also expected to visit the royal court on that occasion with gifts for all the king's servants. "If we miss one of these harpies," Abigail observed caustically, "they will follow you from Versailles to Paris."

Nevertheless, Abigail soon learned to appreciate the French. The men she found charming and attentive, full of flirtatious compliments; and the women were graceful, easy in manner, and interesting conversationalists. Their superiority over American women she attributed to better education. The Adamses enjoyed French cooking and attended the theater regularly. Life in Paris was a world away from Braintree, or even Boston, yet the experience also reinforced their pride in home. When the Dutch minister arrived for dinner in a coach drawn by six horses and attended by five liveried servants, Abigail wished that she was back in America "where frugality and economy are considered as virtues."

England, where the Adamses removed at the end of 1784, charmed Abigail at once. The countryside was clean and tidy, she wrote Jefferson, and London was a magnificent city. She admitted, however, that the English could not compare with the French in cooking and in dress. After lecturing Jefferson on the superiority of English life, she commissioned the Virginian to purchase her four pairs of shoes in Paris.

The stay in England further reinforced her Americanism. Both the Adamses detested the caste system into which English society was divided and the snobbery that it produced. The treatment of women was especially appalling to Abigail, who resented being herded off to a special room after dinner while the men drew port and lit cigars. Cards, the only pastime in which women were included, she considered a waste of time. To improve their manners and widen their horizons, Abigail suggested, Englishmen ought to reside for a time in America. In England, she complained, she had heard "more narrow prejudice, more illiberality of sentiment . . . than I ever saw or heard in my whole life."

Still, she was not one to romanticize her homeland. She criticized Congress for its weakness and fretted over the seeming paralysis that had overtaken Americans since the end of the war. The Shaysites, debt-ridden farmers who interrupted court proceedings in Massachusetts during the fall of 1786, aroused her wrath. They were "ignorant, restless desperadoes, without conscience or principles," she exploded to Jefferson. Nor was she happy with the Virginian's mild reply: "I like a little rebellion now and then. It is like a storm in the atmosphere."

The Adamses greeted with joy the new American Constitution, drafted at Philadelphia in the summer of 1787. The expanded powers given to both Congress and the Executive gave promise of order and stability. The change in government also increased John Adams's desire to return home. A decade of service abroad was enough; besides, he had a good chance of winning a post in the new regime. Adams signified his wishes to Secretary of Foreign Affairs John Jay, and Congress duly recalled him. The Adamses landed in New York in July 1788, just as New York gave it approval to the Constitution (all but North Carolina and Rhode Island had earlier ratified).

First Lady

After the stately mansions they occupied in Europe, Abigail worried that the Braintree farmhouse was too small for her family. When her business agent at home (who superintended the farm, purchased securities for her, and provided funds for John Quincy at Harvard) informed her that a particularly nice house in Quincy was for sale, she quickly instructed him to buy it. She got it for six hundred dollars. The purchase was just the beginning of her new responsibilities. After years of freedom from such mundane concerns, husband John took no interest in their income or expenses.

More than housewife, Abigail was quite literally a home economist. She managed the farm, put the boys through college, and invested their extra cash in securities for their old age. The instructions that she left when she journeyed to New York to attend the birth of Nabby's first baby reveal her many concerns. Briesler, the hired man, was to slaughter a steer and hang it in the cellar, guard the winter stores against rats and mice, bottle the apple cider before it turned to vinegar, and pick through the harvest of pears and apples to remove the rotten ones. If she failed to return in time for Christmas, she authorized John to slaughter a pig so that he could have roast pork for Christmas dinner. He was to save the legs, however, for smoked bacon.

When Adams was chosen vice president in the first federal elections, Abigail supervised the move to New York. She found tenants for the farm, paid their local debts, and saw to the crating of furniture. Richmond Hill, their residence in Manhattan, was a splendid house ("perfectly romantic," exclaimed Abigail), though it was some distance from the center of town.

Adams soon found that his principal job as vice president (a position that he eventually derided as the most insignificant office ever contrived by the mind of man) was to preside over the Senate. Unfamiliar with the role and unable to sit quietly for long periods of time, Adams took an active part in the debates. Enemies were shocked, and even friends were irritated at his lack of presidential impartiality. The early weeks of the first Congress were occupied with a discussion of titles — how to address the president, what to call fellow congressmen, whether to bow upon entering the Senate.

Feeling, as Washington did, that the first essential of the new government was to win the respect of the people, Adams held out for titles and ceremonies of all kinds. Every European government relied on pomp and ceremony, he informed the astonished Senate. Jefferson and other critics of the government began to suspect him of being a monarchist at heart. Abigail loyally echoed John's political views but with garnishment of her own. When a Federalist friend suggested titling her "Autocratrix of the United States," she responded with barbed wit. "I do not know what he means by abusing me so," she wrote. "I was always for equality as my husband can witness."

Abigail did not enjoy the political limelight. Aside from the proximity of her daughter, who lived on Long Island, the only bright spot for her in New York was Martha Washington. The president, the Adamses found, was quiet and reserved, but Martha was a delight. The two "first ladies" quickly became friends. As Abigail had found with Jefferson, the difference between Yankee and Virginian was not a barrier but a source of fascination.

Toward the end of Washington's first term, Abigail's health worsened and she returned to Quincy. Like her husband, she was never robust, and advancing age brought diabetes and a susceptibility to "fevers" (influenza would probably be the modern diagnosis). She remained there until her husband was elected president in 1796. Her interest in politics never flagged, however. When John Jay's accommodation with Great Britain came before Congress for approval, she helped to circulate a pro-treaty petition. Canvassing the town, she encountered a company of militia drilling on the Quincy Common. The captain was reluctant to sign anything, but she brought him around by reading one of her husband's letters, which predicted that anarchy and war would result if the treaty were rejected. To her delight the captain then prevailed upon his entire company to sign.

Washington's retirement she greeted with mixed emotions, for her husband was the logical choice among Federalists to succeed him. "My ambition leads me not to be first in Rome," she wrote John. "If personal considerations alone were to weigh, I should immediately say retire with [him]." For her it meant leaving the peaceful intimacy of her native village for the boisterous pageantry of the capital. And it meant a new sort of confinement. "I must impose a silence upon myself," she said, reflecting on her habit of speaking her mind. She was sure that the presidency would be "a most unpleasant seat, full of thorns, briars, thistles, murmuring, fault-finding, calumny, obloquy." But, she added philosophically, "the Hand of Providence ought to be attended to and what is designed, cheerfully submitted to."

Of one thing she was certain — John must never accept second place should Thomas Jefferson win the presidency. The party battles of the 1790s had utterly destroyed her affection for the lanky Virginian. Jefferson, she now felt, was a cheap demagogue determined to destroy the government. Like Washington and her own husband, Abigail did not understand the function or the value of political parties.

Adams won the election, though by the slimmest of margins — three votes in the electoral college. Jefferson, who placed second in the balloting, became vice president. More flexible than the Adamses, he accepted the job. Tensions within the administration and troubles with France, which had reacted angrily to the Jay Treaty, meant a difficult four years for both president and vice president.

Abigail set out from Quincy at the end of April 1797, some six weeks after her husband was inaugurated. John met her just outside New York and drove her in the presidential carriage to the new seat of government, Philadelphia. The executive mansion had been stocked with their own furniture from Quincy after the Washingtons moved out, and the servants had put all in good order. Within a few days after her arrival Abigail held her first formal reception — "thirty-two ladies and near as many gentlemen."

She adapted swiftly to the role of First Lady. The president relied on her heavily for opinions and advice. He was not inclined to consult his cabinet, a contentious collection of second-rate politicians, who (he later discovered) owed their allegiance to party leader Alexander Hamilton. Abigail usually reflected the president's own views, but the discussion helped him reach decisions. She also kept up an extensive correspondence, mostly with old political allies, explaining and reinforcing the president's public statements. But most important was her function as family economist: she directed a corporate household in Philadelphia while overseeing the Quincy farms by mail.

On a typical day she rose at five and spent the early hours reading, at prayer, writing letters, or watching the sunrise. Family breakfast was at eight, and the remainder of the morning she spent supervising the household. Maids had to be checked, meals planned, and food ordered. Entertaining was part of the daily routine, for she often had thirty or forty guests to dinner. On one occasion she invited the entire Senate. From noon until three she received visitors. Dinner, served in the middle or late afternoon was an elaborate affair, usually lasting two hours. Afterward she "rode out," visiting friends in the city, shopping, or exploring the Pennsylvania countryside.

Philadelphia was a deadly place in the summer, swept annually by yellow fever, and the entire government fled for home. On the road to Quincy in the summer of 1798 Abigail herself was struck by fever, complicated by diarrhea. The common prescription for fever was bleeding, and that, of course, only made her weaker. She recovered slowly and did not accompany John when he returned to the capital city. Indeed, she remained in Quincy for the next two years.

The intervening years were trying ones for President Adams. The French crisis came to a head with the failure of a special commission sent to Paris, and fighting broke out on the high seas. Ultra-Federalists wished for a formal declaration of war against France and were enraged when Adams sent over a new peace mission in 1799. Adams upheld his stand by dismissing two members of his cabinet, but the action left his party bitterly divided. The division helped cost him the election of 1800.

The seat of government moved again in early 1800, this time to its permanent location on the banks of the Potomac, where a city had been carved out of the wooded flats of southern Maryland. No one liked the new capital, except the Virginians, who had contrived the removal. Buildings were unfinished; trees grew in the middle of streets because no one had taken time to remove them. Pennsylvania Avenue, the principal thoroughfare, bogged down in a swamp halfway between the Capitol and the President's house. The executive mansion was a damp and drafty place, barren of furnishings. Mindful of their health, the Adamses kept fires burning in every room.

Nor did Abigail like the South. She had always abhorred slavery, but she had never realized the debilitating effect that the institution had on whites. It was impossible to get them to do anything, she complained, because any sort of manual labor was scorned as "nigger's work." The lower class in white society she considered a step below the slaves "in point of intelligence and ten below them in point of civility."

Abigail greeted Adams's loss to Jefferson in the election of 1800 with sympathy for her husband, but without regret. "Neither my habits, or my education or inclinations," she told a Quincy cousin, "have led me to an expensive style of living. . . . If I did not rise with dignity, I can at least fall with ease, which is the more difficult task." Shortly after his victory became known, Jefferson paid a call on her, offering to be of service in any way that he could. Abigail was gratified at this gracious gesture, but it failed to still her partisan distaste. It would be a decade before the wounds of party strife were healed and the old friendship of Jefferson and the Adamses was restored.

Retirement was a tonic after thirty years of public service, and the health of both Adamses returned. Money was scarce, as ever, but with the cash from the securities that Abigail had secretly bought over the years they lived comfortably enough. The Quincy "mansion" was crowded with grandchildren, first the daughter of Charles, who died in 1800, and then Nabby's children after she died of breast cancer. In 1811 they also took the children of John Quincy Adams after their eldest son, having turned Republican, was rewarded with the post of minister to Russia. There was also a constant stream of visitors and overnight guests. Abigail superintended it all, and when friends suggested that she ought to slow down, she replied: "I had rather have too much than too little. Life stagnates without action. I could never bear merely to vegetate."

In 1818 she suffered a stroke and died swiftly. John survived her another eight years, living long enough to see their son elected president. But the beautiful partnership had ended.

SUGGESTIONS FOR FURTHER READING

Janet Whitney's *Abigail Adams* (1947, reprinted 1970) is probably the best of a rather weak assortment of biographies about the second First Lady. She receives extended and sensitive treatment in Page Smith's splendid biography of *John Adams* (2 vols., 1962). But in many respects Adams herself provides the best insight into her talents and personality. There are several editions of her letters; among the most recent and widely available is Lyman H. Butterfield, Marc Friedlaender, and Mary Jo Kline, eds., *The Book of Abigail and John, Selected Letters of the Adams Family, 1762–1784* (1975). Nancy F. Cott, *The Bonds of Womanhood: "Women's Sphere" in New England, 1780–1835* (1977) discusses the social environment in which Abigail Adams lived.

6

Aaron Lopez: An Immigrant's Story

For the newcomer to America, unfettered by ties of family or custom, Newport was an attractive place to settle. It had a commercial hum, much like that of neighboring Boston, but it also had an air of casual freedom and mannered gentility, reminiscent of Washington's Virginia. Nestled on the southern tip of Aquidneck Island in Narragansett Bay, Newport was born of the sea. Its harbor, one of the finest on the coast, was both natural haven and deepwater anchorage. The largest ocean carriers could tie up at its wharves without the trouble and expense of lightering. Lying almost due east of New York, Newport was closer to Europe by a full day's sail. It also carried on a thriving West Indies trade and competed successfully against Boston for the coastal traffic of New England.

During the Anglo-French wars of the eighteenth century, Newport's ship captains preyed on

Aaron Lopez (1731–1782). *This pastel (measuring in the original 10½ inches by 8½ inches) is the only known portrait of Lopez. It is a miniature, an art form that was very popular at the time of the Revolution.*

enemy commerce in a form of legalized piracy, while smuggling enemy goods past royal customs officials. In peacetime, Newport vessels led the parade of slavers that hounded the coast of Africa. Such enterprise, combined with a leathery conscience, made Newport one of the colonies' busiest seaports on the eve of the Revolution.

The ocean also conditioned Newport's climate and social life. The sea cooled the south winds of summer, making the town a favorite retreat of the wealthy. Carolina rice planters fled to Newport by the hundreds during the fever season, leaving their death-harboring fields to hapless slaves and frightened overseers. From May to October Newport was aglow with the diversions of the rich, and soft Southern accents mingled with Yankee twang.

For a newcomer who had suffered political or religious persecution in Europe, Rhode Island was an idyllic sanctuary. Indeed, the colony was more democratic than Pennsylvania, more open-minded than Massachusetts. Rhode Islanders elected their own town officials, their assembly, even their own governor. Rhode Island and its neighbor Connecticut were virtually self-governing republics only loosely affiliated with the British empire. Religious freedom, decreed by Roger Williams a century before, attracted persecuted sectarians from other colonies and from Europe. Baptists, with their twin roots in Roger Williams and the Great Awakening, were in the majority; but the colony also sheltered sizable numbers of Roman Catholics, Quakers, Huguenots, and the tiniest of American minorities, Jews. Free and flourishing Newport was a powerful magnet to the oppressed, one whose field spanned three thousand miles of Atlantic. Among those feeling the force were a pair of Portuguese Jews, the brothers Moses and Aaron Lopez.

For centuries the Iberian peninsula had been an earthly hell for Jews. In both Spain and Portugal the Roman Catholic church was the dominant force; at times it was even more powerful than the state. When the Protestant Reformation swept across northern Europe, the Church of Rome fortified its bastions on the Mediterranean. The Holy Inquisition, a committee charged with defending the church and eliminating heresy, dictated behavior, speech, and for some, even thought. In Spain and Portugal, Jews, who resisted ethnic assimilation and religious conformity, had never been popular. Both kingdoms, soon after ridding themselves of Arabs (about the time of Columbus) had turned against the Jews. Most Jews fled to less hostile, though scarcely friendly, countries in northern Europe. Those who remained lived under the squinting eye of the Inquisition. To survive, they adopted Christian names and became practicing, if not faithful, Christians.

Among these New Christians, as they were called in Lisbon, Portugal, was Dom Diego Lopez, whose family numbered five sons and a daughter. A well-to-do, respected citizen of Lisbon, Dom Diego wore his Christianity like a cloak, to be shed on entering the sanctuary of his household. His sons shared his pride of birthright, and before long the eldest, José, came under the scrutiny of the Inquisition. Fearing imprisonment (which often ended in execution and burning), José fled to England and then moved on to New York. There he cast off his Christian veneer and assumed the Jewish name Moses. It was some time around the year 1740.

In that year Parliament granted an important concession to Jews and other non-English immigrants in America. It provided that every foreign-born Protestant or Jew could become a naturalized citizen after residing in the colonies for seven years. Parliament's purpose was financial, not humanitarian. It hoped to populate the colonies (and thereby increase imperial revenues) by encouraging the flow of religious dissenters, Germans and Scots-Irish, across the Atlantic. Although Jews were not as yet an important element in this migration, Parliament offered them a special exemption from Christian religious tests. This meant that, once naturalized, Jews had more rights in America than anywhere in Europe, more even than in Britain itself. That meant, however, only that they were free from government harassment. They were not permitted to share in the broad social concerns or political decision making of American society. What was allowed was essentially economic freedom.

Moses Lopez took out his naturalization papers as soon as he was able, formed a mercantile partnership with a cousin who had moved to New York earlier, and was soon on the way to wealth. Newport, which blossomed during the Anglo-French war of the 1740s, soon caught his eye, and in 1748 he took his business partner and his family to the island city in Narragansett Bay. His success was a source of inspiration to other members of the Lopez family in Lisbon, and one by one they began to slip out of Portugal. In 1752 twenty-year-old Duarte, together with a wife and two children, joined Moses in Newport. In his new surroundings the émigré assumed the name Aaron, had himself circumcised, and purchased a Jewish prayerbook. The masquerade was over.

The Rise of Aaron Lopez

A Jew settling in the American colonies did not face the same problems as other non-English immigrants. In some respects his lot was easier, in others more difficult. He encountered, for instance, ethnic and religious discrimination despite the official tolerance. When Aaron Lopez applied to the Rhode Island superior court for naturalization, the court sent him to the assembly. The lower house of the assembly flatly denied his petition on ground that he was a Jew; the upper house suggested that he ask the courts to enforce the 1740 act of Parliament. Back in the superior court, he was once again denied citizenship, this time on the grounds that the colony was already full of people. Lopez ultimately obtained his naturalization papers in Massachusetts, though he had to establish temporary residence in the Bay Colony (one month proved sufficient).

Partly because they were a tiny minority battered by prejudice, Newport Jews were a close-knit community, and they maintained regular contact with the Jewish community in New York. For a new arrival, such as Aaron Lopez, this was a decided advantage. Friends and relatives lent him money on easy terms and introduced him to mercantile contacts in New York, Boston, and London. Within several years after his arrival, Lopez was an international dealer pursuing profit between the Western Hemisphere and Europe.

The outbreak of the French and Indian War just two years after his arrival in America was another streak of fortune. Naval operations interrupted trade, caused shortages of certain goods, and raised prices. The Dutch island of St. Eustacius in the West Indies became an entrepot for European goods evading the British and French regulations. Lopez was soon doing a brisk business in smuggled Dutch tea, which Parliament had prohibited Americans from drinking as far back as the 1720s. At first he hired ships for his various enterprises, legal and otherwise; but by the end of the war he owned vessels of his own, usually in partnership with other merchants. Shareholding, because it spread the risks, was an early form of marine insurance.

Spermaceti was another article made scarce by the war. A waxy substance extracted from the cranial cavities of the sperm whale, spermaceti was used in making candles. For brightness, durability, and cleanliness, spermaceti candles were unequaled by any other kind. Such was the demand for these candles in America and Europe that any hint of shortages drove prices up. As an intercolonial middleman, Lopez bought head matter from the Nantucket whalers, sold it to candle manufacturers, and helped market the end product. Toward the end of the war — exactly when is not certain — he went into candle manufacturing himself.

The war disrupted the whale hunt and caused a shortage of head matter. Candle manufacturers found themselves in a bidding war, while Nantucket fishermen reaped more profit from fewer whales. In 1761, the year after fighting ended in North America, the candlers moved to resolve their problem. Nine of them signed a trust agreement fixing the price of head matter and allocating portions of the annual catch. Among the signers were Aaron Lopez (though whether as candle trader or manufacturer is uncertain) and the largest candlemakers of all, the Browns of Providence. External competition and internal bickering prevented the agreement from working as planned, but in 1763 it was renewed for another year. Such cartels were known in Europe at the time, but this was probably the first to be formed in America. It was hardly the "big business" techniques of a John D. Rockefeller, but the mentality was essentially the same.

Smuggling and cartels suggest that Aaron Lopez was a man of slender conscience when a silver shilling was to be made. His entry into the slave trade furthers the impression. The infamous triangle trade — the corners of which were New England, the Guinea Coast of Africa, and the Southern colonies — was a relatively late development. Through much of the seventeenth century the slave trade was dominated by Europeans, principally Spanish, Portuguese, and Dutch; and the scattered imports into British North America were mainly an overflow from the West Indies. In 1670 England, through the agency of the Royal African Company, swept into the lucrative traffic in human beings, but it was not until after 1700 that American merchants became interested. When they did involve themselves, however, the Newporters were in the forefront, probably because of their well-established West Indies contacts.

The exchange of New England rum and trinkets for African slaves was common practice by the time Aaron Lopez entered the trade in the 1760s. Rhode Island alone possessed thirty distilleries for making rum from West Indies molasses, and the colony annually sent eighteen to twenty rum-laden vessels to the Guinea Coast. Half of Newport's sailing fleet, it has been estimated, was engaged in the rum and slave traffic. Lopez entered the trade in partnership with his father-in-law, and until the Revolution disrupted the trade he sent one or two ships a year to the Gulf of Guinea. That he felt no pang of conscience over such a nefarious way of making money is clear from his correspondence. That he was not alone in his indifference to the tragedy of slavery is equally clear. Men must be judged in part by the moral code of their times.

Merchant Prince

By the end of the 1760s Aaron Lopez was one of the richest merchants in Newport, with agents and business correspondents in every major trading center of the Atlantic community. His waterfront establishment on Thames Street was a city landmark. When the British occupied Newport during the Revolution, a British officer declared the premises capable of housing two hundred men. They included Lopez's own residence, a wharf, and a three-story building that served as warehouse, counting office, and sail loft.

He owned a fleet of about twenty vessels with shares in many others. The number fluctuated constantly as Lopez built and sold, and in ports where timber was scarce he sometimes ordered his ships broken up for lumber. Captains and crews apparently wound their way home in the service of others.

He traded in anything and nearly everything, from Bibles to horses, from barrel staves to violins. Yet there was system in his expansiveness. The loci of his operations were the West Indies, the Atlantic coast of Europe, and New England. His business was chiefly the exchange of colonial staples for European consumer goods, yet he concentrated on products with which he was familiar. Sugar and molasses were mainstays of his trade, but he avoided tobacco, apparently because he knew little of what one English king called "the stynkyng weed." Despite Newport's close association with South Carolina, Lopez did no important traffic in that colony's staples: rice and indigo.

The far-flung ventures of Aaron Lopez concealed a basic conservatism of character. Land speculation, the foundation of many an American fortune from John Jacob Astor onwards, Lopez considered too risky. Nothing about the American West attracted him, whether furs, Indian trade, or mineral riches. Even whaling, which was perhaps the most speculative venture of his life, was tied closely with his other concerns, such as candle manufacturing. He was a merchant, not a speculator, and a man of his own time, not a prototype of the flamboyant nineteenth-century businessman.

Within the context of his surroundings, Lopez was nevertheless a man of boldness and imagination, who literally built an empire on credit. On the eve of the Revolution he owed his London agent the towering sum of £22,600. The size of his operation and the uncertainty of his markets (given the lengthy transatlantic communications lag) meant that he had to have a great deal of flexibility in making choices. Flexibility required substantial lines of instant credit in every commercial center. Credit, in turn, depended on a reputation for fair dealing, to say nothing of paying past debts. A hard-headed conservatism no doubt also played a part. In the eighteenth century, whether in Rhode Island or Virginia, reputation was a person's most valued asset. A traveler passing through Newport four years after Lopez died was informed that the "eminent Jew Merchant" was considered a man of "unblemished character and was universally esteemed." Few of the business captains of the following century could justly put that on their tombstones, no matter how many libraries they endowed.

Though at the height of his career, Aaron Lopez faced a host of troubles as the 1760s drew to a close. The growing conflict between crown and colonies disrupted his trade patterns and forced him into unfamiliar political dilemmas. Lopez eventually came to terms with the Revolution in America, but the transatlantic conflict broke apart his own empire. He might have regained his power and prestige after the war — though his beloved Newport never did — but an untimely death dispelled the opportunity.

Internationalist or Patriot?

The imperial conflict that swirled up in the 1760s, following the French and Indian War, deeply affected Aaron Lopez's interests but failed to provoke his sympathies. With evenhanded indifference he evaded British regulations and American embargoes. He carried on business as usual through the Stamp Act controversy, though he found the London market slow because the trade of others had been disrupted.

Lopez was not alone, for the mercantile community of Newport itself was politically apathetic. There were no riots there following the Stamp Act, and Newporters refused to join the Nonimportation agreements of 1769–70. When in 1770 Boston's Sons of Liberty sent a delegation to persuade Newport to join the agreement, a Tory friend alerted Lopez of their coming. The friend did not doubt that Lopez would "treat them as they deserve." We do not know the outcome of the visitation, except to say that Nonimportation collapsed before Newport did. But the incident also reveals Aaron Lopez to have been at best a very reluctant rebel.

Why this apparent indifference in such exciting times? In Samuel Adams's Boston or Washington's Virginia scarcely anyone could avoid an early commitment, to one side or the other, in the imperial controversy. Newporters, with some exceptions, were dragged into the patriot cause. One explanation, perhaps, is that Newport was a polyglot community, full of religious and ethnic minorities who had little in common with the Sam Adamses and George Washingtons who dominated the Revolutionary movement. Jews, such as Aaron Lopez, saw little in the American political system to command their loyalty. Lopez's only contact with the government was in the humiliating episode of naturalization papers. As a rich merchant, moreover, he had much to fear from lower-class disorders, and he disliked the interference of the Sons of Liberty in his business affairs.

There was still much of the European in Aaron Lopez. After coming to America, he seemed more interested in Europeanizing his surroundings than in absorbing American ways. His shiploads of imports seemed designed to bring European amenities into American life. After the early years when friends in Newport and New York helped get him started, his chief line of credit came from London. Yet a return to the Europe from which he had fled presented other problems. In America he was at least legally free. He became a patriot in 1775, it seems likely, because there were no visible alternatives.

The outbreak of war in the spring of 1775 found Lopez undertaking a characteristic business-as-usual venture into the South Atlantic. One of the whaling captains reported that the hunting off the Falkland Islands was yielding spectacular results. Brazilian ships had taken a thousand whales in the vicinity of the islands in the previous year. For years the whale hunt had been drifting southward as the waters of the mid-Atlantic were cleared of whales. The Brazilian coast, moreover, was a dangerous one politically. To be forced ashore there, by storm or accident, was, moaned one captain, to fall into the hands of "whores and rogues fiercer than the infernal devils."

So promising did the Falkland venture seem that Lopez invested every available penny, forming a temporary partnership with two Boston adventurers. Oblivious to the imperial conflict, he sent one vessel out in April

1775, within days of the Battle of Lexington, and several more in September while Washington's army was digging in around Boston. To ignore the obvious risks was strange for one of Lopez's cautious temperament. Even if his whalers managed to escape British men-of-war, the market for head matter was bound to be unsteady. Most curious of all, in his sailing orders Lopez warned his captains to steer clear of Spanish and Portuguese warships but never mentioned the British. He would pay dearly for his political naïveté.

The predictable disaster came in November 1775, when British warships seized five of Lopez's southbound whalers off the Azores. Lopez's partners promptly sailed for London to secure release of the vessels. In a petition to the ministry of Lord North, they claimed that the whalers were ultimately destined for Britain with their cargoes of oil and head matter. They even averred that Lopez himself was bound for London to set up a candle factory. That point was not true, though it may at one time have been under consideration. It may have been a bit of insurance had Lopez decided to side with the Loyalist cause. At the least it reveals him as an international dealer with few, if any, political loyalties.

The promises, however, paid off. In February 1776 the British government released the five whalers, and three resumed their voyage to the South Atlantic (two proved unseaworthy). Then nature intervened, as it had so often before on such hazardous waters. Only one of Lopez's whalers survived the Atlantic storms and made it back to London with a cargo of oil and head matter, and that one was so broken that it had to be scrapped. It was a costly failure that left Aaron Lopez in financial straits for some years.

Miraculously, Lopez's political trimming never incurred the wrath of radicals. The urbane tolerance of Newport was part of it, for he almost surely would have been in trouble in Sam Adams's Boston. But his smuggling activities no doubt also helped. Lopez had evaded British taxes and regulations long before the imperial hostilities began; the new impositions, such as the Townshend duties, merely increased the variety of his illicit cargoes. In 1772 Samuel Ward, former governor of the colony and soon to be a member of the Continental Congress, wrote Lopez a friendly letter concerning a cask of wine that had washed up on Ward's beach. Although by law the wine was his, Ward had learned that it was part of a cargo thrown overboard by one of Lopez's captains evidently under threat of British search. Ward returned it to Lopez, asking only that the man who had rescued it from the sea be rewarded. It was a sign of the general esteem that Lopez commanded.

When the war came, Lopez, whatever private doubts he may have had, publicly endorsed the patriot cause. His hesitation is scarcely surprising. Jews never participated in European wars; not since ancient times had they fought as a people. They had, moreover, been well treated by the British, both at home and in the colonies. But the heady promises of the Declaration of Independence were too alluring. They joined a cause that promised freedom and respect for all men. And American governments had already begun the never-ending process of redeeming those promises. Several of the state constitutions drafted in the early years of the war permitted Jews for the first time to vote and to hold political office.

Endorsing the patriot cause by no means ended the troubles of Aaron Lopez, however. In December 1776, while Sir William Howe's army tightened its grip on New Jersey, a British amphibious force landed in Rhode Island and captured Newport. Some two thousand townspeople fled the British advance, among them the Lopez family. In contrast to his political naïveté of the previous year, Lopez was prepared for this intrusion of world affairs into his life. Some months earlier he had begun transferring his property and business records to Providence at the upper end of the bay. By the time the British arrived, he had nothing to leave the marauders but his house and wharf.

Lopez conducted his business from Providence until the summer of 1777 and then moved farther inland. He ultimately settled in the town of Leicester in southern Massachusetts. There he purchased some land and built "a large and elegant mansion," the size of the house bespeaking an improvement in his financial circumstances. He resumed his mercantile operations but with changes dictated by the war. His domestic trade increased considerably and with it the amount of traveling he had to do, making contacts and collecting debts. He even kept open the European connection, even though all goods had to be smuggled now because of the British blockade. He bought and sold through the Dutch, transshipping goods through Sweden to avoid British scrutiny. Even so, only about half his cargoes got through, and the war so disrupted the American economy that he was never sure of his market.

Lopez's letters from Leicester during the war years nevertheless spell contentment. Others of the Newport Jewish community settled in Leicester as well, and they apparently encountered no overt hostility. The Jews for their part were cautious not to offend local customs, notably by closing their stores on Protestant holidays. Aaron Lopez's personal fortune mended, and he paid off most of his past debts.

He was no doubt looking forward to a prosperous future in the spring of 1782, as fighting faded in the wake of Yorktown. On a springlike morning in May, the Lopez family decided to visit an ailing relative in Providence. Riding in a two-wheeled sulky while his family rode in a carriage, Lopez paused at a pond to water his horse. Something startled the horse, and it plunged into deep water overturning the sulky. Aaron Lopez, who had never learned to swim despite a lifelong connection with the sea, was drowned.

He had lived through the birth of the republic without taking part in the drama. In that respect he may have been more typical of his fellowmen than were Washington, Franklin, or Adams. His devotion to business and its profits — pursuits at which he excelled in the way that Adams excelled in politics — were not unusual for his time, nor later. In his own way this Portuguese refugee helped build the new nation.

SUGGESTIONS FOR FURTHER READING

There is only one biography of the Newport merchant, but it is well crafted: Stanley F. Chyet, *Lopez of Newport, Colonial American Merchant Prince* (1970). The story of another prominent Jew of the Revolutionary period is Madison C. Peters, *Haym Salomon, the Financier of the Revolution* (1911). For the social milieu in which Lopez lived and worked, the reader might consult Samuel Rezneck, *Unrecognized Patriots: The Jews in the American Revolution* (1975), and Carl Bridenbaugh, *Cities in Revolt, Urban Life in America, 1745–1776* (1955).

Part 2

Character Builders

"As an independent nation, our honor requires us to have a system of our own, in language as well as government. Great Britain . . . should no longer be our standard; for the taste of her writers is already corrupted, and her language on the decline."

— Noah Webster

7

Noah Webster: The Search for National Identity

"Who in the four corners of the earth reads an American book? Or goes to an American play? Or looks at an American painting or sculpture?" This poisoned dart was flung by an English literary critic, Sir Sydney Smith, in 1819, almost a half-century after America declared its independence. The sneer hurt, but there was much truth in it. Long after it achieved its political freedom, the young republic remained commercially and culturally dependent on Great Britain.

American writers were few and unread. Philip Freneau, the newspaper curmudgeon who assaulted Washington's policies in the 1790s, produced some fine lyrical poetry, and Charles Brockden Brown was a passable storyteller in the Gothic tradition. A handful of New England poets ("Connecticut Wits") struggled with self-conscious epics glorifying the new nation, but it all scarcely amounted to a literary flowering.

Noah Webster (1758–1843). *This oil-on-canvas portrait, done in 1833, presents a benevolent old schoolmaster, seated at his desk with open book and ready pen. The dictionary had been published by this time, but improving and expanding it remained a life's work.*

Benjamin Franklin once blamed the wilderness for the paucity of American literature. Americans, he explained, were so busy taming a continent that they lacked time for plays and poetry. The explanation was plausible but not sufficient. Another factor was the shortage of type, ink, and paper, all of which had to be imported from Europe in the early days. As a result, American printers preferred timely periodicals, such as newspapers and almanacs, which did not tie up their machinery for long periods of time.

Even when these technological problems were solved, publishers ignored American authors. It was cheaper and easier to pirate British works, since there was no international copyright agreement. American readers, too, seemed to prefer the English greats — Shakespeare, Milton, Dryden, and Pope — to their own fledgling writers. Even after the appearance of Washington Irving, the first American writer to win international acclaim, most Americans could be found reading the novels of Sir Walter Scott.

The Blue-Backed Speller

Noah Webster set out to change all that. A nation, he reasoned, needed a feeling of identity, a consciousness of self that bound it together and distinguished it from others. Political independence was important, but no nation was truly independent until it developed a culture of its own. "Every engine should be employed," he declared after the Revolution ended, "to render the people of the country national, to call their attachment home to their own country; and to inspire them to the pride of national character."

A sense of homeland, it must be said, existed even before the Revolution; John Adams referred to it as "the Revolution in the minds and hearts of the people." And it was early reflected in literature and the arts. A century before the Revolution, Americans took pride in a distinctive literary style. New England writers in particular stressed the importance of plain, clear writing, cleansed of aristocratic ornament. Cotton Mather, whose *Magnalia Christi Americana* (1702) was an historical glorification of New England, explained that he wrote "everything with an American pen," avoiding "Ostentation" in order to make his discourse "Profitable for . . . Plain Folkes."

The notion of European decadence was not simply a figment of Puritan clerics. Americans generally subscribed to the theory of the westward movement of the arts. The history of civilization, so ran this concept, followed a grand pattern — imperial domination and cultural leadership had migrated inexorably westward, from Greece to Rome to western Europe. British writers, viewing themselves as the ultimate beneficiaries of this transplanting, prepared themselves for the role of genial host. Americans gloried in this British fortune, but they could see further implications as well. "There is nothing," wrote John Adams in his later years, "more ancient in my memory than the observation that arts, sciences, and empire had travelled westward; and in conversation it was always added since I was a child, that their next leap would be over the Atlantic into America."

Implicit in this assortment of attitudes were several key ingredients for a "national character." Puritanical reform, with its implied moral superiority, the sense of mission, and the inherent faith in the informed individual were part of a feeling of Americanness. A search for national identity was well under way before 1776; political independence only made the search more urgent, more self-conscious. No one felt this more acutely than Noah Webster; and, like Cotton Mather a century earlier, he recognized that linguistic expression was a critical step. To the formation of an American language he devoted his life.

Noah Webster was born in 1758 in Hartford, Connecticut. His forebears were among the first settlers in the Connecticut River valley, but they had not significantly advanced their fortunes. Webster's father, though a man of some importance in the village, possessed a modest eighty-acre farm. He had enough substance to send Noah to Yale, however. After graduating from college in 1777, the young scholar took up the study of law. Legal training then consisted of work in the office of some practicing attorney, while wading through the heavy tomes of Coke and Blackstone. Noah Webster's tutor was Oliver Ellsworth, later to become senator from Connecticut and the nation's second chief justice. It was a good start for a promising career in law and politics.

But something went wrong. His law practice failed within a year. In 1782 he moved to Goshen, New York, and opened a private elementary school. It was a curious decision; schoolteaching was not a profession then, nor were teachers highly regarded. For the ambitious young man, teaching was a brief pause in life while he saved enough money to enter a more rewarding field such as law, medicine, or the ministry. Webster spent a year teaching school after he emerged from Yale. Perhaps he simply enjoyed that more than the law.

Having made teaching his vocation, Webster gave some thought to the art. What disturbed him most was the lack of books. Arithmetic could be mastered with horn and pencil, but spelling and reading required books. The few such books available were published in England, containing English usages and forms. What American children needed, Webster decided, were books that would reflect the American language. Within a year he produced a speller, the first such published in the United States. The many purposes of the *American Spelling Book* (1783) were outlined in the preface:

> *To diffuse an uniformity and purity of language in America, to destroy the provincial prejudices that originate in the trifling differences of dialect and produce reciprocal ridicule, to promote the interest of literature and the harmony of the United States. . . . .*

Webster's motives were as much patriotic as pedagogical. He wanted to give the American form of English a distinctive cast by cleansing it of archaic spelling (such as *publick*) and unnecessary letters (such as the *u* in *labour*, *favour*, and *honour*). A nationally accepted speller, he also realized, would create a uniform language and eliminate the variations that originated in the phonetic spelling of regional pronunciations. Even as a teaching device, the speller was multipurposed. In addition to providing a standard for word usage, it would, Webster hoped, improve the morals of youth. The first sentence in the book, consisting of two- and three-letter words, was: "No man may put off the law of God."

By 1786 Webster was ready with two more texts, the *American Reader* and *American Grammar*. The *Reader* was intended to replace the ancient *New England Primer*, used by generations of young Yankees. Where the *Primer* focused on religious themes, Webster sought to instill patriotism. His reading passages dealt with the events of the Revolution and the lives of American heroes. The *Grammar* battled the pedantry of English grammarians, who persisted in using archaic forms. Webster was one of the first to perceive that language is a living thing, subject to change by common usage. Not only was he willing to let usage guide grammarians, he also sought to simplify and clarify the language — by using a singular verb, for instance, after the second person singular ("you was").

For convenience (and doubtless to promote additional sales) Webster combined the speller, reader, and grammar into a single volume entitled *The Grammatical Institute*. The subtitle promised an entire curriculum:

An American Selection of Lessons in Reading and Speaking; calculated to improve the minds and refine the Tastes of Youth, and also to instruct them in Geography, History, and Politics of the United States. To which are prefixed rules in Elocution, and Directions for expressing the Principal Passions of the Mind.

Patriotism, morality, and advanced pedagogy were a potent sales combination, and *The Grammatical Institute* was an instant success. The *Reader* was the mainstay of American schools until the 1830s, when it was replaced by the *McGuffey Reader* (whose principal contribution was the use of graduated reading passages). The "Blue-backed Speller" was even more durable, lasting through most of the nineteenth century. By the time of Webster's death in 1843, it had sold some twenty-four million copies (only the Bible exceeded its sales record). Webster's royalty was a half-cent a copy, enough to keep him in comfort for the rest of his life.

Realizing the ease with which his books could be pirated, Webster instantly began a campaign for American copyright laws. Webster spent much of the 1780s touring state capitals in the effort to secure laws that would guarantee authors' rights. Little could be achieved, however, without national legislation. The Federal Constitution authorized just that; and in

1790, Webster, working through his old mentor Oliver Ellsworth, secured passage of a federal copyright law. Forty years later the law was renewed through the efforts of another friend (though no relation), Daniel Webster. His motives were not entirely selfish. Without protection for its authors, he felt, the new nation would never be able to develop a distinctive literature. Other writers agreed. Charles Brockden Brown pointed out that there was not a single full-time professional author in the entire country because American publishers found it more profitable to pirate English works.

Political unity, symbolized if not fully established by the Federal Constitution in 1788, reinvigorated Webster's crusade for cultural identity. Simplicity, he came to argue, was the virtue that best befitted a republic. To survive, a republic required patriotic citizens willing to subordinate personal interests to the public good. Allusion, indirection, and ornament were the devices of the factious and the corrupt. "America must be as independent in literature as she is in politics," he insisted. By "literature" he meant more than fiction or poetry; he was thinking of learned publications of all kinds — artistic, scientific, even historical. He had in mind an aesthetic and moral creed for the young nation, one as true and guileless as nature itself.

The youthfulness of America was a decided advantage, Webster felt, because cultural achievement was cyclical. Nations, like human beings, grew from infancy to maturity and eventually to senility. England, he felt, had already passed that meridian when "language and taste arrive to purity." America, still in her infancy, thus had little to learn from Europe except "folly, corruption, and tyranny." By returning to "first principles," by developing "original" ideas, the new nation could establish a luminescent cultural identity of its own. "Americans," he cried, "unshackle your minds and act like independent beings."

Partisan Unionist

In 1783 Webster returned to his Hartford birthplace and rented rooms from the lawyer-poet John Trumbull. For the next ten years, despite wide travels, he would regard Hartford as home. It was a small village, perhaps three hundred houses, perched on the west bank of the Connecticut River, but it was a hive of commercial and intellectual activity. The Connecticut Valley offered some of the best farmland in New England; its sturdy proprietors had some time since earned the appreciative title "river gods." As the chief market town for the valley, Hartford was booming at the end of the war. Shopkeepers grew unexpectedly rich; factories, making everything from textiles to clocks, sprouted on the village outskirts.

The newfound wealth transformed the somber "land of steady habits," as Connecticut liked to consider itself. Hartford glowed with social activities every night of the week, and Webster moved easily into its gay routine. Oliver Wolcott, a classmate of Webster's at Yale (and later U.S. Secretary of the Treasury), introduced the rustic schoolteacher to the more fashionable ladies of Hartford; the two young bachelors were soon to be seen everywhere.

Hartford also became during these years the most active literary center in the new nation, home of "the Wits," poets, essayists, and diarists who sang the glories of the new republic. Trumbull introduced Webster to this circle, the center of which was Timothy Dwight, staunch defender of Congregational orthodoxy and, somewhat later, president of Yale. The vehicle for the Wits' ponderous poems and heavy satire was *The Echo*, a literary digest that combined culture with strong Federalist politics. Webster's ardent nationalism made him a Federalist too. Publication of his books earned him a national reputation and requests for lectures from all parts of the country. More often than not, his lecture topics were political, pleas for a stronger national government. He was in Philadelphia when the Federal Convention met in 1787, serving temporarily as headmaster of an Episcopal Academy. He obtained a copy of the Constitution on the day it was published, and a month later he was in print with a pamphlet explaining and defending it.

During his brief sojourn in Philadelphia, Webster met Rebecca Greenleaf, the vivacious daughter of a wealthy Massachusetts landowner. The courtship was swift, primed no doubt by Webster's social baptism in Hartford. A week after he met her, Webster was addressing her as "the sweet Miss Greenleaf"; two weeks later she was "the lovely Becca." When Rebecca returned to Boston two months later, the pair had an "understanding" that they would marry, provided her family approved and Webster obtained financial independence. The latter proved the more difficult condition, for it was two years before Webster felt secure enough in the income from his writings to marry. They settled in Hartford in 1789.

It was a happy and fruitful union. During the next seventeen years, they had eight children, all but one of them girls. A second son died shortly after he was born; the rest of the children survived their father. Webster, brimming with educational theories, took an active part in their training. He could not, however, surmount the eighteenth-century view of female roles; hence most of their education centered on household management and such skills as playing the harpsichord. The few family letters that survive reveal a happy household. Webster's only son, William, was one of the last to be born and hence was hopelessly spoiled by parents and sisters alike. In later life he experienced a succession of misadventures in business and had to be repeatedly rescued by his father.

On moving to Hartford, Webster once more put out his plaque advertising himself as attorney-at-law, but it is doubtful that he ever intended to make a living at the law. Instead, he undertook a series of publishing ventures, none of which turned out very well. He retained his political interests as well, lending his pen freely to the service of the Washington administration. In 1793 he moved his family to New York to found a newspaper, the *Commercial Advertiser*. This venture was a success, and before long Webster was the chief journalistic voice of Federalism in the city. A series of letters he wrote in defense of the Jay Treaty under the pseudonym Curtius were so ably drawn that Jefferson thought them to be the work of Alexander Hamilton. Yet Webster was not an unthinking partisan. During the French crisis of the late 1790s he criticized Federalists for abandoning Washington's policy of strict neutrality. He approved of Adams's peace initiatives; and in the election of 1800 Webster openly sided with the president, denouncing the Hamiltonians for undermining him. This was too much for Hamilton, the Federalist leader in New York, and he set out to purge Webster from the party. In 1801 Hamilton helped to finance the establishment of a rival paper, the *New York Evening Post*. Thus rebuffed, Webster sold out and left politics. He would devote the rest of his life to a dictionary.

The Dictionary

A dictionary was a natural outgrowth of Webster's interest in spelling proprieties and national uniformity. He had been toying with the notion since the 1780s when Benjamin Franklin suggested making English more phonetic. Franklin, who had taught himself French by lip-reading (and to improve his proficiency in that art had invented bifocals), thought that an international language, spelled phonetically, would promote understanding and peace. In particular, Franklin wanted to substitute *k* for *ch* and to rid the language of the infamous silent *e* in such words as *knife* and *wife* (though he did not realize, as Webster did, that the *e*, though silent, is not without function, for it lengthens the sound of the *i*). Webster wrote a number of essays in defense of Franklin's concept, pointing out that it would make the language easier to learn for children and immigrants and would help distinguish the American style of writing. The idea certainly appealed to Abigail Adams, a poor speller because of her lack of formal education. To simplify words like *thought* (*thot*) and *through* (*thru*), she felt, would help the many who suffered from the same disadvantage. Otherwise, Webster's crusade unfortunately aroused little attention, but it did start him thinking about an American dictionary.

The most widely used English dictionary was that compiled by Samuel Johnson in the mid-eighteenth century. For Americans the work had serious limitations, of the sort that had induced Webster to undertake his initial textbooks. Johnson, a pedagogical snob, listed primarily words of Latin or Greek origin (though he could not avoid such common Nordic words as *sky*), and he disliked newly coined expressions. The result was a compilation of archaic words, many of which were infrequently used, and it contained no American expressions at all.

Webster started work on the dictionary after selling his newspaper. The project took him almost a quarter-century, including two years in England doing philological research in the library at Cambridge; but in 1825 he finally published it in two massive volumes.

Webster's dictionary represented some philological improvement over Johnson's. He pointed out the French and Anglo-Saxon origins of some English words, though he was still unacquainted with Indo-European antecedents. He also incorporated some of the spelling reforms that he had pioneered in his *Speller*, dropping the *k* from *publick*, for instance, though he conservatively retained *traffick* and *frolick* (these were altered in later editions, however). He dropped the unnecessary *u* from *honour* and *labour*, and he reversed the English (actually French-originated) *re* in *theatre* and *centre*. He retained the order in *massacre* and *acre*, however, realizing that the *re* kept the *c* hard *(er* would have changed the *c* to an *s* sound, as in *acer)*.

But his chief contribution was the introduction of peculiarly American words, which had never before received a philological imprimatur. The New World experience had enriched the English language in many ways. There were unique forms of landscape, such as plains and prairie that required description (often French in origin*). There were new kinds of plants (squash, corn, tomato) and new animals (buffalo, moose, porcupine, caribou, antelope) that demanded names, most of them contributed by Indians. Foreign words introduced by immigrants added further enrichment. In Pennsylvania, western Virginia, and the Carolinas, German expressions, such as *strudel* and *noodle*, were in common use. The Dutch, who first settled New York, added more variety with *crib, boss, stoop, pumpkin,* and *cookie.*

Webster also democratically incorporated American colloquialisms, though he carefully excluded slang. Most were familiar English words to which Americans gave a new meaning. *Calculate* to an Englishman meant "to reason, to put things together mentally"; Americans often used it as a synonym for *intend* or *propose. Clever* in old English applied to body movements, meaning "graceful"; Americans applied it to the mind, making it synonymous with *shrewd.* Finally, Englishmen raised *windows;* Americans raised *kids,* or occasionally *hell.*

Such linguistic flexibility inevitably ran afoul of some of the more conservative literary critics. Joseph Dennie, arch-Federalist editor of the *Port Folio,* denounced any effort to form a dictionary of the "American vulgar tongue." Such Americanisms as *lengthy, belittle,* and *sot* he relegated to a category of "wigwam words" that stemmed from a too-long association with Indians. To recognize such barbarisms as legitimate, he predicted,

---

* Some terms are French in origin because they were devised by French explorers and fur traders, who were among the first to penetrate the interior of the continent.

would subject American writing to world ridicule. Thomas Jefferson disagreed. New expressions, he thought, were the natural result of the diversity and novelty of American life; they enriched the language rather than adulterating it.

Implicit in Jefferson's argument was the cyclical theory of culture, the abhorrence of European decadence and the worship of America's pristine youth. During the 1790s the venerable imagery of the cultural nationalists had been adapted to partisan ends. Jeffersonian Republicans effectively portrayed the Federalists as decadent monarchists, while clothing themselves in republican simplicity. After 1800 Federalists would retaliate with a claim that Jefferson's election to the presidency brought a decline in moral standards, a laxness of social behavior, and (presumably) an "Indian vocabulary." The political cannon fire redirected, but did not halt, the efforts of the linguistic nationalists. In the field of architecture, as we shall see, there was a similar interaction of politics and art.

Webster, who credited American farmers with speaking the purest English in the world, was willing to accept any usage that was in "general practice." But he also recognized that a dictionary had to set some sort of standard. So he compromised his democratic and nationalistic inclinations by agreeing to follow the usage of the "best English writers." His solution — reminiscent of his moderate Federalism in politics — became standard practice for American dictionaries.

Like *The Grammatical Institute*, the dictionary was an instant success, though its size and cost precluded wide sales. Reproduced in countless editions, and published today by Charles Merriam and Sons, it is still the widest-selling dictionary in the United States. Because Webster himself realized the need to keep language abreast of the times, he devoted the rest of his life to the project. He was in the midst of a revised edition when he died in 1843.

Appearing at a time when spelling and pronunciation were not fully settled, when there was wide regional variation, Webster's dictionary set a national standard. It had an incalculable impact on the development of a national consciousness. And, by giving its blessing to American expressions, his dictionary helped free American writers from the straitjacket of European classicism. American literature came into full flower shortly after his death, with the essays of Emerson, the poems of Longfellow and Whitman, and the novels of Hawthorne and Melville. Noah Webster, it can justly be said, planted the seed.

SUGGESTIONS FOR FURTHER READING

A recent, rather commendable essay on the Yankee schoolmaster is John S. Morgan's *Noah Webster* (1975). Older but more detailed is Harry R. Warfel, *Noah Webster: Schoolmaster to America* (1936, reprinted 1966). Homer B. Babbidge, Jr., has collected some of Webster's own essays in *Noah Webster: On*

Being American (1967). Benjamin T. Spencer, *The Quest for Nationality* (1957), traces the search for an American style in literature. A splendid book, relevant to all the sketches in this section, is Kenneth Silverman, *A Cultural History of the American Revolution: Painting, Music, Literature, and the Theatre in the Colonies from the Treaty of Paris to the Inauguration of George Washington, 1763–1789* (1976). Silverman skillfully blends literary and artistic criticism with historical fact. It is a book that will instruct the scholar and entertain the dilettante.

8

Charles Willson Peale: Patriotism in Color

The literary talents of the Revolutionary generation were invested in political themes, rather than creative or imaginative writing. Yet there was an abundance of cultural creativity. It simply appeared in the visual arts rather than in literature. In the field of painting, for instance, no generation of Americans has excelled the genius of Benjamin West, John Singleton Copley, and Gilbert Stuart.

Unfortunately, all three of these giants were Americans only in name. Benjamin West went to London at an early age and remained there all his life. Copley became a Loyalist in the Revolution and joined West in London. Stuart spent his best years in Britain, returning to the United States only when he ran short of money. America gave birth to great artists, but it did not nurture them.

The exiles, it is true, formed a

Charles Willson Peale (1741–1827). *Entitled "Self-Portrait with Spectacles," this oil was done in 1804. Peale was a versatile individual, like so many others of his time. He combined a talent for painting with entrepreneurial skill. For him, art was a business.*

distinctively American school in London. West painted scenes from the American past, and his masterpieces — *Penn's Treaty with the Indians* and *The Death of Wolfe* (1771) — started a vogue of historical painting. John Trumbull, an officer in Washington's army, earned the title Painter of the Revolution by recording epochal events, such as *The Declaration of Independence* and *The Surrender of Cornwallis*. Trumbull's work was done, however, in West's London studio after the war, and the scenes he depicted sprang mostly from imagination. Perhaps a better claimant to the title Painter of the Revolution was another soldier, who carried brush and canvas along with his gun, Charles Willson Peale.

A portrait artist, Peale recorded the visage of every political and military figure of his day. By preserving the Revolutionary generation for posterity, he hoped to inspire patriotism and national pride. Like Noah Webster, he set out to mold an American character. His vehicle was the brush and canvas. The finished paintings were exhibited in his Philadelphia museum, alongside fossils, stuffed animals, and writhing reptiles. Entertainment, instruction, and a sense of national pride were all under one roof.

The Planter-Artist

Charles Willson Peale's family was English. His grandfather and great-grandfather were ministers of the Church of England. Peale's father, though educated at Cambridge, did not enter the ministry; indeed, his one talent seems to have been handwriting. Along with some family influence it landed him a job in the London post office. Unhappily he abused both his talent and his position by forging signatures that enabled him to embezzle several thousand pounds of sterling. He was arrested and sentenced to death, the normal punishment for forgery. Family political influence instead won him a sentence of transportation to the colonies.

Death or transportation was a common choice for British criminals. To confine them in jail for any length of time was considered an unnecessary burden on the public. For some time Maryland and Virginia were the favored targets of transport until they formally objected. The colonists feared a criminal element in their midst, although there is good evidence that most transportees mended their ways. Benjamin Franklin informally suggested that Americans transport their rattlesnakes to Britain in exchange. After Americans won independence, Britain bestowed her penal custom on Australia.

After landing in Virginia, Peale made his way north to Annapolis, where he obtained a job as a schoolmaster. (It was evidently considered a fit position for a felon.) Successful at that, he married and moved across the bay to Maryland's eastern shore to open a school of his own. There Charles Willson Peale was born in 1741.

Upon the father's early death, the family returned to Annapolis, the lovely provincial capital nestled on the banks of the Severn River. It was a small village, numbering perhaps a hundred houses and a half-dozen stores and warehouses. Government traffic and the law courts were its chief profit and pleasure. It boasted a theater and various open-air entertainments. Maryland's tobacco gentry took their leisure there, giving the place a resort atmosphere — the "Bath of America" some called it. Samuel Adams would not have enjoyed the place, but it was a natural environment for a young man with artistic talent.

At the age of fourteen Peale was apprenticed to a saddler to learn a trade. Before long, he was decorating his saddles with ornaments and buckles of his own design. They sold well and brought in money enough so that he could open a shop of his own. He did a brisk business in ornate saddles and decorated harnesses, for Maryland was prospering in the 1760s. Tobacco was selling better than usual, and Maryland's planters enjoyed high living. Some with a taste for English customs asked him to paint the family arms on their coaches. From there he branched into portraying the gentry themselves.

Peale was a natural tinkerer, somewhat like Benjamin Franklin. Among his sidelines were furniture upholstery, silversmithing, and watch repair, in all of which he was self-taught. Painting was for him another form of manual art. He shared Franklin's deistic curiosity about nature, probing its mysteries with oil and canvas, and later collecting specimens for a museum.

He taught himself painting in the same way that Franklin taught himself reading. Knowing nothing of colors, he journeyed to Philadelphia, bought a book on painting in a bookstore, studied it for four days, and went to a color shop to load up on supplies. Back in Annapolis, he swapped one of his best saddles for lessons with a local portraitist. His instructor first demonstrated his technique while Peale watched and then painted half a face, leaving Peale to finish the other half.

Peale's own efforts were clearly amateur. He was able to achieve likenesses, but the subjects were stiff and formal, bent in unnatural postures. Some, because of the poor quality of his oils, faded after a few years. Worst of all, they failed to provide much income. Never able to manage money, he soon found himself over nine hundred pounds in debt and pursued by the sheriff. In the summer of 1765 he fled to Virginia to escape his creditors — he claimed that they had secured court judgments to punish him for having joined the Sons of Liberty. From Virginia he journeyed on to Boston, making his way evidently by giving lessons in drawing.

In Boston, Peale made his way to the studio of John Singleton Copley, already regarded as the best portrait artist in America. Copley showed him his latest productions and may even have thrown in an informal lesson or two. Whatever the details, Peale seems to have profited by the experience, for his own portraits became noticeably more lively. He returned to Virginia (selling his watch to finance the voyage), taking up residence with an art-loving family that he met on the ship.

Then fortune, at last, intervened. John Beale Bordley, prominent Maryland planter (also famed for his agricultural experiments) and member of the Governor's Council, took a liking to one of his paintings and offered to finance a trip to Europe "to get improvement." Peale accepted, though it meant leaving behind a wife and two children (who had somehow weathered his earlier misfortunes). He sailed in the spring of 1766 on the same vessel that carried Maryland's unused stamps, left from the defunct Stamp Act.

The Artistic Whig

The American painter's mecca was the London studio of Benjamin West. A founder of the Royal Academy, West was one of the best-known painters of the day. Though an exile, he never forgot his Americanness, and he offered lodging and advice for every young artist that came his way. Peale remained with him for almost three years, learning the rudiments of portraiture — how to select and mix oils, to prepare canvases, to pose subjects, and to render lighting. His major work in London was a portrait of William Pitt, a hero among Americans for his opposition to the Stamp Act. Following the rules of neoclassicism, Peale dressed Pitt (who did not sit for the portrait in any case) in a Roman toga with Roman ruins in the background. In his hand was a scroll listing the rights of Englishmen. It was more political cartoon than work of art, but the king's opponents liked it.

The only other surviving work from Peale's London sojourn was a pencil sketch entitled *London Lovers*. The man, seated with a girl in his lap, closely resembles Benjamin Franklin. The sketch may well have originated in a visit that Peale paid to the venerable doctor. Admitted by a servant and sent upstairs, Peale found Franklin in deep embrace. The conversation, he reported, later turned to the subject of electricity.

On his return home in 1769, Peale found himself something of a celebrity. His Pitt portrait had been reprinted in colonial newspapers, instant advertising for both his talents and his politics. Portrait commissions flowed in, especially from persons of political import. A portrait of Pennsylvania's John Dickinson done at this time shows, in the relaxed poise of the subject and the exquisite use of lighting and color, how much Peale had learned in the school of Benjamin West.

In 1772 Martha Washington asked him to render George in oil (evidently to balance the portrait she had of her first husband). She also wanted him in military uniform, a reminder of the glory days. Though reluctant, George finally agreed. The result is the first known portrait of Washington, and it was the first of five done by Peale.

For the next few years Peale traveled extensively, living variously in Philadelphia, Baltimore, and Williamsburg. He understood his limitations as a painter. In 1772 he told his patron, John Beale Bordley, that he lacked the skill and dedication to be a first-rate portraitist but hoped to "improve myself as well as I can while I am providing for my support." Though never fully free of financial worries (partly because his family expanded faster than his income), Peale did acquire a few acres of land and some slaves.

Despite his financial straits, he freed his slaves as quickly as he could, often after training them for work. (Too many critics of slavery freed their bondsmen only at death, without providing for the slaves' education.) The most famous of Peale's black protégés was Moses Williams, who learned to draw profiles from shadows. It was mass-production art, which Peale later put to good use in his Philadelphia museum. Williams was said to have done 8,880 shadow profiles in a single year, at a royalty of eight cents apiece. He ultimately married Peale's white cook and settled in Philadelphia with a modest fortune.

When the Revolution began, Peale was settled in Philadelphia. It was a wonderful position for a patriot-artist, set amidst momentous events, mingling with the country's great. Peale, a radical since the days of the Stamp Act, wore his politics on his sleeve. Though he was not in the army, he had a military uniform in his wardrobe and practiced shooting his rifle in the yard behind the State House where Congress was sitting. John Adams found Peale's dress (which included sword and gold lace) a bit ostentatious but liked him personally as a "tender, soft, affectionate Creature." Adams paid several visits to what he described as Peale's "Painter's Room." He admired the portraits, though he considered Peale inferior to Copley.

In the spring of 1776 Congress commissioned Peale to do a portrait of Washington in honor of his having expelled the British from Boston. It was indeed an honor, since this was the first bit of artistic patronage undertaken by what was yet to be the United States. John Hancock, who as president of Congress transmitted the commission, asked Peale to do a portrait of Martha Washington as well. Martha, in turn, asked him to render a miniature of George. Before it was over, Peale also did one of Hancock — who ended by paying for the entire lot out of his own pocket (twenty-eight guineas).

When the British chased Washington across New Jersey and menaced Philadelphia in the fall of 1776, Peale's militia company was called to arms. He joined Washington's forces shortly after the raid on Trenton, and painted the army recrossing the Delaware River, returning to Pennsylvania with its prisoners. Though not the *Crossing* of fame and legend, Peale's sketch was far more accurate than the romantic extravagance (complete with Washington standing in a boat) done by the German Emmanuel Leutze seventy-five years later.

He continued to paint in the army, doing portraits of countless generals and colonels. He also experimented with the miniature, a portrait so tiny that it could be carried in a locket. He offered to do another one of Washington during the summer of 1777 (for free, he said), but the commander in chief declined. Because General Howe was on his way to Philadelphia, Washington was busy preparing defenses at the Brandywine. That winter, at Valley Forge, while the army shivered in snowbound tents, Peale found time to portray the likenesses of over forty officers.

In 1780, after the war in the North died down, Washington agreed to another sitting, this one commissioned by General Rochambeau, commander of the French army in America. Though completed before Washington's final triumph at Yorktown, the portrait contains an aura of victory (see p. 37). Washington, resplendent in continental uniform, stands leaning casually on the muzzle of a cannon, a confident smile brightening his face. The American flag, symbol of the newborn nation, reaches skyward to the rear. This, incidentally, was the first pictorial representation of the American flag, which had been authorized by Congress in 1777. Earlier battle flags either included the British Union Jack in a corner or featured Rattlesnakes and Pine Trees.

Ever alert to profit, Peale made nineteen oil copies of the painting for distribution in both America and Europe. The copies varied some in both dress and background (some showed Trenton; others showed Princeton, and even Monmouth), but public-spirited citizens and state legislatures scooped them up (although the five consigned to Europe never sold). Until Gilbert Stuart rendered his famous bust portrait some fifteen years later, Peale's version was the Washington familiar to the public — a tall, narrow-shouldered man, fighting a middle-age paunch, benevolent in look, self-confident in his manner.

In the latter stages of the war Peale busied himself with Philadelphia. During the British occupation, Loyalists and neutrals had come into the open and had dominated the city's social and economic life. When the British evacuated the city, they marched overland to New York (risking Washington's attack at Monmouth) so that their Tory sympathizers could leave by ship. Even so, a number of British sympathizers remained in the city, braving patriot wrath. Peale, a 1776 radical and member of the Constitutionalist party (supporters of the state's ultra-democratic constitution), was among the leading Tory-baiters. He soon ran afoul of the Republicans, a party organized by Robert Morris and other city merchants for the purpose of revising the state constitution. The subtle distinctions between patriotism and partisanship, criticism and subversion became blurred, and at times the fighting got rough. Peale took to carrying a hardwood club, which he dubbed Hercules, when he went out by day; he hung it by his bed at night. He credited it with saving his life on one occasion, though it is not clear whether the assault was political or simply street crime. When the war ended, he purchased a house on Second Street, which the government had confiscated from a Loyalist, and returned to his brush and canvas.

The Philadelphia Museum

The museum became Peale's chief interest after the war. The idea originated with a discovery in a Kentucky salt lick of the bones of a prehistoric animal (a mastodon). Never before described by scientists, the animal was called simply the American *incognitum*. Peale purchased the bones to make drawings of them. Lying about the studio, they attracted visitors. A museum of such relics, Peale decided, would make money (he was forever short of funds), and it would assist in the display of his art.

There were few forms of popular entertainment in American cities of the Revolutionary era. The theater was frowned upon because it encouraged idleness. Musical societies were for the wealthy. Public parks were still in the future. The poor, who lived on the perimeter of the city, would have had no use for them, in any case. Museums, which were educational enough to satisfy the puritanical but entertaining enough to attract the multitudes, were among the few available facilities. Peale showed how versatile a museum could be for mass entertainment. P. T. Barnum, who purchased the remnants of Peale's collection years later, expanded the museum into a circus.

Peale collected specimens throughout the postwar years, and — with characteristic timing — opened the museum while the Federal Convention was meeting during the summer of 1787. The place itself was a work of art. Paintings of Revolutionary heroes adorned the walls. Stuffed animals (Peale became an expert taxidermist) were placed in their natural settings, a painted background with real rocks and logs for effect. Members of the American Philosophical Society, with which Peale was closely associated, sent specimens and fossils from all over the country. It quickly became a national institution. A pair of prize European pheasants, which Lafayette had given Washington, were sent on to Peale when the birds died.

After the museum was well established, a European visitor recorded his impressions:

Near the door the American buffalo stands in its huge and natural shape; this aborigine of the western hemisphere may properly be called a substitute for the Cow. . . . A vast variety of monsters of earth and main, and fowls of the air are seen in perfect preservation and in their natural shape and order. Over them are suspended 50 portraits, being complete likenesses of American and French patriots.

At the further extremity of this room are to be seen a great collection of bones, jaws, and grinders of the incognitum, or non-descript animal, royal tiger, sharks, and many other land and marine animals hostile to the human race — shields, bows, arrows, Indian and European, scalps, etc.

In an adjacent room Peale had a snake collection. For special visitors he would pick up the slithery creatures and let them wrap themselves around his neck. The chief feature was a rattlesnake, an animal unknown in Europe and widely feared. In the museum's yard was a veritable zoo, with eagles, owls, monkeys, baboons, and, most curious of all, a five-legged (six-footed) cow.

The museum, in short, was a microcosm of the world, all of nature's wonder brought under one roof. It was a union of art and science, "a new kind of painting" in the words of one of Peale's biographers. It reduced the Enlightenment to common understanding, spreading knowledge while encouraging artistic taste.

The museum netted Peale a steady income, but it was also expensive. Expeditions to recover new wonders had to be financed out of his painting. The Federal Convention appeared at first to be a rich source of commissions, and Peale took advantage of the occasion to ask Washington for another sitting. Washington obliged, coming to Peale's house for several mornings in succession before attending the day's session of the convention. Reproducing the painting by a mezzotint process, Peale offered copies for sale at a dollar apiece. He hit the market just as the convention was ending (a good time, one would suppose, for the sale of souvenirs), but the prints did not do well, even when he cut the price in half. Thus his money troubles continued. In 1789 he asked Washington for a post in the government, specifically as postmaster general, but was turned down (was Washington acquainted with Peale's family history?).

Peale's first wife, a Maryland woman, died in 1790. She had borne him four sons — Raphael, Rubens, Rembrandt, and Titian. Seeing an opportunity to cure his financial troubles, Peale set out to find a wealthy dowager, scouring first Maryland and then Pennsylvania. In New York he finally found a partner both willing and suitable, a De Peyster whose lineage and lands went back to the earliest settlements (she was twenty-five, he fifty). In honor of her ancestry he named his first child by her Van Dyke Peale. He ultimately had three wives and sixteen children.

Financially secure at last, Peale expanded the museum in the 1790s. It quickly outgrew its quarters, and in 1794 he moved into the hall of the Philosophical Society at Fifth and Chestnut, occupying the whole second floor. In 1802, when the state capital moved to Harrisburg, the legislature rented him the old State House. Informative, entertaining, and patriotic,

Peale's museum had become almost a public service. It was one of the landmarks of Philadelphia.

Preoccupied with the museum, Peale's portrait work became less frequent, though there was a fifth and final rendering of Washington. The occasion was the return of Rembrandt Peale, the only son with sizable artistic talent, from a European tour. To help secure the young man's reputation (he was only seventeen), Peale asked President Washington for a sitting. It was 1795, nearly the end of Washington's term, and the aged hero agreed. Taking advantage of the opportunity, Peale brought every member of his family with a talent for drawing. He himself did one from a three-quarters angle, Rembrandt painted a full view, Raphael did a pencil sketch, and the youngest, James, dabbled. When Gilbert Stuart, who had already done several renditions of Washington, learned of the exercise, he warned, with heavy-handed pun, that the president was "in danger of being Pealed all around." The remark also had a political sting, for Peale was by then a firm adherent of the Jeffersonian Republicans.

Peale became acquainted with Jefferson through their mutual scientific friends in Philadelphia — David Rittenhouse, astronomer; Joseph Priestley, discoverer of oxygen; and Benjamin Rush, the celebrated physician. All three were, like Peale, Pennsylvania democrats and firm Jeffersonians. The Jefferson connection became of service to Peale, when the skeleton of another *incognitum* was found by a farmer in Ulster County, New York. Although the bones were broken in the digging, Peale bought them for two hundred dollars and got permission to explore the pit further.

The job was not easy, for the twelve-foot pit, where the farmer had been digging marl for fertilizer, was full of water. Peale obtained money from the American Philosophical Society, and President Jefferson asked the navy to lend him bilge pumps and tackle. Peale's painting of the operation indicates that most of the labor force was his own family (see p. 118). The results at first were disappointing, but in a second marl pit they found a virtually complete skeleton. Mounted in the museum, it stood eleven feet high, with tusks eleven feet long. It was popularly called a "mammoth" (creating a short-lived fad for oversize products such as mammoth bread and mammoth cheeses), but scientists eventually named it "mastodon" after its peculiar teeth.

Peale considered the beast long extinct; scientists agreed. This produced some philosophical problems, however, since the Darwinian theory of evolution had not yet been formulated. God, it was commonly assumed, had created all living things in one gesture, arranging them by order of complexity and intelligence in a "great chain of being." But if that was truly the order of creation, why would God have permitted one link in the chain to expire? That was a question that neither Jefferson nor Peale could resolve.

In 1810 Peale purchased a farm near Germantown and retired to the

"Exhuming the First American Mastodon" (1806–1808).

country, leaving the museum in the hands of his son Rubens. Rubens dressed up the place and introduced gas lights, the first to be used in an American building. More of a businessman than his father was, Rubens added entertainment features to attract crowds. One of his most popular acts was a one-man band, an Italian who, with hands, elbows, and knees, played a viola, cymbals, a drum, and a set of pipes simultaneously, and by wagging his head could ring chimes with a crown of Chinese bells. Rubens also set up a branch museum in Baltimore and moved the main operation to New York. When P. T. Barnum purchased the New York museum in 1841, it formed another link in the evolution of mass entertainment.

Peale disapproved of his son's methods but did not interfere. Instead, he devoted his declining years to tinkering with inventions. Among his devices was a "fast walking machine," a sort of two-wheeled scooter that anticipated the bicycle. The toy became so popular in Philadelphia that it menaced pedestrians and had to be outlawed. Peale also found a way of making false teeth out of porcelain, a vast improvement over the wooden or ivory ones that had plagued the aged. Ever mindful of money, he advertised himself as a dentist who could fit false teeth, though his price ($150) was too high for most.

Peale lived to see the golden anniversary of independence and Lafayette's celebrated tour. The French aristocrat stopped with Peale to pay his respects and was delighted with a portrait of himself as a nineteen-year-old general. Peale contracted a fever shortly thereafter, and, like his friend Washington, died of the bleeding prescribed by his physician. It was Washington's birthday, February 22, 1827.

SUGGESTIONS FOR FURTHER READING

Charles C. Sellers, *Charles Willson Peale* (1969), an edition graced with many fine examples of Peale's work, is the standard biography. Good accounts of some of Peale's fellow artists include James T. Flexner, *America's Old Masters: West, Copley, Peale, and Stuart* (1939); and Irma B. Jaffe, *John Trumbull: Patriot-Artist of the American Revolution* (1975). J. Meredith Neil, *Toward a National Taste: America's Quest for Aesthetic Independence* (1975) traces the efforts of Americans to free themselves from European styles of painting.

9

Charles Bulfinch: An American Style in Building

The Atlantic community was more than the economic interdependence of Europe and America. A community of ideas, of cultural interchange, it was a tie that political independence could not break, nor could cultural nationalists, such as Charles Willson Peale and Noah Webster. Artistic styles know no national boundaries. The best that Americans could hope for was to make some contribution of their own to the Western community. In painting and eventually in literature they certainly did. So, too, did they in architecture.

Massachusetts-born Charles Bulfinch lacked the self-conscious nationalism of Webster and Peale. He was content with British forms, indeed with a style of building that the British had borrowed from Italy. Yet his buildings, though they followed the rules of European classicism, had a distinctively American flavor. Bulfinch was an

Charles Bulfinch (1763–1844). *This oil portrait by Mather Brown was completed in 1786, just before Bulfinch departed on his European tour. And prepared he was for European society, with well-tailored coat, ruffled lace, and powdered wig. This was a pedigreed gentleman, not a rustic colonial.*

artist in his own right, the first professional American architect. And his works were an important thread in the Atlantic community.

The Neoclassic Revival

Colonial American builders copied their plans from British architectural handbooks. Every British style found its echo in America. Early in the century, Christopher Wren, who had rebuilt much of London after the Great Fire, was the acknowledged master. His crisp, stocky style can be seen today in the Wren building of the College of William and Mary or in Harvard's Massachusetts Hall. A little later the baroque came into fashion, influenced by Inigo Jones's masterful Blenheim Palace in England. Baroque designers broke the face of a building into planes, employed curved or broken lines, and varied the texture and color of their walls. All of these devices were used by Virginia's William Byrd in constructing Westover on the banks of the James River (1730).

Later still, a Palladian fad swept Britain and America. A sixteenth-century Italian, Andrea Palladio, had discovered the decorative possibilities in Roman and Greek columns. He boldly posted columns and pilasters around doors and windows, and added columned cornices to his structures for their effect. Palladian art crossed the Atlantic in English architectural handbooks. Peter Harrison, a Newport merchant-designer, used a Palladian model for his famous Redwood Library (1750), and Thomas Jefferson's Monticello (1772) is Palladian in essence.

In the middle of the eighteenth century, Western Europeans discovered the ancients for themselves. French archeologists unearthed the city of Pompeii, buried under volcanic ash since A.D. 79; other scholars poked through the ruins of ancient Greece. Greek civilization, overshadowed for centuries by the lingering memory of Rome, won new esteem. French archeologists were so bold as to suggest that Greek designs were even superior to Roman. Doric temples, such as the Parthenon in Athens, previously considered primitive, came to be admired for their pristine simplicity. A classical revival swept the Atlantic community, influencing building styles in Europe and America for the better part of the next hundred years.

A Scot, Robert Adam, was the leading proponent of neoclassicism in Britain and, indirectly, in America. Touring Italy's archeological treasures, Adam absorbed the Roman mode of design. What impressed him most were the Romans' public buildings, such as the baths of Diocletian. Sturdy and immense, they conveyed a sense of hardihood, that they would endure for a millennium. The form could also be ponderously dull; so, to overcome that, Adam added Roman arches and domes, supported by Palladian columns. On the interior he introduced oval-shaped and octagonal rooms.

The result was an orgy of design, an architecture that was more pictur-
esque than functional. It was also a form well suited to institutions that
wished to convey an impression of durable magnificence — government
offices, for instance, or universities and banks. Adam's best-known works
were of this sort: the law library at Edinburgh University, for example, or
Somerset House in London (1786), which is today a government records
depository.

The Adamesque style, as it was called in Britain, was brought to America by Charles Bulfinch. But Bulfinch, unlike his American predecessors,
was not content to apply British plans to American needs. He evolved a
distinctive style of his own, one that reflected the strict, disciplined environment of New England. With Bulfinch came the beginnings of an
American style in architecture.

Yankee Designer

Charles Bulfinch, born in Boston in 1763, came of good Yankee stock. His
father was one of the leading physicians in town; his mother was the
daughter of a wealthy merchant. He attended the Boston Latin School,
which offered the finest elementary education in the country, and attended
Harvard. After the Revolution he went on the Grand Tour, the finishing
touch on a young gentleman's education. Minister Jefferson, to whom he
carried a letter of introduction, showed him the sights of Paris and recommended a tour of the Roman remains in southern France and Italy. In
1786 Bulfinch visited England, just as Adam was finishing his famous
Somerset House. The style apparently made a lasting impression, although
Bulfinch at the time had no intention of entering the field of design.

He had been bred to the world of trade, and on his return in 1787 he
opened a mercantile house in Boston. For a few years things went well, and
in 1791 he was elected one of the town selectmen, a position he held until
he moved to Washington, D.C., in 1817. He had the imagination and
enterprise for financial success. Seeing a housing shortage in the town
(there had been little construction since before the war), Bulfinch planned
a housing complex. It was to be financed by a tontine, a form of life an-
nuity. A group of persons contributed to an investment pool, and the
annual return for each increased as the number of survivors diminished,
with the last survivor inheriting the whole.

Bullfinch undertook to design the housing development himself, and his
plan was both bold and original. Called the Tontine Crescent, it consisted
of two crescent-shaped lines of row houses, which together formed an
oval. At one end of the oval was a theater, at the other a marketing center.
The oval form was undoubtedly borrowed from Adam, as were the arches
and columns with which Bulfinch adorned windows and doors. But the
concept itself was pure Bulfinch. It was certainly unlike anything ever

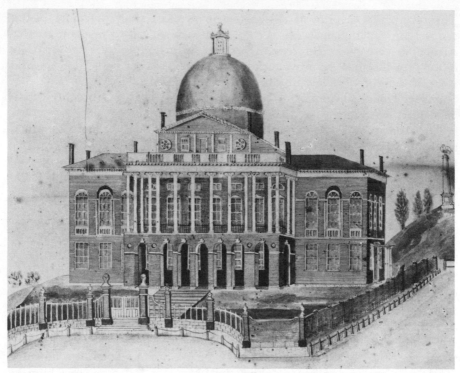

The Massachusetts State House, Boston (1797).

seen in Boston, whose principal architectural landmarks were century-old churches designed by Christopher Wren.

Financially, however, the experiment was a disaster. Only half the oval, consisting of sixteen houses, was completed before a brief commercial depression struck the city. The tontine went bankrupt, taking Bulfinch's mercantile firm down with it. His business ruined, he turned increasingly to architecture to support his growing family.

The Massachusetts State House established his reputation in his new profession. The construction of government houses after the Revolution presented everywhere a rare opportunity to give architectural expression to American ideals. Jefferson's design for the Virginia state Capitol (1786) was deliberately Roman, as a reminder of history's grandest republic. Bulfinch was less self-conscious in his choice of styles, but when he won the commission for a state house in Boston, he turned to British classicism for a model.

Completed in 1797, the Massachusetts State House (shown above) was clearly inspired by Robert Adam's Somerset House, but with important changes. By using brick instead of stone, Bulfinch avoided some of Adam's ponderousness. Heightened arches and slim columns holding the front portico gave Bulfinch's structure a light, airy appearance. The dome, another feature of Adamesque style, Bulfinch made of wood, finely spliced to present a smooth appearance and coated with gold leaf. The use of brick and wood gave the building a fine-textured appearance, quite in contrast to the heavy ornamentation of the Adamesque, and allowed it to blend with its Boston surroundings.

The State House in Boston was an ingenious adaptation of the imperial Adamesque to the American environment. Nowhere was this more evident than in the interior. Slender columns and unadorned woodwork gave the hall of the House of Representatives the virtuous simplicity of a congregational meetinghouse. The decorated domed ceiling was a reminder of Adam, yet even there Bulfinch managed an impression of restrained elegance.

The State House was instantly acclaimed a masterpiece; together with the Tontine Crescent it ranked Bulfinch as the leading designer in New England. Imitated elsewhere in New England and across the North, it started a new vogue in architecture, often called the federal style because it coincided with the formation of the federal government under the Constitution. There was political innuendo in the term *federal* as well. Federalists, particularly in New England, were fond of things British, and they approved of Bulfinch's model. Bulfinch himself was a lifelong Federalist. Thomas Jefferson, on the other hand, wished instead to cleanse America of all British influences. He hoped that the architects of the new republic would turn to Greece and Rome for inspiration. Thus, the party warfare of the 1790s spilled even into the domain of architecture.

A Federal Style in Building

Establishing Bulfinch's reputation, the Massachusetts State House earned him numerous commissions for the design of private townhouses; thereafter he devoted full time to his art. He did more than draft plans: he supervised the construction of buildings to ensure that his plans were met. Because of his total commitment to his craft, as well as the number and variety of buildings that he designed, Bulfinch qualifies as America's first professional architect.

Like his public works, Bulfinch's townhouses were Adamesque in inspiration. Robert Adam designed an entire square (Portland Place) in his native Edinburgh and numerous country seats for Scottish and English aristocrats. Among his trademarks were the columned hood over the front entryway, often with curved ironwork, the alternation of square and semicircular windows, and the use of pilasters for decoration. Adam's interiors (usually done by his brother James) were excessively ornate, a maze of ovals and octagons, false arches supported by false columns, and domed ceilings with a plethora of artistic detail.

*Harrison Gray Otis
House, Boston (1796).*

Such opulent splendor would have been entirely out of place in stern New England, as Bulfinch well knew. So he tempered Adam's style, eliminating the frills, yet retaining basic elements, such as the spatial juxtaposition of squares and circles. The more he worked with the art form, the more he bent it to the New England environment, where wealth was earned, but never outwardly displayed. The houses he built for Federalist leader Harrison Gray Otis were starkly functional, as businesslike as an accounting office. The Adamesque is only hinted — in entryway and in windows — the rest is pure New England.

Boston's thriving merchants avoided external displays of wealth, but they indulged themselves more openly on the inside of their houses. Like Adam, Bulfinch sought artistic help with interiors. In Samuel McIntyre of Salem, a woodcarver who could make everything from furniture to fireplaces, he found authentic genius. McIntyre's best pieces, such as the fireplace in the Otis house, managed to convey both an opulent warmth and a restrained elegance, and compares favorably with the artistic saturnalia of an Adam fireplace.

Bulfinch also designed a number of churches in New England. In fact, his finest piece may have been the meetinghouse in Lancaster, Massachu-

*Lancaster Meeting
House, Massachusetts
(1817).*

setts. Though basically federal in design, and reminiscent of the State House, the Lancaster meetinghouse was bare of ornament, except for the McIntyre-style cupola. The bell tower, as square and simple as a Wren church, was supported by graceful arches, with columns only two bricks thick. The church's interior was determinedly spartan, as Puritan custom demanded, except for the pulpit, a decorative climax that commanded the attention. The stairway, an intricate blend of geometric planes and lighting effects, bespoke an exquisite austerity. When compared with an Adamesque staircase, it presents a symbolic declaration of American artistic independence.

In 1817, the year in which the Lancaster meetinghouse was completed, President Monroe invited Bulfinch to Washington as Capitol architect. It was a signal honor, especially coming from a Republican and a Virginian. It reflected, perhaps, Monroe's wish to heal the wounds of party warfare and to draw the nation together. A Federalist newspaper in Boston dubbed the new climate an "era of good feelings."

Bulfinch replaced Benjamin H. Latrobe, who had been Capitol architect almost from the inception of the federal city. Although born and trained in England, Latrobe had no feeling for the Adamesque style. He preferred a closer imitation of Greco-Roman forms, a style that suited Secretary of State Jefferson, who superintended construction of the federal city in the 1790s. As a result, Washington was a classical city; the Capitol was a Roman building. Its grand porticoes, held up by Ionic and Corinthian columns, and its splendid dome, reminiscent of the Roman Pantheon, spoke a classical grandeur that Latrobe and Jefferson found befitting a republic that was also, in its Western dominions, an empire.

The Capitol was virtually finished by the time Bulfinch took command, and he had the good sense to leave it alone. He disliked its slavish classicalism, but he also realized that alterations at that juncture would result in nothing but an ugly hybrid. He did remove the corncob capitals, which Latrobe had placed on the columns outside the House of Representatives in a misplaced burst of patriotism. And he made some alterations in the interior, introducing his own unique blend of intimacy and elegance.

Bulfinch returned to Boston in 1830, having made little impact on the nation's capital. But by then his main work was done; indeed, his federal style was already yielding to a new form of classicism, known as the Greek Revival. Even so, his style remained the vogue in the Yankee settlements of the upper Middle West, where every market town boasted its own variation on the Otis house (for instance, William Tecumseh Sherman's house in Lancaster, Ohio). And the Massachusetts State House also had its Western replicas, such as Bascom Hall (1851) at the University of Wisconsin.

The Greek Revival, on the other hand, found its principal adherents in the South. Massive porticoes supported by sweeping columns contributed a stately elegance to the plantation homes of the gentry. The architectural finery seemed to reinforce their dominant political and social position.

The contrasting styles, well developed by the time Bulfinch died in 1844, reflected the growing sectional rift between North and South. There was no "national style," nor had there ever been. But Bulfinch and his compatriots had made a telling contribution to the Atlantic community of design.

SUGGESTIONS FOR FURTHER READING

A good new assessment of Bulfinch is badly needed. The best available at present is *Charles Bulfinch, Architect and Citizen* (1925) by Charles A. Place. William H. Pierson, Jr., *American Buildings and their Architects: The Colonial and Neoclassical Styles* (1970), is splendidly detailed, clearly written, and lavishly illustrated. Talbot F. Hamlin treats Bulfinch's contemporary designer, *Benjamin Henry Latrobe* (1955). Harold and James Kirker, *Bulfinch's Boston, 1787–1817* (1964), discuss the homeland of the "federal style."

10

Isaac Backus, Crusader

The first settlers came to New England to establish a Godly community with a true church. They soon found that righteousness was a never-ending struggle against apathy and evil. Their

descendants were still carrying on the struggle in the Revolutionary generation. By then itinerant evangelists had fanned out from New England bearing the Word into every part of the country. Revealed religion was in every fiber of the American character.

The settlers of early New England called themselves Puritans because they wanted to eliminate from the Church of England the lingering vestiges of Roman Catholicism — the ranks of bishops and archbishops, for instance, the colorful vestments worn by the clergy, and symbolic gestures such as the sign of the cross and kneeling at Communion. All of these were "relics of popery" that had no foundation in the Bible.

Isaac Backus (1724–1806). *The Spartan informality of this sketch, done apparently in Backus's middle years, is somehow fitting. He would have been as out of place in an elegant painting as he would have been in ministerial raiment. A plain dark suit, probably home-made, was the working apparel for this much-traveled evangelist.*

Puritan theology originated with John Calvin, one of the great intellects of the Protestant Reformation. Calvin's theology, eminently logical, derived from his concept of God as all-knowing and all-powerful. If God was truly all-powerful, reasoned Calvin, then only He could determine the population of Heaven — that is, which beings would be His saints. It followed, too, from the fact of his omniscience that he must *know* at the beginning of time who all the saints would be. This, then, was the Covenant of Grace, the doctrine of predestination — that God chose certain individuals as saints, long before they were even born, and that He did it out of His grace alone without any thought or deed on their part. When those individuals chanced to be born — becoming thereby "visible saints" — they would, of course, lead meritorious lives, for that was the sign of grace. Their upright lives *merited* Heaven but did not *earn* it.

The covenant, or contract with God, was an important part of this theology. The Biblical foundation for it was God's bargain with Abraham and the promise to watch over his "seed." On this rested the ancient Jewish notion of the "chosen people," protected by God but obliged, in turn, to follow His way. English and American Puritans, as "visible saints," similarly regarded themselves as chosen. Those who came to America came not only to escape persecution in England but to found a Godly community, a "Wilderness Zion," a society so perfect that it would serve as a model to the world.

In practice, of course, they ran into some difficulties. In any community the saints were certain to be in a minority, especially as it prospered and attracted newcomers of uncertain morals. In the daily routine of this earth, how was one to identify true saints? There might be many law-abiding individuals who had simply not been among the chosen. Early Puritan ministers evaded the issue by suggesting that, while only a few persons could reach Heaven, it was the duty of all to act as if they might. And it was the function of the church to point the way.

Still, there were some, like Roger Williams, who remained troubled. What happened to the saint, Williams wondered, if he or she might chance to take Communion side by side with a sinner? The difficulty with sanctity was that it was so easily tainted. The slightest mote of evil was sufficient to bring damnation. Williams was also troubled by the union of church and state, which was implicit in the concept of a Zion. The Puritans' intent was to govern by God's law, but in practice it meant political interference in the church — another source of pollution. Because his critique struck at the very foundation of the Puritan community in Massachusetts, Roger Williams was exiled to Rhode Island in the 1630s. Establishing a colony of his own there on the shores of Narragansett Bay, Williams separated church and state so as to leave each individual free to pursue his or her own conscience. Williams's conscience eventually led him into adult baptism as a symbol of rebirth in righteousness. A few English Puritans had followed a similar path, just as another group, the Anabaptists, had done in Switzerland a century before.

Baptists remained a minor religious sect in both Britain and America until the eve of the Revolution. Then another religious revival set anew the search for a way to distinguish the saints. The leader in this cause — and founder of the modern Baptist Church — was Isaac Backus.

The Great Awakening

The Puritans' Zion suffered chronic backsliding and cleansed itself with periodic revivals. The intent of each revivalist was to awaken people to a realization of their sanctity, to induce them to shed their past sins and to experience a rebirth. By so doing, they hoped to restore the original ideal — the community of saints. In the mid-1730s one extraordinary minister, Jonathan Edwards, succeeded in doing just that, converting his entire community of Northampton, Massachusetts. By the end of the decade Edwards's revival became merged with an intercolonial religious awakening, with zealous converts spreading the word in every hamlet and byway.

The climax of this Great Awakening came in 1739 when George Whitefield stormed onto American shores. Whitefield came out of English Methodism, a religious revival started by John Wesley in an effort to bring the church to the ordinary Englishman, and vice versa. Wesley would eventually steer the Methodist church away from strict Calvinism, but Whitefield adhered to the Calvinist creed. He preached the doctrine of original sin, that the vast majority of mankind was condemned to perdition. But he also offered redemption to those who would shed their sins and seek salvation through Christ. It was a simple formula — "experimental religion" he called it — a plea that his listeners experience conversion, with the certainty that they would lead upright lives thereafter.

Whitefield was a magnificent speaker who could hold an audience of thousands in rigid attentiveness. And he was a new breed. Protestant services had always centered on the minister's sermon, usually a soporific exploration of fine points of theology. Whitefield was a one-man show — he raved and ranted, he shouted, sang, wept, and roared. He could describe hell so vividly that one could almost find it on a map. And he made converts by the thousands. When he arrived at last in New England in September 1740, the Congregational ministers invited him into their pulpits. Piety swept the land, and echoes of Whitefield's visit reverberated for years afterward.

Isaac Backus grew up in this atmosphere of intense spiritualism. Born in 1724 in Norwich, Connecticut, he came of a fairly prominent family, which could trace its lineage to the first settlements. His father, a prosperous farmer and owner of several flour mills, was a church communicant but not a member. The atmosphere of the Backus household was one of industry and rectitude but not of intense piety.

It was sometimes said that evangelists like Whitefield appealed primarily to the down-and-out of American society, to the ignorant and the uneducated. That may have been true generally, but it was not the case with Isaac Backus. He was educated in local schools, and though he did not attend college (a number of his relatives went to Yale), he was a well-informed young man. He was to have a bright future.

Then in 1740, when Backus was only sixteen, his father died. The loss was devastating. Many of the great religious figures of the past experienced that sort of psychic crisis before their spiritual awakening. Backus and his mother attended a few revival meetings, and then in 1741 he experienced conversion himself. He was out in the fields when it happened — a sudden flood of light, a warmth that suffused his inner being, and an overwhelming certainty that he had been saved, that he was one of the chosen few destined for heaven.

For Backus the life of a saint was a demanding one. Inner piety and outward rectitude were not enough. It was a calling, an obligation to do God's good work. That meant involvement in the world instead of monastic withdrawal; and involvement, in turn, ran risks, for the world was a cruel and sinful place. Thus the saint had to be constantly on guard. The most dangerous foes of all, because they were the most insidious, were the hypocrites — people whose outward piety masked an evil heart. To admit such people into one's church, especially to share with them the Communion of the Lord's Supper, was to risk corrupting the whole. Isaac Backus soon faced the dilemma that had puzzled Roger Williams a century before.

The saints, fortunately, could recognize one another. The inner light itself was an infallible guide. "The Saints," wrote Backus, "by virtue of Grace in themselves, know the certainty of Grace in another." A circle of the righteous formed naturally within the Norwich congregation, and to preserve their purity they soon began taking Communion separately from the rest. Not satisfied with this halfway arrangement, Backus in 1746 formed a separate congregation. The communicants took turns conducting services and preaching to one another. To gain admission, a new member had to relate in convincing fashion the details of his or her conversion experience. Strict Congregationalists was what their neighbors called them, because they followed the New England system of congregational autonomy but with strict entrance requirements.

Discovering that he had a gift for speaking, Backus took to the road, seeking new converts all over New England. The itinerant ministry was as old as Christianity itself, but during the Awakening it got a bad name. Circuit riding converts, with nothing but faith to guide them, exhorted the masses in the Whitefield style, causing theological confusion and institutional chaos. Orthodox clergy found themselves in a hideous dilemma. If they opened their pulpits to itinerants, they subjected themselves and their congregations to ferocious examination; if they denied the itinerants, they were accused of protecting sinners. Backus was critical of such methods, and he worried much about the confusion shown by ignorant exhorters. But it did not deter him from his own travels. There was still God's work to be done.

In 1747 a separated congregation in Middleborough, Massachusetts, invited him to be their pastor. Although it was another decade before the group could afford a meetinghouse, Backus made Middleborough his home. As the Separatists formed permanent congregations they found themselves in a familiar dilemma. A congregation of saints was certain to be a small one; indeed, it might die out altogether if the rate of conversions, for whatever reason, should decline. A related problem was what to do with the children of saints? Was sanctity heritable, and, if not, could the children be baptized in the church without polluting it? On the other hand, the admission of halfway members, allowed to attend service but not to take Communion, put them right back where they started. Backus, ever insistent upon perfection, ruled that halfway membership was not permissible.

The obvious solution was adult baptism. Only an adult was old enough, or experienced enough, to make a moral choice, a "decision for Christ," as a modern evangelist would put it. The baptism ritual would then symbolically cleanse the convert of past sins, leaving him or her pure enough to participate in the congregation. It was a path already marked out by Roger Williams, and Backus was moving along it when he met and married Susanna Mason in 1749. She was an old-line Baptist, a descendant of those who had followed Williams. She crystalized his thoughts, and he, in turn, converted his Middleborough congregation. From that point on, his chief mission in life became the gospel of adult baptism. In 1754 a convention of Separates endorsed the principle, and a new church was born. Those who rejected Backus's creed drifted back into orthodox, "old light" Congregationalism.

Beginnings of the Baptist Church

The name Baptist was slow to come into use. Many congregations called themselves Strict Congregationalists or Separate Baptists for some years. All, however, considered themselves a new church, and they early applied to colonial authorities for tax exemption. Under the Massachusetts charter of 1691 the Congregational church was established by law: everyone was obliged to pay taxes for its support — everyone, that is, except recognized dissenters such as Quakers and Anglicans. These people were permitted to allocate their assessments to their own churches.

Separate Baptists wanted the same privilege. Orthodox Congregationalists objected, accusing the Separates of breaking away in order to escape their tax obligations. The dispute became especially bitter when congregations broke down the middle. Each side claimed to be the legitimate church, and neither wanted to pay taxes for the maintenance of the other. In the 1760s the courts began ruling that the Separate Baptists were an identifiable church, entitled to toleration and hence the privilege of allocating their own religious assessment. The decision gave them new status in New England society; they had been considered fanatics and curiosities. It also made them virtually indistinguishable from old-line Baptists, a long-recognized, if not entirely accepted, sect. Backus promptly set out to unite new Baptists with old, a job largely completed by the time of the Revolution.

His church established, its ranks trimmed, Backus set out after new converts. He was constantly on the road, an indefatigable traveler. Until his death in 1806 he averaged about 1,200 miles a year by horseback. His carefully kept journal reveals a total of 918 journeys in the cause, and a total of 9,828 sermons (an average of about four a week). The results were evident in the dramatic increase in membership. There were some 1,500 Baptists in the colonies on the eve of the Awakening. At the outbreak of the Revolution there were about 5,000; by 1800 they numbered 25,000. In the southern Appalachians, where itinerants carried the gospel in the years after the Revolution, Baptists became the dominant church. Methodists and Presbyterians met the competition with circuit riders of their own; from New England forests to Western prairies, the fires of revivalism burned on for years.

Legal recognition and social acceptance brought new responsibilities for the Baptists. A church, after all, is an institution, and institutions have a habit of carving identities of their own. In 1764 church leaders founded Rhode Island College for the training of young ministers. Untutored exhorters had given the church a bad name. To saintliness must be added some theological expertise. The school was later moved from Warren, Rhode Island, to Providence, and in 1804 it was renamed Brown University, in honor of its principal benefactor.

In 1767 Backus and other leaders organized the Warren Baptist Association to provide some organizational unity, while retaining the principle of local autonomy. The Warren Association had advisory powers only, but it did provide the church a vehicle for intercolonial communication.

Concern for heresy was another sign of institutional development. It implied a doctrinal standard from which heretics had deviated. In the early days of the movement there were no agreed-upon standards, for each convert was feeling his or her own theological way. With no central authority to provide guidelines, there was a natural tendency to spin off onto theological tangents. Backus came to recognize that, unless some order was imposed, the church would dissolve into chaos.

Perfectionism was the most common heresy because it was a logical extension of the conversion experience. Having attained the status of "visible saint," the convert might naturally consider himself free from sin, or "perfect." Such a person had no need for laws or other social constraints. Laws and penalties, some said, are made to restrain the wicked, not the righteous. Nor did such persons feel obliged to yield to earthly authority, unless the authorities themselves could demonstrate perfection (it was the same antinomian heresy for which Anne Hutchinson had been banished from the Massachusetts Bay Colony in 1638). Backus recognized the danger in such a doctrine. "Visible saints" themselves might be law-abiding, but if their anarchism were widely imitated, all authority would break down. It struck at the very roots of society.

Perfectionism had other side effects that caused Backus headaches. One was cohabitation between spiritual soulmates. What could be sinful, some thought, about two saints lying together? The result, presumably, would either be perfection or nothing. One father refused to let his daughter enter into such a liaison until the couple promised to keep a Bible between them. She became pregnant anyway.

Backus also objected to the practice of saints baptizing one another and therefore admitting new members to the church. To maintain entrance standards, Backus would not admit new members officially until he had baptized them himself. The ministerial function was another sign of institutionalization. In the early days of the movement every convert ministered to others.

Rules and regulations, however, did win the Baptists social respectability. By the time of the Revolution the church was beginning to attract the educated and the wealthy. Evangelical fervor yielded to a punctilious orthodoxy. Except for their adherence to adult baptism, Baptists, at least in New England, became virtually indistinguishable from neighboring Congregationalists and Presbyterians.

The Fight for Religious Freedom

The American Revolution brought a new dilemma for Isaac Backus and his friends. The Congregational establishment was in the forefront of the Revolutionary agitation, so much so that some dissenting churches feared that a patriot victory might bring an end to what few rights they had. A number of Anglicans sided with the empire and fled to Britain or Canada when fighting started. Baptists generally fought on the Revolutionary side, but some of them without much enthusiasm. Their fears seemed justified when they saw the religious article of the Massachusetts constitution, drafted by Samuel Adams. Congregationalism would remain established by law and supported by the State. Other churches were to be tolerated with the right to collect their own taxes. But toleration was a far cry from religious freedom, in which all churches would be on an equal footing. Connecticut, which did not even bother to draft a new constitution, also held fast to Congregationalism. Only in Rhode Island, which had a tradition of religious freedom dating back to Roger Williams, and in newly emancipated Vermont and New Hampshire could New England's Baptists feel comfortable.

It started Isaac Backus on a new crusade, stumping the country in behalf of religious freedom. His efforts paralleled those of religious liberals, such as Jefferson in Virginia, but they stemmed from different motives. Jefferson wanted to sever the connection of church and state in order to leave individuals free to worship as they chose — or not to worship at all. Backus wanted separation because he felt that political connection polluted the church — and because the state backed the wrong church. Jefferson succeeded, ironically with the help of southern Baptists. The Virginia assembly adopted his Statute for Religious Freedom in 1786. Isaac Backus failed. Not until 1833, long after his death, did Massachusetts finally shake the grip of Congregational orthodoxy.

The last years of this tireless propagator were spent defending Baptist theology and practices in sermon and pamphlet. By the 1790s his movement faced new competition in the appeal to the down-and-out. Methodism gained by the Revolution, for it severed the Anglican connection and established itself as an American church. Better organized than the local-minded Baptists, the Methodists employed professional missionaries, circuit riders who poked into every farm and hamlet of the West. Not burdened by Calvinist concepts of sin and redemption, Methodist evangelists could preach a vague and universal salvation. Conversion was simple; the Methodists' appeal was broad.

Attracted by the success of the Methodists and Baptists, Presbyterians, too, began employing itinerant evangelists. With all three churches using the same methods, the theological distinctions among them became blurred. In 1801 evangelists of all faiths cooperated in Kentucky's massive Cane Ridge revival, taking turns preaching around the clock for days on end to a transfixed multitude. So stupendous was the Cane Ridge revival — attended by thousands — that Isaac Backus thought that it heralded the Second Coming of Christ. He was premature, it seems, but he did not live to find out. He died in 1806.

SUGGESTIONS FOR FURTHER READING

William G. McLoughlin has compressed his considerable knowledge of early American religion into a fine essay, *Isaac Backus and the American Pietistic Tradition* (1967). The best study of the Great Awakening in New England is C. C. Goen, *Revivalism and Separatism in New England, 1740–1800* (1962). In a more recent piece, *Religion and the American Mind: from the Great Awakening to the Revolution* (1966), Alan Heimert establishes (not very successfully, I think) a relationship between revivalism and political radicalism. Conrad Wright, *The Beginnings of Unitarianism in America* (1955), discusses the other end of the theological rainbow, the religious rationalists.

11

Benjamin Rush, Patriot Physician

William Byrd of Virginia, writing in the early part of the eighteenth century, claimed that colonial proprietors attracted settlers to America with two promises — one that they would be safe

from religious persecution, the other "that it was a place free from those three great scourges of mankind, priests, lawyers, and physicians." Not that such professions were prohibited in America, Byrd added, it was simply that "the people were yet too poor to maintain these learned gentlemen."

Byrd's barbed wit aside, the fact was that American society was curiously unspecialized, blissfully unprofessional. There were neither law schools nor medical schools in America until the end of the colonial period, and a mere handful of practitioners journeyed to Europe for training. Most lawyers and doctors received on-the-job training as apprentices. Specialization was rare; the jack-of-all-trades,

Benjamin Rush (1745–1813). *This portrait, by Thomas Sully, shows Rush in characteristic pose, at his writing desk surrounded by manuscripts, rather than in a laboratory surrounded by microscopes. It was painted in 1810, when Rush was hard at work on his last and most important treatise,* Diseases of the Mind.

epitomized by Benjamin Franklin, was the norm. Physicians doubled as pharmacists, barbers performed surgery, and ministers dispensed medicines along with faith.

In the field of medicine there were advantages to bedside training. American physicians often prescribed local herbs and home remedies that had proved useful in the course of time. When their medicines failed, they often resorted to such commonsense therapy as bed rest, a mild diet, and fresh air. Such remedies, even if they did not help the patient, rarely did harm. In Europe, by contrast, physicians were immersed in theory, doled out by schools of medicine. There were various theories about bodily illness, each with its staunch adherents, but none of them had any foundation in clinical experience. Thus their remedies, chiefly purging and bloodletting, did no good and often resulted in much harm. The ill survived, when they did so at all, in spite of their physicians.

Even so, there was much to be said for medical training and professional specialization. Without it no real progress could be made in the scientific identification and cure of disease. By the last quarter of the eighteenth century, Europeans were undertaking clinical analyses that laid the foundation for modern medicine. About the same time Americans, ironically enough, fell under the spell of the outmoded European doctrines.

Americans trained in European medical centers disseminated the twin ideas of professional standards and doctrinal conformity. In the vanguard of this promotional effort was Dr. Benjamin Rush, whose voluminous writings made him the best known, if not the most influential, physician of his day. He was also the most doctrinaire practitioner of the age, staunchly defending European theories of disease long after his contemporaries began to make clinical observations. A staunch patriot, Rush even attempted to formulate an American doctrine by blending the various European theories. The result was a monistic explanation for disease, from which he concluded that all fevers, regardless of their symptomatic differences, were susceptible to the same treatment — purges, vomiting, and bloodletting. His system, imparted to thousands of students through his lectures at the University of Pennsylvania, caused untold injury and delayed for years the development of clinical pathology in America. Seldom has patriotism been so ill used.

Rush's activities showed the medical doctrinaire at his worst, yet even he could not escape the experimental temper of the new nation. He campaigned for waste disposal and clean water in Philadelphia, even though there was no theoretical connection between pollution and disease. He campaigned for more humane treatment of the insane, insisting upon cleanliness and comfort, again without any doctrinal foundation. Nor was he wedded to a narrow professionalism. He took up arms against every threat to human well-being, whether it be strong drink or vermin-filled slums. He had a hand in the founding of nearly every social crusade of the nineteenth century, from temperance, to female education, to care of the insane, to antislavery. And therein lay his contribution to the developing nation.

The Education of a Physician

Cities, Benjamin Rush once told Thomas Jefferson, are like "abscesses on the human body." His own Philadelphia, he admitted on another occasion, was "a seat of corruption," yet he rarely left it. Like Samuel Adams, Rush was bred to city life, and, like Adams, he devoted much of his life to elevating his city's morals to rural standards.

Rush had deep roots in the Pennsylvania countryside, even though he visited his rural birthplace only twice in his life. His Quaker ancestors had been among the first settlers in the colony; father and grandfather combined farming with the trade of gunsmith. The family farm was ninety acres of fertile bottomland a few miles north of Philadelphia. Benjamin, fourth of seven children, was born on the second floor of the old stone farmhouse on Christmas Eve, 1745. When he was but a few years old, the family moved into Philadelphia, where his father, John Rush, took up gunsmithing full time. John Rush died shortly thereafter, though he was only thirty-nine, and his widow, Susannah, opened a grocery store to finance her family of seven. She was successful enough to afford a fair education for all of them.

Time and prosperity had tempered the Quaker piety that had originally brought the Rushes to America; John Rush had his children baptized in the Church of England. After his death, however, Susannah switched to the Presbyterian church, in which she had evidently been reared. In 1754, at the age of eight, Benjamin was sent to an academy run by a Presbyterian minister, the husband of his mother's sister. There he encountered the heady spirit of the Great Awakening, which was to influence his entire life. Rush's Presbyterian uncle was himself a student of William Tennent, founder of the "Log College"* that had helped inspire the revival. Central to the faith of "new light" Presbyterians, as with the Separate Baptists, was the conversion experience, the feeling of rebirth. Both groups believed that regeneration was available to all who opened their hearts to God, that it was the duty of the reborn in turn to carry on God's work by improving this earth. Such a faith impelled Isaac Backus to become an itinerant minister; in Benjamin Rush it instilled a lifelong interest in social reform.

Orthodox "old light" Presbyterians were content with giving lip service

* The "Log College" was an informal seminary for Presbyterian evangelists in New Jersey.

to the Calvinist concept of rebirth. Simple rectitude and outward piety were for them enough; it was not necessary to investigate the inner springs of sanctity. "Old lights" also tried to preserve the church as they had known it in Scotland and northern Ireland. They insisted on bringing ministers over from the mother country, and they wanted the church ruled by a central governing body, or synod, as it was in Scotland. "New lights" railed against coldhearted clergy and foreign domination; they wanted each presbytery to control its own affairs, including the choice of minister. In a sense, they would Americanize the Presbyterian church. Thus the religious conflict came to have political overtones. This, too, would influence the young Benjamin Rush, who was already a flaming patriot by the time the world became acquainted with the name of Samuel Adams.

The conflict between old and new in the Presbyterian church also influenced Rush's later education. The College of Philadelphia would have been a natural choice, since it would have enabled him to save money by living at home, but the Reverend William Smith (Franklin's choice as head of the college) had given that institution an Anglican flavor. Thus Rush's uncle sent him to the College of New Jersey at Princeton, where the Reverend Samuel Davies held sway. Davies was justly famed for having carried the Presbyterian church into Virginia during the Great Awakening, but he was a scholar as well as preacher. He introduced courses in science and mathematics at Princeton and added English literature to the classic diet of Latin and Greek. The new curriculum was in the main current of the Enlightenment, and Rush absorbed it eagerly though he remained at the college only a little more than a year. Perhaps that short span was as far as he felt he could stretch his mother's pocketbook.

In 1761, Rush, newly turned fifteen, apprenticed himself to Dr. John Redman, a staunch Presbyterian who had one of the largest medical practices in Philadelphia. He was given room and board in the doctor's house and the promise of elementary medical training. In return he served as a nursing aide, ran errands, and kept the doctor's accounts. Occasionally he accompanied the doctor on house calls and visits to the Pennsylvania Hospital. After some time spent in simple observation, he was allowed to share in some of the simpler tasks, such as bleeding infections and dressing wounds.

Medicine in the eighteenth century had made little progress since the Middle Ages. A few diseases had been identified and given names — scarlet fever, whooping cough, or syphilis, for instance. Each of these had symptoms peculiar enough to be readily identifiable. But in most diseases physicians simply accepted the laymen's descriptions. "Pleurisy" was a catchall for chest pains, though the disorder might vary from pneumonia to tuberculosis. Many diseases went by the name of their most obvious symptom — fever. The various fevers, in turn, were distinguished by their severity, regularity, or other associations. A "bilious remitting fever" (usually a reference to yellow fever) described one that came and went irregularly, accompanied by discoloration of bile. A fever succeeded by chills was called an "ague." Thus an "intermittent ague," i.e., one that came and went at regular intervals, usually meant malaria. Fevers accompanied by dysentery went by the name "flux." The "bloody flux" was probably typhoid or cholera. Finally, the common cold was known and had already earned its somewhat ambiguous name. "Epidemic cold" connoted influenza.

Early in the eighteenth century the Dutch physician Hermann Boerhaave had tried to bring some order to this descriptive pathology. Boerhaave's system was as neat and all-embracing as Newton's laws of physics. It was the medical counterpart of the Enlightenment, and like Newtonian rationalism it pervaded European — and hence American — thought. Boerhaave described the human body as a hydraulic mechanism full of pumps and pipes. When any of these tubes, such as a blood vessel, became obstructed, the blood flowed more rapidly past the obstacle, causing friction and thus heat or fever. The physician's task was to regulate this "tension," usually by bleeding the patient. Such ethereal rationalism, however, did not prevent Boerhaave from adopting the empirical methods of the physical scientists. He insisted on careful observation and examination of patients, and he taught his students at the University of Leyden to record their observations and treatments. Boerhaave was thus the bridge from medical scholasticism to modern clinical pathology.

A one-time student of Boerhaave's at Leyden, Dr. Redman introduced Rush to the system and provided the apprentice with the master's weighty treatises. Redman also encouraged Rush to venture abroad himself to absorb the most recent doctrines and discoveries. Susannah Rush's remarriage along about 1765 may have provided the opportunity, for Benjamin's new stepfather was a prosperous distiller. Rush cautiously delayed his departure for a year in order to prepare himself for the venture. He attended the college lectures of Dr. John Morgan, newly returned from five years of study in Europe, and he brushed up on his Latin and Greek. He soon found an excuse to drop his language exercises, however, when "public commotions" distracted his mind. The "commotion" was the Stamp Act violence. The act was a political awakening for Rush, and he was an ardent patriot from the outset. Even residence in Edinburgh and London failed to temper his radical politics.

Rush sailed for Britain in August 1766 in sorrowful mood, dreading the sea and uncertain of his future. Yet in later years he was to look back on his years in Edinburgh and London as the happiest and most fruitful of his life. Pleasureful they may have been, but professionally they were of little value, except to add to Rush's collection of famous acquaintances. He became more thoroughly imbued than ever with erroneous medical theory and more resistant to American criticism of it.

The preeminent figure at the University of Edinburgh was Dr. William Cullen, whom Morgan called "the Boerhaave of his age." Cullen had set out to modify the Boerhaavian system, though he ended unfortunately in only compounding its errors. Where Boerhaave stressed the tension in body fluids, Cullen called attention to its solids. Disease, he claimed, originated in a malfunction of the brain, which caused the body to be either too tense or too relaxed. The job of the physician, then, was to regulate nervous energy by building it up with drugs or relieving it through bleeding and purging. Neither the theory nor the remedy had any foundation in clinical experience, which seems odd in view of the importance that Cullen otherwise attached to empirical observation. Rush nevertheless swallowed it in toto and adhered to it for a quarter-century, until he finally discarded it in favor of an equally fallacious doctrine of his own.

The "Medical Business"

In 1769 Benjamin Rush returned to Philadelphia to take up the "medical business," as he candidly called it. He moved into a house on Front Street within view of the city's bustling wharves. It was a fashionable part of town, for the wealthy then lived in the inner city. The poor lived on the outskirts where they combined part-time occupation with small-time gardening.

Rush had no difficulty building a medical practice, for the colonial city was a filthy place where sewage was thrown into the streets, and piles of refuse lay everywhere. Epidemics of smallpox, scarlet fever, and influenza were endemic. Seaports like Philadelphia also suffered from various ship-borne maladies. The most dreaded of these was yellow fever, which periodically swept in from the West Indies. Rush later estimated that the annual death rate in Philadelphia was one person in every twenty-five.

Rush's practice grew steadily. Within a year he was seeing an average of thirty-five patients a month, and his monthly income was about forty pounds. The buildup was not without effort, however. Quakers and Anglicans, the city's elite, preferred the established practitioners of their own faith. Rush built up some clientele among the Presbyterians by attending his own church faithfully, but that group was not numerous enough to sustain him. So he turned to the poor. There was less money there, but the opportunities were unlimited.

Rush soon became a familiar sight in every wooden shanty and tenement in the city. Many was the time that he had to shake lice and bugs from his clothes before entering his own house. He charged only those who seemed able to pay (at times no more than one in ten). This sort of charity appealed to Rush's religious need to serve, and it had some practical advantages. He came into contact with a wide variety of ailments and their symptoms; and, since patients could not pay anyway, he was able to experiment with various medicines and dosages. Even the most dogmatic physicians could not avoid the ultimate empirical test — whether a patient lived or died.

He succeeded more often than he failed evidently, for Rush's reputation spread by word of mouth. Before long, members of the city's elite were knocking at his office door. Dr. John Fothergill, one of the best known among Philadelphia's physicians, once admitted that he had "crept over the backs of the poor into the pockets of the rich." Rush, though never quite so frank, followed the same path. But he never forgot the poor. In 1772 he became medical consultant to the city almshouse to provide better care for the indigent, and two years later he was one of a group of eight physicians who formed a Society for Inoculating the Poor against smallpox.

Teaching was another, and at first important, source of income. Before Rush departed for Edinburgh, Dr. Morgan had hinted that he might, on his return, qualify for the newly created post of professor of chemistry in the College of Philadelphia. To select such a young, not to say untested, individual for such a post was unusual, but Rush, even then, had powerful friends. Morgan, named professor of physic in 1765, was hoping to expand medical studies in the college, and among the college trustees was Rush's first patron, Dr. Redman. In Edinburgh, Rush sat twice through the lecture series presented by the famous Scots chemist, Joseph Black, and on his return to Philadelphia he was duly elected to the chemistry professorship. His lectures were enormously popular — Rush was a gifted teacher — but they never strayed far from the classroom notes recorded at the feet of Dr. Black.

Rush was not a creative scientist, but he was a curious one whose interests ranged widely across the field of medicine. He was also an indefatigable worker, who could return home after a day in the Pennsylvania Hospital to spend an evening scratching out an essay. His publications ranged from cold remedies to an examination of the medicinal qualities of the mineral springs around Philadelphia. A few of Rush's productions were published by the American Philosophical Society, but others were little more than newspaper fillers. Not one, except possibly an essay on asthma in children, pushed back the frontiers of science. His analysis of mineral water, for instance, failed to uncover the fact that it was contaminated with sewage. It would have been better had he rested his quill for a time and dusted off the chemical apparatus given the college by the Penn family.

Rush's literary productions failed to enhance his standing among his colleagues in Philadelphia, but they did earn him intercolonial renown. By 1773 he had published more medical essays than had any other physician in America, and his circle of correspondents extended from New England to South Carolina. He was, when the Revolution broke out, probably the best-known physician in America; his fame, in turn, enabled him to branch out into the field of politics.

Rush's first literary venture outside of medicine was a bold one, and it momentarily threatened his career. In early 1773 he published *An Address to the Inhabitants of the British Settlements in America, upon Slave-Keeping.* Although the arguments, as Rush himself admitted, were nothing new, the pamphlet was a landmark. Previous assaults on slavery had been religiously inspired, nearly all written by Quakers. Rush's attitude, though conditioned in part by his evangelical zeal for reform, was essentially secular. It was inspired by the imperial contest and the new meaning that was coming to be attached to the word *liberty*. Always in the forefront of American radicalism, Rush by 1773 felt that the contest involved more than the rights of Englishmen; it was a struggle for the rights of all mankind. "Remember," he warned his countrymen, "the eyes of all Europe are fixed upon you to preserve an asylum for freedom in this country, after the last pillars of it are fallen in every other quarter of the globe." Three years later Rush's friend Tom Paine would pick up this imagery, reworking it into one of the most memorable passages of *Common Sense*.

Rush's remedy for the evil of slavery was a comparatively mild one, perhaps because he himself owned a black servant (and did so for many years after the Revolution). Rush wanted to prohibit the further import of Africans, and he would limit the terms of slaves while preparing them for freedom with education. Moderate though this program was, it raised a storm of controversy in the Philadelphia press. Rush had published his pamphlet anonymously, but his authorship was an open secret, especially after he answered critics with *A Vindication*. This follow-up essay was even more political in its appeal. Americans, he pointed out, had no right to complain of British tyranny so long as they tolerated racial tyranny among themselves. It was a piece of logic that would eventually spawn a number of antislavery societies during the Revolution, but for the moment it earned Rush only vilification. Even his medical practice suffered; his monthly average of visitations dropped from eighty to under forty. By the summer of 1774, however, it was back to normal.

The controversy failed to dampen his impulse to publish; indeed, it widened his critical horizon. The Tea Act brought him back into the newspapers, this time under the politically rich pseudonym Hampden. Writing in October 1773 — before even Samuel Adams was fully alive to the partisan value of tea — Rush predicted that if the East India Company ships were allowed to land their tea, "We are undone forever." Those tea chests, he reminded the timid, "contain something worse than death — the seeds of SLAVERY." In a subsequent essay he put medicine to the cause of patriotism by offering recipes for tea substitutes. One concoction, which combined dried oak twigs with myrtle leaves, he claimed was effective even against "wasting diseases and fluxes."

Troublesome Revolutionary

Rush's polemical efforts brought him to the attention of radical politicians, notably Charles Thomson, leader of the Sons of Liberty, and John Dickinson, head of the Presbyterian party. These he added to his social circle, surrounding himself with power, as he had earlier enveloped himself among the medically prominent. Rush made friends easily, for he was a naturally sociable being, talkative to a fault, and his wide-ranging mind no doubt made him a fascinating companion. When the First Continental Congress assembled in September 1774, Rush provided rooms in his own house for Samuel and John Adams. That gesture was the beginning of another friendship. Indeed, Benjamin Rush is the only prominent figure of the age who remained all his life on good terms with both John Adams and Thomas Jefferson.

When fighting broke out in Massachusetts in April 1775, Rush made another step to the left. No longer were the rights of Englishmen the issue, he concluded; it was now a contest for independence. He promptly took up his quill to bring others to the new line of thought. He was the first essayist in Pennsylvania and one of the first in any colony publicly to advocate independence. He hovered around the edges of the Second Continental Congress, striking up friendships with Patrick Henry (whom he inoculated against smallpox) and Thomas Jefferson. When Congress took up the question of a military commander, Rush (urged on, perhaps, by John Adams) promoted Washington's candidacy with a newspaper essay. He kept his identity hidden under pseudonyms, however, having learned the price of nonconformity in the antislavery episode.

Throughout these months his most important acquaintance was Thomas Paine, a radical young Englishman who had come to Philadelphia in 1774 armed with letters of introduction from Benjamin Franklin. Paine was made editor of the *Pennsylvania Magazine*, and in that capacity he soon encountered the city's most prolific columnist, Benjamin Rush. The two saw eye-to-eye on political matters, and by the fall of 1775 Rush was urging Paine to write a pamphlet on independence. Rush himself could not do it, for fear of losing his professional standing and social connections; but Paine, he pointed out, had nothing to lose. It was hardly a tactful argument, but Paine accepted the challenge. He even accepted Rush's suggestion for a title, *Common Sense*.

On January 11, 1776, the day after *Common Sense* appeared on the streets, Rush was married. The courtship was a brief one, although Rush was no stammering novice. He was often in female company and still maintained a correspondence with his first love, a titled heiress in Scotland. His choice was Julia Stockton of Princeton, whose father, Richard Stockton, represented New Jersey in the Continental Congress. Rush celebrated the occasion by having their portraits done by Charles Willson Peale, who had recently hung out his sign in the city. The marriage was a good one. He later referred to Julia as "a perfect wife," and he was a man who could be hard to please. She bore him thirteen children, of whom nine lived to maturity. Two of their sons became physicians; one, Richard, became a lawyer, serving as attorney general under President James Madison and minister to Great Britain.

In February 1776, a month after his marriage, Rush dropped the anonymity that had masked his pen and formally entered politics. He was elected to Philadelphia's Committee of Inspection and Observation, one of a network of extra-legal authorities (called committees of safety in most other colonies) that had been created to enforce the trade embargo adopted by the First Continental Congress. As royal authority dissolved, the committees undertook new duties. They were the vanguard of revolution, filling the power vacuum until constitutional state governments could be created. The makeup of the Philadelphia committee revealed the unsettling effect of revolution. Absent were the conservative merchants that had controlled city and provincial affairs for years. The new power bloc was made up of artisans and shopkeepers, outsiders who had never wielded influence or power. Rush, who considered himself a social outsider in Philadelphia, slipped easily into this new democracy.

Rush was only one of thirty-two new men chosen to the committee in the February election, and nearly all were warm for independence. Their first target was the assembly, still dragging its feet on the issue. A week after the city election the Philadelphia committee called for a Provincial Convention, its delegates to be chosen by the inspection committee throughout the state. The committee was deliberately vague about the function of the convention, but it was almost certain to weaken the authority of the assembly. In a belated effort to keep control of events, the assembly in June altered its instructions to its congressional delegates, thereby enabling Congress to approve the resolution for independence.

The assembly's tactical retreat failed to stem the democratic tide. A new political force was forming in the state, just as it had in Philadelphia. Delegates from the conservative eastern counties of the Delaware Valley had long controlled the assembly, and they were largely responsible for its moderate stance. Western counties and the city of Philadelphia, underrepresented in the assembly, were the leading advocates for independence. Regional interest and political radicalism went hand in hand, and evangelical religion helped to cement the alliance.

Assembling in mid-July, the convention instantly usurped the authority of the assembly. It began by naming a new congressional delegation, with Benjamin Rush among its number. It then began drafting a constitution for the new state, one designed to ensure maximum popular input into governmental decision making.

Rush arrived in Congress in time to put his name to the Declaration of Independence when the signing ceremony came in early August. He attended sessions regularly but without interrupting his medical practice. The summer sickly season increased his daily load of patients, and the war added new burdens. In September, a month in which he saw fifty-seven patients of his own, he received £138 from Congress for treating soldiers and prisoners of war. "I was willing to be poor, that my country might be free," he wrote with apparent reference to his excursion into politics. "The latter I hope will be granted, and contrary even to my wishes I find I am growing rich."

Rush's practice deteriorated along with the American military position in the fall of 1776. When Washington abandoned New Jersey and crossed into Pennsylvania, Philadelphians braced themselves for a British attack. Shopkeepers boarded their windows and fled into the hinterland. By December the city was but "a dark and silent wilderness of houses," as one transient put it. On December 20 Rush himself departed, but not in fear. He went instead to offer his services to the American army, then camped along the river opposite Trenton. He was assigned to General Cadwalader's regiment and thus missed the dramatic raid on Trenton. Cadwalader's force was not able to make it across the Delaware until the day after the battle.

When Washington retired to winter quarters at Morristown, Rush (who had never formally joined the army) journeyed to Baltimore, where Congress had taken up temporary residence. He emerged from his brief tour of duty convinced that the medical department of the army had to be completely reorganized. The military hospitals that he had visited were overcrowded and short of supplies; the physicians in charge spent most of their time bickering with one another. Complaints about the medical department had reached Congress from other quarters, and in April 1777 the whole apparatus was reorganized. Congress named Dr. William Shippen, Jr., director general and made Rush surgeon general of the middle department, the theater that had seen most of the recent military action. Shippen, professor of anatomy at the College of Philadelphia, was part of the city's medical elite; his relations with Rush had been distant but cordial.

Rush brought to his new position the zeal of the reformer. His first instinct, as usual, was to take up his quill. On April 22 the *Pennsylvania Packet* devoted its entire front page to an essay addressed "To the Officers in the Army of the United American States: Directions for Preserving the Health of Soldiers." For once, Rush's prescriptions were in advance of his time and on the right track. Noting that soldiers died more from diseases than from combat, Rush urged a military cleanup. Officers should see to it that their men dressed properly, were fed well, and were not exposed "to unnecessary fatigue." Soldiers he told to bathe at least twice a week, change underclothing frequently, and never sleep in wet clothes. Eating utensils were to be washed after every use. No modern physician could give an army better advice. In an age that feared bathing and invented perfumes to hide body odors, Rush's stand was truly remarkable.

He soon found a cause on which to vent his crusading urge. An epidemic of "hospital fever" swept through the army hospitals in the spring of 1777. Blaming the sickness on overcrowding, Rush asked Shippen to find more room. Shippen refused to open more hospitals and declined Rush's request for medicines. Shippen probably had no choice; there were few public buildings available that could be turned into hospitals, and to place the sick in private homes would have risked spreading the contagion. Shippen may have had access to wine (Rush's favorite tonic for fevers), but other medicines were always in short supply. Rush was not the only physician who had to make do with what he had.

Convinced, nevertheless, that Shippen was either corrupt or incompetent, Rush began a personal investigation. He toured army hospitals looking for signs of mismanagement, and, not surprisingly, he found some. In the summer of 1777 the medical corps was swamped with casualties from the battles of Brandywine and Germantown, and the loss of Philadelphia deprived it of its best facilities. The wounded were carted around in wagons from town to town until they found a place that could accommodate them. Rush saw confusion and shortages everywhere that he went, and he peppered his friend John Adams with complaints. In the winter of 1777 a committee of Congress examined Rush's allegations, listened to his testimony, and then exonerated Shippen. Rush promptly tendered his resignation; Congress accepted it unanimously.

Not content with his vendetta against Shippen in the fall of 1777, Rush also joined the movement to displace Washington. The American army, he felt, was as bad as its medical corps — undisciplined and poorly equipped. After the Battle of Brandywine he was one of several physicians sent into the British camp to treat American prisoners. To him it seemed a model of efficiency. Sentries looked as though they were actually guarding something; soldiers were trim and well-fed. "Order and contentment" prevailed in the hospital. By contrast, the American force was an unruly mob.

If fault was to be found for such conditions, it was natural to blame the commander in chief, though common sense should have told Rush that Washington was the most professional-minded, self-disciplined feature of the army. A visit to Washington's headquarters a few days after the Germantown defeat confirmed Rush's suspicions. The commander, he felt, was surrounded with incompetents. Colonel Alexander Hamilton was too young, Nathanael Greene was a mere "sycophant," and the rest were drunks and cowards. The one staff officer that Rush found he liked was Thomas Conway, evidently because Conway shared his hypercritical views.

Rush communicated his feelings to John Adams and to Patrick Henry. Adams wisely burned the letter, but Patrick Henry relayed his to Washington. Washington already had troubles enough — a winter at Valley Forge, a congressional move to make Horatio Gates his superior, and the sinister intrigues of Thomas Conway. Rush's barrage seemed part of the "cabal," and Washington was understandably furious. He kept silent, however, and let the storm blow itself out. Rush's resignation removed one gadfly from his hair.

Rush's departure from the army also ended his direct role in the Revolution. His contribution had been neither noble nor notable. Indeed, his excessive vanity, tactlessness, and indiscretion simply caused trouble for those with clearer heads. Resignation ended a rather dismal chapter in his life.

Toward a Regenerate Society

When the British evacuated Philadelphia in 1778, Rush returned to the
city and resumed his medical practice. His return to private life, however,
did not end his interest in public affairs. Rush was ever concerned not just
with the illnesses of individuals but with the ills of society as well. Conditioned by his early evangelical training, Rush saw the Revolution as an
opportunity to sweep out social corruption and to establish the kingdom
of God upon earth. No one, save perhaps Thomas Jefferson in Virginia,
saw so clearly the dual nature of the Revolution: more than a colonial war
for independence, it was a popular struggle for political democracy and
social justice. "The American war is over," Rush wrote in 1786, "but
this is far from being the case with the American revolution. On the contrary, nothing but the first act of the great drama is closed. It remains
yet to establish and perfect our new forms of government, and to prepare
the principles, morals, and manners of our citizens." The latter task, he
added in a note to a friend, "is the most difficult part of the business.
. . . It requires more wisdom and fortitude than to expel or to reduce
armies into captivity."

Slavery, among the most obvious of social cankers, had caught his attention as early as 1773. After the war he joined the Quakers' abolition
society, soon becoming its secretary; and, when the Federal Convention met
in 1787, he presented it with a petition condemning slavery. Throughout
these years, however, he owned a black house servant. He finally freed
the man in 1794, by which time he felt he had been reimbursed for the
servant's price. He clearly lacked the moral indignation of a later generation of abolitionists, yet he was far ahead of his own time, far ahead even
of Thomas Jefferson.

During the 1780s Rush widened his social concerns. In the year 1782
alone he lectured Congress on the value of national honesty and the payment of debts; he also wrote essays on the need for a navy to enhance the
nation's international standing, on the evils of drinking spiritous liquors;
and he initiated plans for a new college in western Pennsylvania.

In common with most men of his time, Rush felt that the success of a
republic depended on the virtue of its citizenry. By "virtue" he meant
disinterested patriotism. Without it, a republic (which history had proved
a fragile form of government) would dissolve into warring factions. Virtue,
then, was the balancing staff that enabled a people to avoid the twin pitfalls of tyranny and anarchy. To attain such virtue, Rush concluded, Americans had to be cleansed of the monarchical manners and morals acquired
from Great Britain. How? Education was the answer. Public schools, open
to all, would instill in American youth an ethical code and a civic consciousness proper for a republic, and in so doing they would shape a uniform national character. "One general and uniform system of education,"
Rush wrote, would "render the mass of the people more homogeneous, and

thereby fit them more easily for uniform and peaceable government." Homogeneity, in short, would eliminate a major cause of factions and thus help preserve the republic. Noah Webster reached much the same conclusion; so did Jefferson.

Rush's first target was the College of Philadelphia, which, though secular in conception, had been under the influence of the Church of England and catered to the whims of Philadelphia's worldly elite. Even the school's recharter as the University of Pennsylvania in 1779 and the replacement of its Anglican provost did not satisfy Rush. He wanted a fresh institution, staffed by "prophets" of virtue and located in the backcountry free from the temptations of Philadelphia. The site that he eventually selected was Carlisle, in the rolling farmland of the Cumberland Valley. The people there were a mixture of Scots-Irish and Germans with a sprinkling of English. The intermingling of sects, Rush felt, would encourage homogeneity and prevent any one church from dominating the school. A western location, moreover, offered opportunities to those who might otherwise not go to college. Thus it would "soften the tempers of our turbulent brethren in the West." Rush's faith in education, it must be said, was boundless.

Rush enlisted the help of some wealthy friends in the project, and the legislature issued a charter for Dickinson College in 1783. Rush served on the board of trustees, found a suitable provost (imported from Scotland), and designed the curriculum. The curriculum reflected his prejudices as well as his liberalism. First-year students would concentrate on English, French, and German, instead of Latin and Greek. The classical languages, which Rush had always detested, were left for later years. Verbal eloquence, "the first accomplishment in a republic," was given a prominent spot, as was history. Rush also desired a course on international trade, an early recognition of the work of European free-trade rationalists who were carving out a new intellectual discipline, economics.

The college was only the beginning. In 1786 Rush sent the assembly "A Plan for Establishing Public Schools in Pennsylvania." Similar to the scheme outlined a few years earlier by Jefferson to the Virginia assembly, Rush's plan envisioned an educational hierarchy. At the top was a university to be located in Philadelphia (he was by then on the outs with Dickinson's provost). Beneath that were four junior colleges, fed in turn by schools in every township in the state. Rush's plan differed from Jefferson's in significant ways, however. Rush's hierarchy of schools was designed to provide more intellectual challenge and opportunity for scholarly expertise. Jefferson's was a screening process concerned with leadership ("raking geniuses from the rubbish"). And Rush's school system was free from top to bottom. He was the first American to advocate publicly financed common schools.

He also proposed schools for girls. (Coeducation was too advanced a notion, even for Rush.) In a speech to the Young Ladies Academy in Philadelphia a month after he addressed the assembly, Rush outlined a broad curriculum for female education. It included the standard disciplines, from natural philosophy to history, plus music and dancing, and even bookkeeping (for household accounts). The rationale throughout was to make women better wives and mothers, but, even so, Rush's program went well beyond the standard cooking-and-sewing clichés.

Rush was better at conceiving plans than at putting them into action. His educational reforms, set adrift on hope, sank in a morass of legislative indifference. Even Dickinson College, the one institution he fathered, failed to produce the desired results. Given a measly five hundred dollars and ten thousand acres of land by the state assembly, the college suffered acute financial difficulties. Trustees and provost fought one another, and Rush's interest in the school slowly evaporated. In 1788 he took up a new project, a federal university to prepare young men for public office. Mercifully, that idea never got beyond the paper stage.

Although not all of Rush's dreams were fulfilled, his accomplishments in the field of education are impressive indeed. One biographer summarizes them in this way:

> *Benjamin Rush . . . wrote more often and more fully than perhaps any American of the day on education. Others, notably Jefferson, contemplated colleges, but Rush was the first to create one after the Revolution. Others talked about a free public school system, but Rush alone developed a detailed plan for one. Others spoke of educating women, but only Rush prepared a syllabus. The first six Presidents of the United States called for a federal university, but only long after Rush had advanced the idea.*

The Frontiers of Medicine

Shortly after the Revolution ended, Rush wrote to William Cullen, his old Edinburgh teacher: "One of the severest taxes paid by our profession during the war was occasioned by the want of a regular supply of books from Europe, by which means we are eight years behind you in everything." Given the doctrinal rigidity of European medical texts, the intellectual blockade may have been an unseen blessing. Rush himself seemed to become less doctrinaire as his Edinburgh experience dimmed, more given to experiment and observation. When a certain brand of cancer pills came on the market, for instance, he subjected them to chemical analysis. Discovering that the principal ingredient was arsenic, an element long used in the treatment of cancer, he dismissed the pills as nothing new.

Early in his career Rush had observed the relationship between stagnant or polluted water and the various fevers that hit Philadelphia. In the 1780s he initiated a cleanup campaign. An early target was Dock Creek, an open sewer that ran through the heart of the city. At Rush's urging, the legislature ordered the creek covered over and turned into a street. Residents almost immediately noticed a reduction in pollution-associated fevers (typhoid and cholera). In 1786 Rush extended his program into the countryside with an essay demanding that farmers drain their marshy lands or cultivate them. Rush's explanation of why swamps were deadly (putrid "exhalations") was off the mark, but his observation was accurate enough. And his remedy amounted to an early expedition into the field of preventive medicine.

The mentally deranged also caught Rush's attention in these years, and in this field too he brought his newly developed penchant for clinical observation. He came into contact with the mentally ill on his hospital rounds, and in 1784 he began keeping records on them. He recorded the reasons for their afflictions, whether alcohol, disappointed love, grief, or religious melancholy; and he noted how many were cured, how many showed improvement, how many "received no benefit."

After several years of such observations, he broke into print with an essay on "The Influence of Physical Causes upon the Moral Faculty." By moral faculty he meant that part of the mind responsible for behavior. Deviant behavior, he argued, was caused by some physical oddity in the individual's environment — poor diet, for instance, excessive noise, or even certain medicines. Thus, mental illness could be cured like any other disease, simply by identifying the cause and correcting it. Rush failed to take into account some of the more obvious causes of mental illness — notably human interrelationships — yet his notion that insanity was a sickness curable by medical treatment was an important step. It opened the door to a new field of medicine, psychiatry.

Rush's emphasis on the physical causes of disease also gave a theoretical underpinning to medical empiricism. Physical abnormalities, after all, could be diagnosed only by clinical observation. Even so, Rush was not quite willing to shed his European doctrines. The external stimulus, he explained, affected body tension; this, in turn, affected the mind, much as it might instill a fever. Thus his most common prescription for mental illness was alternating hot and cold baths. There was still much of the doctrinaire in the aging doctor.

There is no indication that Rush saw the potential inconsistency between his medical schooling and his medical practice, between untested doctrine and practical observation. He applied the two interchangeably in the greatest trial of his life — Philadelphia's yellow fever epidemic of 1793.

The slave revolt in Santo Domingo started it all. White French refugees fled to America, many of them landing in Philadelphia. By August 1793 the already overcrowded city was trying to make room for more than two thousand homeless and destitute refugees. Yellow fever, a disease endemic in the West Indies, came with them; mosquitoes spread it through the city. On August 5 Rush was called to a house near the city docks, where a young girl suffered from a "bilious fever" and had a yellow skin. She died two days later, and in the interval Rush lost another patient with similar symptoms. Neither case, he later admitted, "excited the least apprehension" of an epidemic.

Rush was no stranger to yellow fever, but his diagnostic skills were blunted by doctrine. An epidemic of influenza had already struck the city, and among Rush's theories was the notion that one fever superseded or suppressed all others. As the death toll mounted, however, he could not ignore the evidence. After conferring with several other physicians and tracing the spread of contagion from dockside to central city, he concluded that it was yellow fever and of epidemic proportions. As was his custom, he published his findings and, as usual, suffered the scorn of his medical confreres. They, too, had difficulty identifying the disease, and they wanted to avoid alarming the public. Alarm, even panic, was not long in coming as the death rate mounted and physicians themselves began succumbing to the disease. Those who could afford to do so boarded up their shops and fled into the countryside. Sending his family to Princeton, Rush opened his house to student aides and the sickly poor who could not afford to go to the hospital. For weeks he barely ate or slept, attending personally to more than a hundred patients a day, while daily expecting to contract the sickness himself. The exhausting pace did bring him down, not with yellow fever (which he thought he had), but with tuberculosis, which troubled him the rest of his life.

Rush's remedy for the fever was the classic one — doses of calomel (a mercury compound that worked as a laxative) and drawing blood. Such treatment only weakened the patient further, unfortunately, and undoubtedly contributed to the death rate. It is a sad irony, however, that Rush's methods did relieve many of the fever's symptoms; so experience reinforced error.

The yellow fever virus attacks the liver, causing jaundice, the symptom from which the illness derived its name. The destruction of liver tissue permits body wastes (bile) to escape into the bloodstream, causing vomiting and a slowing of the heartbeat. Eventually the blood vessels weaken, and blood leaks into the lungs, stomach, or intestines. The result often, but not invariably, was death. Indeed, the most peculiar feature of the disease was its variant effect on individuals. Thus, no matter what Rush did, he could always point to a success, a patient who survived after treatment.

So far as Rush could tell, the bile was the main cause of trouble; thus the laxative purges, administered three times a day, were designed to eliminate bile as fast as it was produced. The simultaneous bloodletting reduced the fever, quickened the pulse rate, relieved tension, and induced sleep — all this, of course, because it simply depleted the patient. It might be said that anyone tough enough to survive such heroic treatment probably could have survived without help. Rush, of course, had no way of knowing how many people recovered from the fever without medical attention (the best test of his prescriptions) because there was no one around to keep such statistics.

By the time that November frosts ended the epidemic, Rush's methods had created a storm of controversy. Most of the city's physicians, having been trained in the same system, followed the same diagnosis and treatment. But toward the end of the epidemic a few began to have misgivings, particularly in regard to bloodletting. Any systematic observer could tell that bleeding had only a temporary impact on symptoms and no long-range effect on the ailment. The most devastating of Rush's critics was a West Indies physician familiar with yellow fever; he recommended quinine bark, cold baths, and bedrest instead of purges and bleeding. This treatment at least had the practical advantage of doing the patient no harm.

Rush stoutly defended his views, and controversy raged for months. When the quality of the debate deteriorated into name-calling, Rush's practice suffered. (It was commonly said that his violent purges were meant for horses, not people.) Before long, politics intruded as well. Rush, though a supporter of the Federal Constitution in 1787–88, became a Jeffersonian Republican in the 1790s, as did other friends of 1776, Samuel Adams and Peale. In 1797 Federalist newspapers began attacking Rush; leading the pack was William Cobbett, who published (under the pseudonym Peter Porcupine) the newspaper *Porcupine's Gazette*. A recent émigré from England, Cobbett was evidently acquainted with the latest British medical opinion, which had begun to steer away from bloodletting. He called Rush a "potent quack" whose disciples had slain "tens of thousands" with their bloody purges. When someone pointed out that Rush was a well-intentioned, useful member of society, Cobbett replied: "And so is a mosquito, a horse-leech, a ferret, a pole-cat, a weasel: for these are all bleeders, and understand their business full as well as Dr. Rush does his."

To protect his reputation, Rush sued for libel. The trial, coming in December 1799, coincided with the Adams administration's prosecution of Jeffersonian newspaper publishers for seditious libel. With unintended irony Rush was mirroring the government. And he won his suit: the court ordered Cobbett to pay eight thousand dollars in damages. The assessment ruined Cobbett, though it did not silence his vitriolic pen. In 1800 he returned to England, having paid Rush only half the sum. Rush gave the money to charity.

Rush's reputation recovered quickly from the nadir of the Cobbett affair. His history of the yellow fever epidemic won him international acclaim. In 1805 the king of Prussia awarded him a gold medal for his courage during the crisis, and a few years later the tsar of Russia gave him a diamond ring. The king of Spain, impressed by the clinical details in the account, ordered it translated into Spanish. European philosophical societies offered him membership diplomas, although Britain's Royal Society (the one membership he truly coveted) continued to ignore him. The international recognition eased his late years, and a diminished medical practice (Philadelphians never fully regained their faith in him) left time for thought and writing.

The problem of mental illness occupied his last years. During the 1790s he had continued to improve the facilities for the mentally deranged at the Pennsylvania Hospital. At his urging, the hospital staff provided simple tasks — sewing, carpentry, or gardening — for those capable of working. Such occupational therapy, to use modern terminology, was another step toward humane treatment.

In 1812 Rush published his last and most important essay: *Medical Inquiries and Observations upon the Diseases of the Mind.* The first comprehensive examination of the causes and cure of mental illness, it remained for many years the only textbook on the subject in Europe or America. Characteristically, Rush stood in error on both cause and cure. Mental illness, he argued, as he had in 1787, was caused by tension in the blood vessels of the brain, a variant of his theory that all disease had a single cause, bodily tension. Hence, his remedy for madness was essentially the same as that for yellow fever — bleeding and purging. The important contribution of the work, however, was in Rush's plea that insanity was an illness capable of treatment. As with so much of his work, it laid the foundation for a nineteenth-century reform movement, in this case the establishment of special hospitals, or asylums, for the mentally deranged. His archaic penchant for bloodletting could be — and was — ignored by an increasingly sophisticated medical profession. Rush was ever a man of two worlds, the medieval and the modern.

In sending a copy of his book to John Adams, Rush expressed the hope that time and experience would vindicate his theories of mental illness, for "I believe them to be true and calculated to lessen some of the greatest evils of human life. If they are not, I shall console myself with having aimed well and erred honestly." It was a life summary that could have been inscribed on his tombstone when he died, a year later, of tuberculosis. When the end came in April 1813, he diagnosed the ailment himself, and in the final professional act of his life he sent out for a specialist — a bleeder.

SUGGESTIONS FOR FURTHER READING

The biographies of Benjamin Rush are almost as numerous and varied as the man's interests. The most complete is by a physician: Carl Binger, *Revolutionary Doctor, Benjamin Rush, 1746–1813* (1966). David Freeman Hawke's study, *Benjamin Rush, Revolutionary Gadfly* (1971), is splendidly written and surprisingly critical, but it stops in the middle of Rush's career. Donald J. D'Elia focuses on the influence of evangelical religion in *Benjamin Rush: Philosopher of the American Revolution* (1974). A tolerant view of Rush's medical techniques can be found in Richard Shryock's essay "Benjamin Rush from the Perspective of the Twentieth Century," in *Medicine in America: Historical Essays* (1966).

Part 3

Empire Builders

"Westward the course of empire takes its
    way:
  The first four acts already past,
A fifth shall close the drama with the day;
  Time's noblest offspring is the last."

— *George Berkeley*, On the Prospect of Planting Arts
and Learning in America (*1735*)

12

Pioneers of Business: Eli Whitney and John Jacob Astor

Business was an American word that was just coming into use when Webster compiled his dictionary. Derived from the mundane word, *busyness*, the expression would gain rich meaning in

the American experience. Business was something new; it was more than the mere exchange of goods. It was an occupation, a profession, sometimes a consuming passion. The businessman was part entrepreneur and part promoter, developer, inventor, manufacturer, trader, and speculator — and sometimes all of them at once.

The evolution of merchant into businessman resulted, in part, from the growth of the country — the development of worldwide trade, the coming of industry, and mechanized transportation. But it also was the result of changes in business organization, from the simple partnership to the stock corporation. The corporation pooled large amounts of capital under cen-

Eli Whitney (1765–1825). *This study of Whitney was done by Samuel Finley Breese Morse, who was a highly regarded painter before he took up the study of electromagnetism. That the inventor of the cotton gin chose, in commissioning a portrait, the future inventor of the telegraph reveals much about the talent and versatility of Jeffersonian America.*

tralized management. It could afford developmental risks, such as canals and railroads. If one venture failed, another would succeed. Corporations created modern America, for better and worse. "The business of America is business," President Calvin Coolidge declared in the 1920s, and there was a grain of truth in it.

At the threshold of this development two men stand out. Different from each other, each had his own contribution to make: Eli Whitney was an inventor turned manufacturer who conceived the basic techniques of modern mass production; John Jacob Astor, a fur trader with a gift for organization, constructed the prototype of the modern international conglomerate.

Eli Whitney: Yankee Tinkerer

It took hard work and ingenuity to make a living in backwoods New England. Between the seacoast and the rich Connecticut River valley was a stretch of barren land good mostly for lumber. The soil was rocky, thin, and unyielding; winters were hard and long. Eli Whitney's father scratched a meager living from a small plot of land in the vicinity of Westborough, Massachusetts. Eli grew up on the farm and tended its many chores, but early in life he showed promise of escaping its tedious routine. He sparkled in mathematics at the village school; at home he tinkered with things mechanical.

He was ten years old when the Revolution broke out, in his late teens by the time it ended. And he spied business opportunity in the shortages that the war brought. When imported nails ran short, he began making his own on the farm forge. Demand was brisk, so he hired a helper. This was no lemonade-stand operation; Whitney was a born entrepreneur. Since each nail had to be handcrafted — which seemed an extraordinary amount of effort — Whitney devised a machine for drawing wire. When the end of the war ruined his nail industry, he switched to making hat pins, altering his machine to make finer wire for cutting.

The family forge might tender him a living, but it hardly promised a fortune; so Whitney decided to get an education. To earn money, he taught school for a year and then entered Yale. He emerged in 1792 with both a degree and the offer of a job. He was to become a tutor in the household of the widow Catherine Greene, whose late husband, General Nathanael Greene, had been awarded a plantation by the state of Georgia for his war services. Whitney sailed for Savannah in the fall of 1792.

Georgia and its neighbor South Carolina had been in economic doldrums since the end of the war. The great rice plantations, the glory of the colonial economy, were heavily damaged in the fighting; by 1790 they were barely back to prewar production levels. Indigo, the other great staple of the southernmost colonies, vanished with independence. It was profitable only with a government subsidy, and Parliament understandably terminated that. Some cotton was grown in the Carolinas and Georgia, but separating the fiber from the seed was a problem. The long-fiber variety was fairly easy to "gin," since its seeds could be squeezed out with a wringer. But the plant was so susceptible to frost that it could be grown only on the sea islands along the coast. Short staple cotton was a hardier plant, capable of surviving almost anywhere in the South, but its seeds had to be picked out by hand. As a result, it was grown only for home use. From the moment that he landed in Georgia, Whitney heard talk about the possibilities of cotton if only it could be commercially ginned.

The potential market for cotton was greater than Georgians even dreamed. A succession of technological innovations in Britain over the past quarter-century heralded the dawn of the industrial revolution. And textile manufacturing led the way. The flying shuttle and spinning jenny had vastly improved the spinning and weaving processes, so that a single worker could produce ten or twenty times more cloth in a day than previously. Then in 1769 Richard Awkright invented a water-powered spinning machine. Such a contrivance was too large for the home and required special facilities; with it, textile manufacture moved from home to factory. In that same year James Watt perfected a steam engine that could be used to propel machines. Mechanization brought a new leap in productivity. Indeed, Britain's production potential soon exceeded the supply of raw cotton. Britain imported raw cotton from Egypt and India, but transportation costs were high. The American South was close at hand and rich in soil — if only its short staple cotton could be ginned.

Under conditions such as this, it was inevitable that someone somewhere would have invented a cotton gin. The commercial pressures were that intense. One ingenious Yankee just happened to be in the right place at the right time. Whitney sketched out plans for a gin within days after his arrival in Georgia. By the spring of 1793 he had a working model. He worked fast because the idea was basically simple, so simple that it is a marvel no one had thought of it before. He began with a box with a roller inside and a crank to turn the roller. On the roller he inserted fine wires arranged in rows. Opposite the rows of wire were slats in the box, into which he inserted cotton. When the roller turned, the wires pulled the cotton through the slots, leaving the seeds on the outside. Brushes whisked the fiber off the wires, and the person turning the crank could pull it off the brushes and pile it. With such a device a single worker could gin ten times as much cotton in a day than he could separating it by hand, and with a bigger machine turned by horsepower a worker might turn out fifty times as much.

The invention had only one flaw — it was so simple that it could easily be copied. One look at it and any handy farmer could bang together a gin of his own. Realizing this, Whitney kept the gin secret until he could obtain a patent. He formed a tripartite partnership with the widow Greene (who provided financing) and the plantation overseer, Phineas Miller (another Yale graduate with a head for business). Whitney then sailed for Philadelphia seeking a federal patent.

The national patent law, adopted by Congress along with Webster's copyright law, offered inventors exclusive rights to the proceeds from their inventions for a period of fourteen years. And obtaining a patent was relatively easy. The State Department handled that along with its other duties, and it did not have the clerical staff to investigate new devices. An inventor had only to file a request for a patent and a model of his invention. Whitney had an especially easy time of it, for Secretary of State Jefferson himself took an interest in the gin, aware of its commercial value to the South. Whitney obtained his patent in the spring of 1794.

The partnership then made a mistake that would trouble it for years. They decided against large-scale production of cotton gins, probably because there were neither facilities nor craftsmen available in the South. Instead Whitney purchased a machine shop in New Haven, Connecticut, where he planned to produce only a few gins. The idea was to locate these at strategic crossroads in the South, and, like flour millers, they would gin cotton brought in by planters.

This effort to maintain a monopoly, not only of gins but of ginning, was doomed to failure. Market pressures were much too strong. Planters simply put together crude gins of their own and dared Whitney to sue. Cotton culture spread like wildfire into the Georgia and Carolina backwoods. Production leaped from 190,000 pounds in 1790 to 35 million pounds in 1800. Whitney and Miller sued to protect their patent rights, and the litigation dragged on for years, eating up their meager profits. In the end, planter-dominated courts refused to do anything, while politicians denounced them as monopolists.

When Miller died in 1803, Whitney changed the system. He decided to permit anyone to use a gin, charging only a small license fee. In that year he got his first break when North Carolina paid him a lump sum of fifty thousand dollars for the unlimited use of gins by citizens of that state. Later in the year Whitney negotiated a similar settlement with Tennessee.

Those agreements changed the whole picture. They vindicated Whitney's patent rights and made Georgia and South Carolina planters seem like penny-pinching interlopers. In 1805 South Carolina negotiated a settlement, and the following year Whitney finally won a favorable court decision in Georgia. It was only a moral victory, however, for his patent expired a year later. In 1807 the cotton gin entered the public domain, to be manufactured, bought, and used by anyone.

Machines to Make Machines

By the time that his patent expired, Whitney had long since lost interest in the manufacture of cotton gins. In 1798, five years before his first victory in the patent fight, he decided that he never would make any money out of the cotton gin. Turning that business over to his partner Miller, Whitney went into a new line — the manufacture of firearms. In the process he unearthed a vital principle that would prove even more important to the world than the cotton gin.

Firearms, like most mechanical devices, were made by skilled artisans. Each, with his own shop and tools, sometimes with journeymen helpers, constructed guns one at a time. The pieces might be beautifully designed and tooled, but each, because it was handmade, was unique. The parts of one gun rarely would fit into another. Thus, they were slow to assemble and expensive to buy; moreover, when one part broke, the entire weapon was worthless.

While making cotton gins in his New Haven shop, Whitney learned the value of standardized, interchangeable parts that would fit into any machine. Such parts could then be quickly assembled, even by someone without skill or experience. But Whitney also learned that he could not obtain such precision by hand; he had to use another machine. Machines that made machines — the idea was the germ of the modern machine tool industry and, beyond that, assembly line production. The idea was not completely new with Whitney. The British and Dutch had long experimented with interchangeable parts in the construction of ships. But Whitney was the first to apply the principle to an ordinary device in common use. From Whitney to Henry Ford there is a clear line of descent.

Whitney also recognized that with such techniques his productive potential would quickly outstrip market demand. Outlets for mass production today are created by advertising. In Whitney's day there was only one large-scale, reliable customer — the government — so he went to the federal government with an offer to sell it firearms. His timing, as usual, was perfect. President Adams faced a crisis with France in 1798; Congress had authorized an army of fifty thousand volunteers. The war in Europe had halted arms imports. Adams's Secretary of the Treasury Oliver Wolcott was delighted when Whitney came in with his offer. They signed a contract for the delivery of ten thousand muskets, four thousand by September 1799 and the rest by September 1800.

Whitney's audacity was breathtaking. A manufacturing enterprise of that scale was unknown in America. And he did not, as yet, even have a factory. Nor had he even invented the machine tools to make the guns!

Actually, it was a rash bargain, and Whitney doubtlessly hoped that the government would take pride in his enterprise and not hold him to the letter of the contract. The first delivery date passed before he even got his factory at New Haven built, and the second came and went while he devised machines to stamp out parts of the flintlock. The gun barrels at first were hammered and bored by hand, though he later invented a metal lathe to do the job. Fortunately for him the French crisis faded, and the army authorized by Congress never materialized. Secretary Wolcott, himself a Connecticut Yankee, was sympathetic; he extended the contract deadline and even advanced Whitney money.

The Adams administration departed, and Thomas Jefferson was president by the time that Whitney turned out his first muskets. When he went to Washington to demonstrate one for the new president, Jefferson was impressed and as eager as Adams to encourage American manufactures. He transferred supervision of the contract from the Treasury to the War Department, which was more interested in quality weapons than in financing details or deadlines. Whitney finally delivered the first batch of five hundred muskets in September 1801. The entire ten thousand took him until 1808. Thereafter he kept his operation going with sales to various states for their militia arsenals, until the War of 1812 created a new federal demand. In 1820 the Monroe administration granted him a third contract. The government contracts assured him a steady market and enough profits to improve his methods. He continually worked on the process, making it more efficient by adding new instruments. Improved efficiency even allowed him to reduce the price of each gun, from fifteen to twelve dollars.

After the War of 1812 Whitney spread his investments into shipping and marine insurance. He was a fairly wealthy man by the time that he died in 1825. By then cotton culture had spread into the black belt of the lower South, and cotton was the nation's leading export. By that date, too, machines and factories were beginning to transform the North. It has been said that the cotton gin helped to bring on the Civil War by making slavery profitable to the South. If so, Whitney also helped the North to win it by pointing the way to massive industrial production. Seldom has one human being been able to influence so profoundly the impersonal forces of history.

John Jacob Astor: Immigrant Trader

John Jacob Astor was a different sort of man. Eli Whitney was a tinkerer, a doer, an inventor, who also happened to have a head for business. Astor was a trader, a buyer and seller, a promoter and speculator, who turned everything into money. He represented another side of the new American businessman. And he had a talent for organization that made him a pioneer in the evolution of the modern corporation.

He was born in 1763, in the tiny Black Forest village of Waldorf, Ger-

John Jacob Astor (1763–1848).
Astor was a man widely disliked as a humorless miser. When he presented himself to posterity, however, he spared nothing. He hired Washington Irving to write his life story, and for this portrait he commissioned Gilbert Stuart.

many. His family was originally French, Protestants who had fled the persecution of Louis XIV (the name was originally spelled d'Astorg). His father was a butcher by trade and a man of some substance in the community. But he was also mean and penny-pinching (traits that would also come to be Astor's). John Jacob's elder brothers escaped as quickly and as far as they could. One sold musical instruments in London; another became a butcher in New York. John Jacob, as the youngest, was expected to stay home and to learn the family trade. But he feared his father, quarreled with his stepmother, and hated butchering. He resolved to flee.

The Revolution awakened interest in America among Germans. The mercenary soldiers hired by the British wrote home glowing accounts of the new land. They were impressed with the bounty of the land, as well as a climate and topography much like western Germany. Their letters were passed from hand to hand or posted on tavern walls. John Jacob's brother, too, told of success in New York. Wartime prices were such that a young man's fortune in trade was almost guaranteed.

John Jacob started for America at the end of the war, going first to London, where he worked for a year in his brother's music shop. There he learned English and how to play several instruments, including the flute. From his wages he managed to save seventy-five dollars. The Atlantic passage cost him twenty-five dollars; the remainder he invested in flutes, to be peddled in New York as a start in business. Those flutes were the beginning of the Astor fortune.

Astor had no interest in his brother's butcher shop. After hawking pastries on the streets for a time, he got a job as a clerk in a fur trading house. The fur trade was booming after the war. Demand in Europe was high, and beaver pelts were plentiful with the frontier at peace. For a century the Iroquois had been the middlemen in the trade, buying furs from the Western tribes and bringing them to the English at Albany, New York. French traders, operating from Montreal, penetrated into Western waters to do business directly with trappers, but the fierce Iroquois forced them to stay north of the Great Lakes.

With German thoroughness Astor set out to learn every aspect of the fur trade. He journeyed into western New York himself to visit the Iroquois villages. He learned their language and customs, and he entertained them at campfires with his ever-present flute. He visited Montreal and discovered that it was cheaper to ship to London from there, rather than from New York. Then he returned home and poured through the account books. Within a year he mastered the fur trading business.

In 1785 he married and used his wife's dowry of three hundred dollars to buy a shop of his own. It was a general store, featuring at first musical instruments imported from his brother in London. But he made an annual trip to the Iroquois country, while his wife tended the store. Initially he brought the furs home by packhorse, but within a year or so he made contact with Montreal shippers. Canadian fur traders disliked Americans, but Astor's German ways gained him an entry. He made more money working through Montreal, and gradually furs came to dominate his business.

He lived thriftily, pouring all profits back into the business. By 1789 he had a smooth organization. Avoiding the Iroquois, whose power waned after the Revolution, he made arrangements with white trappers, who fanned out over the region between the Ohio River and the Great Lakes. Traveling by wagon, he would meet them at appointed places, purchasing their annual harvest and trucking it home. The whole operation was held together by simple verbal agreements. Trappers, in any case, had little choice.

Astor's main competition was the British-owned Northwest Company, operating from Canada. The Northwest Company's agents brazenly trespassed on American territory, backed by British military forces stationed illegally in outposts south of the Great Lakes. By securing British agreement to evacuate these posts, Jay's Treaty of 1794 was a boon to Astor, for it left him the dominant power in the West. Jefferson's purchase of Louisiana in 1803 was a further benefit because it excluded British-Canadian competition from the central Rockies.

Astor's competitive vision did not stop there, for it was already extending across the Pacific. In the year of his arrival, 1784, a syndicate of New York merchants had sent a vessel to China, the first such venture undertaken by Americans. Loaded with ginseng, a root-herb that the Chinese thought prolonged life, the ship returned its owners a profit of 30 percent on the voyage. Other ships followed, and by 1800 the nation had a lively trade with the Far East. When the ginseng market became glutted, Yankee traders switched to furs.

Especially prized in China were pelts of the sea otter, which Americans obtained from the Indians of the Pacific Northwest. The voyage involved a trip around Cape Horn, a stop at the mouth of the Columbia River for a cargo of otter pelts, and then a long sail across the Pacific to China. They returned (often by coming around Africa and across the Atlantic) with holds full of tea, silks, and gold. Losses, of course, were high. Pacific typhoons splintered wooden sailing ships like matchboxes, and pirates infested the Chinese coast. But, for those with capital to risk, the profits were even higher.

Astor entered the China trade in 1800. He cautiously avoided the newly opened sea otter trade, sending instead a cargo of ginseng, lead, and scrap iron. The ship captain invested the proceeds in tea and returned a year later with a net profit of fifty thousand dollars. Characteristically, Astor reinvested the profits in a ship of his own and sent it back to China. By 1803 he was building ships and sending them into the more lucrative sea otter trade. His fortune continued to mount.

The European war, which matched Napoleonic France against Britain and her allies, was both a blessing and a curse to American merchants. Distracted by war, European powers could not meet the needs of their West Indies colonies. American captains moved into the gap, carrying West Indies products to Europe. Losses in this trade too were high, for jealous European countries frequently seized American ships and confiscated their cargoes. But prices also were high and profits fabulous. Merchants simply hedged their risks by taking shares in different vessels.

The government was more excited about ship seizures than American traders were, for the nation's pride and honor were involved. In 1807 Congress, at the request of President Jefferson, enacted an embargo in retaliation for British and French transgressions on the high seas. The law cut off all foreign trade and confined American ships to port — even those involved in the China trade.

Astor, unconcerned about honor when there was profit to be made, found ways to evade the law. On one occasion he informed customs officials that he had a special permit to sail. His ship *Beaver* was to carry a Chinese minister back to Canton. The officers never got to see the permit, but they were allowed to peer through the cabin windows of the *Beaver* where a Chinese, clad in silken robes, sat drinking tea. Astor, it appears, had simply hired a Chinese dockworker to play the role. The *Beaver*, with a virtual monopoly of the China market, netted him a profit of a quarter of a million dollars.

The American Fur Company

In 1808 the New York legislature granted a charter to the American Fur Company. Corporations could be created only by special legislative act. The charter spelled out its organization, its capital requirements, and its powers. The American Fur Company was capitalized at one million dollars, all of it supplied by Astor. He had simply incorporated himself, but the device gave him greater flexibility. A corporation had limited liability: if it went bankrupt, the owner lost only his investment. An unincorporated businessman, even a partnership, was liable for all its assets in the event of bankruptcy. The corporation could thus undertake riskier ventures and hence an expansion of operations.

Astor subdivided the American Fur Company into three branches, each with its own director. One branch operated a string of outposts along the Great Lakes where trappers, both whites and Indians, could bring their pelts for sale. The second managed outposts along the Missouri River, directed from St. Louis. The third operation was a fort at the mouth of the Columbia River for the sea otter trade.

The last venture was the most ticklish because the Oregon country — as the Pacific Northwest was called — was claimed by Britain, Spain, and Russia as well as by the United States. Agents of the British-Canadian Northwest Company, moreover, had already penetrated the region. In a later day a venture such as Astor contemplated would need the sympathetic understanding of the State Department. In Jeffersonian times (James Madison succeeded Jefferson as president in 1809) the government was too small to be informed and too weak to interfere.

Astor dealt directly with the Canadians. In 1810 he organized the Pacific Fur Company as a subsidiary of American Fur. Astor supplied half of its $200,000 capital; Canadian partners, former employees of the North-west Company, supplied the rest. Astor supplied the ships for the Oregon venture and agreed to absorb initial expenses; the Canadians offered knowledge of the country and contracts with the Indians. And the arrangement eliminated any possible competition.

Corporate devices of this sort became standard procedure with Astor. When a new fur company appeared in St. Louis a few years later, vying for the Missouri River trade, Astor quickly bought it out. He then reorganized it as a subsidiary of the American Fur Company, retaining the same management. It brought enterprising people into his own organization and preserved his monopoly. The business methods, the organization, even the ethical standards were similar to the giant trusts that appeared later in the nineteenth century. Astor was not ahead of his time, he simply invented the game.

The Oregon venture was the one failure of his life, though it had an important long-range effect on the rising American empire. Astor sent out two expeditions in 1810 to establish a fort at the mouth of the Columbia

River. One went overland, following the Lewis and Clark route along the Missouri River; the other went by sea around Cape Horn. The ship arrived at the Columbia River first, and its crew began constructing a palisade in the spring of 1811. The land expedition got lost and almost starved before it finally blundered into the Columbia River valley.

The outpost, named Astoria, functioned well for a time. Canadians manned the fort and traded with the Indians; Astor's ships profited by having a stock of furs awaiting their arrival. Then war disrupted the cozy relationship. Humiliated by Britain's maritime regulations and angered by British-Canadian meddling with Ohio Valley Indians, the United States declared war in 1812. Using her superior naval power, Britain blockaded the American coast, cutting Astor from contact with his Pacific outpost and wrecking his trade. When a British warship appeared in the mouth of the Columbia River in 1814, the Canadians seized control of Astoria and ran up the British flag. Renamed Fort George, it was turned over to Astor's old rival, the Northwest Company. Astoria was a failure, but it did awaken American interest in the Northwest. After the war, in 1818, the United States and Britain signed an agreement for the joint occupation of Oregon. Ultimate ownership would depend on who settled it. Empire builders, following in Astor's footsteps, would see to that.

The war nearly ruined the American Fur Company, but peace brought new dividends. When the British and American governments drew a boundary line at the 49th parallel from the Lake of the Woods to the Rocky Mountains, Canadians were excluded from the beaver-rich waters of the upper Missouri, leaving Astor with a virtual monopoly. Indeed, his only competition was from the government itself, which maintained a string of trading posts in the West. Begun under President Jefferson, this government enterprise was intended to protect the Indians from sharp traders, though in a later generation it might have served as an experiment in socialism. The government, in any case, sold its posts in 1822, leaving Astor the unchallenged czar of the fur trade. His mastery did not last long, for by the mid-1820s Western businessmen, such as William H. Ashley of St. Louis and Jedediah Smith of the Mountain Men, were devising new and more efficient means of decimating the continent's beaver population. Astor cared little, for by then he had all but lost interest in the fur trade. He retired in 1834, leaving the American Fur Company in the care of his managerial associates. He was seventy-one then and would devote the rest of his years to a passion that had been only a hobby — land speculation.

The Land Game

Land speculation was the commonest business game in early America. Everyone with money indulged in it, from George Washington to the village physician. Nor was it the result of excessive cupidity. In a preindustrial age, when economic growth was almost unknown, land was one of the few outlets for surplus capital.

The irony is that few made money in the game. Land was plentiful and cheap. It could be bought from the government for two dollars an acre ($1.25 after 1820). Many Western settlers simply "squatted" where they wished without paying anybody. Few speculators came away rich; some went broke. The Revolutionary financier Robert Morris ended in a debtor's prison after overcommitting himself in land.

Urban real estate was the exception. Cities grew at a phenomenal rate after the Revolution, gobbling immigrants and sprawling over the landscape. The value of urban land did not always go up, but it never went down. A speculator with a little capital and a lot of foresight could make millions. And Astor did. He bought his first lots in New York City in 1789, only five years after he landed on its docks. He always paid cash for his acquisitions, so market dips and credit squeezes did not bother him. And he never bought Western lands.

He benefited also from the rapid growth of New York. A city of 25,000 when he settled there, it doubled by 1800 and nearly doubled again by 1810 when it overtook Philadelphia as the nation's largest city. With an eye for strategic locations, Astor got some phenomenal bargains. In 1797 he paid twenty-five thousand dollars for a Dutch farm in the middle of Manhattan. Later the site of Times Square, it was selling for that much per square yard by the time of his death. When Aaron Burr fled the state after his duel with Hamilton, Astor bought his home near Greenwich Village and divided the land into city lots.

Astor did not always sell his holdings. He sometimes used the German custom of leasing land for twenty-one years. Tenants would erect a building, and after twenty-one years Astor or his heirs could take it over — or negotiate a new rent.

He was a money-making machine, disliked by all who knew him. Penny-pinching to a fault, he went steerage class on trips to Europe when he could have rented the captain's cabin. In later life he spent most of his time in Italy, mingling with Europe's aristocrats. When his daughter fell in love with a local dentist, he rushed her off to Europe and married her to a Swiss count. When he died in 1848, he left a variety of philanthropic bequests, including $400,000 to the New York Public Library; but the greatest part of his millions went to his family. His descendants would live in princely splendor, intermarrying with the money-shy aristocrats of Europe. In the 1890s, a half-century after his death, the upper echelon of New York society was known as the Four Hundred. Four hundred was the number of persons who could fit into the ballroom of the Astor mansion. By that time, too, the business corporation, which he had done so much to develop, was the most important institution in the country.

SUGGESTIONS FOR FURTHER READING

Constance M. Green, *Eli Whitney and the Birth of American Technology* (1956), is a brief, readable biography that places less stress on the cotton gin than on Whitney's other contributions to American development. Of the Astor biographies, Kenneth W. Porter's *John Jacob Astor, Businessman* (1931) is one of the volumes in the Harvard Studies of Business History; John U. Terrell, *Furs by Astor*, is a little better reading. Roger Burlingame's *March of the Iron Men* (1938), a story of American invention from colonial times to the Civil War, is especially recommended. A broad picture, done by a master craftsman, is Thomas C. Cochran, *200 Years of American Business* (1977).

13

Conqueror of the Northwest: George Rogers Clark

A republic possessed of an empire — this idea seemed absurd, even dangerous, to those who gave thought to such matters. Republics, it was commonly assumed, were inherently fragile

forms of government, inclined to degenerate into mob rule, demagoguery, and tyranny. A republic could survive — so ran the eighteenth-century assumption — only in a tightly confined, socially homogeneous country where civic consciousness and patriotic devotion could overcome the splintering forces of factionalism and greed. An extended empire, by contrast, could be held together only by the unified authority and symbolic power of a despot, whether crowned or simply armed. The history of Rome, the classical model familiar to all educated Americans, bore out this theory. When Rome expanded from city-state to Mediterranean empire, the republic gave way to the tyranny of the Caesars.

George Rogers Clark (1752–1818). *This watercolor, dating probably from the 1790s, shows a mature Clark. His distinctive red hair is gone, but there remains an air of command. Resplendent in a general's uniform, he ponders a map of the West. Is he remembering old campaigns or dreaming of new ones?*

Prepared for it or not, America was an empire. The vast interior of the continent, claimed by several states on the basis of colonial grants, was a land mass greater than anything ruled by Caesar or Charlemagne. Populated only by Indians and a handful of whites, the continental heartland was a richly endowed virgin, awaiting dominion. Settlement might eventually entitle it to equality in the American federation, but for the foreseeable future it would have to be treated as a colony.

Republican theory yielded to imperial interests with scarcely a spoken misgiving. States fortunate enough to have Western claims took pride in their imperial scope. The sale of Western lands promised politicians a never-ending source of income, enabling them to pay debts without levying taxes. Land companies hungrily eyed the virgin lands of the West; even before the Revolution, several had negotiated legally dubious purchases from the Indians. None of these interests worried much about the fate of the republic; the republic could — and eventually would — take care of itself. Politicians and land exploiters asked only for a soldier and a sword. The soldier was George Rogers Clark; the "long knife" was his monument.

The Lure of the West

George Rogers Clark's ancestors came to Virginia about the same time as Washington's, in the latter part of the seventeenth century. They came from Scotland — this is all that is known of them. The name Clark (derived from the medieval Latin *clericus*, meaning anyone who could read and write) is simply too common for genealogists to trace. John Clark, great-grandson of the immigrant, settled with his young wife Ann Rogers in Albemarle County, which was then on Virginia's frontier. There, on November 19, 1752, was born their second son (they ultimately had six sons and four daughters).

Newborn infants are remarkable for little but a pitiful wail, but George Rogers Clark at least had flaming red hair, a vestige of his Scottish ancestry. The trait was regarded as a good omen, for family tradition had it that Clarks with red hair always made something of themselves. It was a tradition not easy to live up to, for, despite its common name, this was a family of uncommon pride. Of George Rogers Clark's five brothers, four were officers in the Revolution. The sixth son, William, missed out on the fighting because, at the age of five when Lexington was fought, he was considered, even by Clark standards, too young to serve. He made up for it by undertaking in later life the exploration of the Northwest, in company with his Albemarle County friend and neighbor, Meriwether Lewis. That pair, Lewis and Clark, traveled in the service of another red-haired Scot from Albemarle, Thomas Jefferson.

Braddock's defeat in 1755 brought warfare to the Virginia frontier, and John Clark took his young family back east to a plantation that he had inherited on the banks of the Rappahannock River. There George Rogers Clark spent his boyhood, schooled in the tutorial boarding house of a local minister. The training made little impression — like Washington, Clark never fully mastered the English language — except to instill in him a life-long interest in history and geography. When his liberal arts studies came to an end, probably after about two years, Clark learned the surveyor's trade. Surveying, like the law, was a promising form of employment in land-hungry, suit-prone Virginia.

In 1772, at the age of twenty, George Rogers Clark left home, having borrowed money from his father to purchase surveying instruments and a geometry book. He was soon in Pittsburgh looking for a boat going downriver to Kentucky. There were as yet no white settlements in that "dark and bloody ground," as the Cherokee chief Dragging Canoe called it, but Virginians had grand ideas. In 1768 they persuaded the Iroquois to cede their claims in the area south of the Ohio River. Having no legitimate claim to Kentucky, the Iroquois were quite willing to sell, especially since the agreement deflected white land hunger away from their own preserve in western New York. The treaty blandly ignored the interests of the Ohio tribes, notably the Shawnees and Wyandottes, who regarded Kentucky as a private hunting ground. An attempt to occupy the cession, without further diplomatic negotiations, was sure to bring trouble.

Clark knew it, and so did everyone else in Pittsburgh in the summer of 1772. But farmer-pioneers, searching ever for cornucopia, paid no heed. Rumors of rich bottom lands (yielding ten bushels to the acre uncultivated and twenty when put to the plow) drove them on. Courage, however, did not overcome caution. The boatload that Clark joined slipped quietly past Indian villages along the river, halting its journey somewhere near the mouth of the Kanawha in present-day West Virginia. In the fall of 1772 Clark returned to the Ohio, having staked a claim to some fine bottom lands "about forty miles below Wheeling." By spring the process of land clearing was going "pretty well," so he informed his father, and he was making "a good deal of cash by surveying" plots for others.

The Ohio tribes naturally resisted the white intrusion onto their lands. Indian raids brought white reprisals in dreary succession. Neither side in this guerrilla war obeyed the rules of military civility, but the whites were guilty of the most barbarous act of all. In the spring of 1774 a group of Indians — three men, a woman, and a baby — visited the camp of a Pennsylvania trader named Greathouse. The trader, with help from some neighboring whites, got the Indians drunk, tricked them into emptying their rifles in a target shooting match, and killed the entire lot.

The murdered woman, it developed, was the sister of Tah-gah-ju-te, a man who may have been part-white himself and had always been on good terms with the English. He had even adopted the name of a prominent Pennsylvania official, John Logan. One individual who knew him called him "the best specimen of humanity he ever met with, either white or red." Though a Mingo (a branch of the Iroquois) and not really a chief, Logan had considerable influence among the Shawnee, whom he summoned to war, vowing to kill ten whites for each Indian victim. He succeeded.

Virginia's governor, Lord Dunmore, himself involved in a scheme to create a fourteenth colony on the upper Ohio, called out the militia in the summer of 1774. Two armies converged on the Ohio country; one, led by Dunmore, headed for Pittsburgh while the other, under Andrew Lewis, moved down the Kanawha. On October 10 Lewis smashed the Shawnees at Point Pleasant, the mouth of the Kanawha River. A conference at Chillicothe, Ohio, brought an end to the fighting and two years of peace to the frontier. Logan refused to attend the conference, sending instead an eloquent protest against white savagery.

George Rogers Clark was in the thick of the fighting throughout. Although he was not involved in the Greathouse Massacre, he participated in other raids that burned Indian homes and cornfields. In Dunmore's War, as the 1774 expedition was called, he served as an officer of militia. It was said that he so distinguished himself that the governor suggested he apply for a commission as a British regular. Dunmore's War reached a climax while the First Continental Congress was meeting in Philadelphia. At the time, the border warfare on the Ohio seemed fairly remote from the political tension of the seaboard. It was not long, however, before the racial hostility of the border became merged in the British-American quarrel.

The Border Captain

The spring of 1775 found George Rogers Clark in Kentucky. He came, so he informed the first Kentuckian he encountered, "to lend you a helping hand if necessary." The Kentucky settlements, for the moment, were not in need of help. So new were they that they had not yet attracted the Indians' attention. Only that spring Daniel Boone had blazed a trail north into Kentucky from the Cumberland Gap, a route that offered prospective settlers a safer passage into Kentucky than did the Indian-haunted Ohio River.

Boone's employer, North Carolina speculator Richard Henderson, had purchased a huge slice of eastern Kentucky from the Cherokees. Henderson's purchase had even less validity than the Virginia cession obtained from the Iroquois; but British authorities, who never permitted such private transactions with the Indians, were too preoccupied to dispute it. Henderson followed Boone up the "Wilderness Road" with a party of riflemen and a packtrain of provisions. In the heart of the Bluegrass Region they set up a wooden palisade and called it Boonesborough. Henderson planned to make Kentucky into a fourteenth colony, with himself as chief proprietor.

Other settlers arrived in Kentucky about the same time, notably the Harrod brothers of Harrodsburg, who had established an earlier claim and then left it to fight in Dunmore's War. These people disputed Henderson's title, but for the sake of unity they submitted to his leadership. In May 1775 representatives of the various settlements met under a great elm in Boonesborough, where they set up a court system, organized the militia, and — perhaps most important of all — adopted regulations for the proper breeding of horses.

Into this political maelstrom dropped George Rogers Clark. He promptly organized a popular meeting of transplanted Virginians, which sent a memorial to the Virginia assembly protesting Henderson's claims to ownership. When news of the battles at Lexington and Concord reached Kentucky in June, a popular meeting in Harrodsburg, styling itself "a Respectable Body of Prime Rifle Men," declared its loyalty to the American cause and asked Virginia to make Kentucky into a county with representation in the assembly. With a blend of optimism and enthusiasm the meeting chose Clark and John Gabriel Jones the new county's delegates.

Thus by the fall of 1775 Clark was back in Virginia after a miserable trek through rain-sodden forests (the Indians, Cherokees probably, were too numerous for him to risk using the trail). He arrived too late for the assembly session, but he pushed on to Williamsburg anyway to beg from governor and council some gunpowder for Kentucky. With the enthusiastic support of Governor Patrick Henry (a vicarious Westerner who never in his life strayed west of the Blue Ridge), Clark got his powder. After sending an express to Kentucky friends telling them to pick up the powder in Pittsburgh, he then settled in to wait for the reopening of the assembly to present Kentucky's claim to representation. On that assignment he got the support of Thomas Jefferson, who favored Western representation. His main opponent was Henderson, but the speculator had lost his influence. Henderson was a hero among Virginians when he was bucking the king on Western lands; now that independence was nigh, he looked more like a nuisance — and one from North Carolina at that.

Kentucky was given county status in December 1776, and Clark hurried to Pittsburgh, only to find the gunpowder still there. Clark's message had miscarried; the bearer no doubt had been waylaid by Indians. Shipping the gunpowder was an adventure even by Clark's standards — a four-hundred-mile dash down the Ohio, pursuit by Indians, burial of the powder, secret retrieval, and a new flight for safety. The entire saga took the better part of a year, but, thanks to Clark, the Kentuckians were at least armed when the blow fell in 1777.

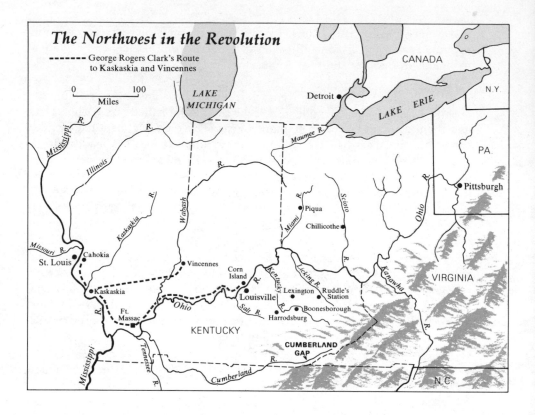

The Northwest in the Revolution

------- George Rogers Clark's Route
to Kaskaskia and Vincennes

    Indians harassed the Kentucky settlements throughout 1776, but their forays were sporadic and short-lived. British officials at Detroit gave the Ohio tribes a few supplies but no encouragement. In March 1777 Lord George Germain, directing the British war effort from the colonial office in London, ordered his commanders in America to form alliances with the Indians and to encourage their raids on the settlements. That same month Shawnees under Blackfish descended on Kentucky. Abandoning the weaker outposts, white settlers crowded into Harrodsburg and Boonesborough. In those stockades they were relatively secure, for the Indians lacked cannon to breach the walls. In the past, an impasse of that sort had been sufficient to discourage the Indians and send them home, but with British supplies (Germain's order reached Detroit in June) the Shawnees extended their siege into the autumn. Then, after a brief and mild Kentucky winter, they were back early the following year. Inside the forest palisades, hunger became part of life.

    In Harrodsburg, George Rogers Clark considered alternatives. Governor Henry made him a major of militia in March 1777, giving him command of Kentucky's defense. Though he lacked military training, Clark instinctively knew that offense was sometimes the best defense. A raid on British outposts might halt the flow of supplies and discourage the volatile Indians.

During the summer of 1777 a pair of Clark's scouts slipped through the Indian encirclement to head for the old French settlements in the Illinois country. They returned with a full report on Kaskaskia, a Mississippi River town just south of St. Louis. There were no British in the village, they reported; it was guarded only by French militia. And while the French at the moment had little use for Americans, they might be won over. Clark's scouts did not examine Vincennes, 120 miles to the east of Kaskaskia on the Wabash River. They had heard rumors (which later proved false) that a regiment of British regulars was stationed there. To Clark it mattered little. Vincennes and its garrison could be dealt with in due time; defenseless Kaskaskia was, for the moment, prize enough. Its capture would damage British prestige, boost American morale, and intimidate the Indians.

Mission: Kaskaskia

The scheme, of course, was preposterous. Clark did not even have enough men to defend Kentucky, yet he proposed to divide his meager resources in order to lead an expedition across 450 miles of wilderness without supplies, bases, or allies. The Indians alone, should they become alerted, could muster an army ten times his number. Yet in its very absurdity lay the plan's chance of success. No one — neither British nor French nor Indians — expected a foray from beleaguered Kentucky. Surprise was Clark's main weapon.

In October 1777 he left for Williamsburg to sell the idea to Patrick Henry. The governor was enthusiastic. Virginia, after all, had little to lose in this high-stake game. After consulting secretively with an inner circle on the council, Henry commissioned Clark a lieutenant colonel, authorized him to raise seven companies of militia, and granted him twelve hundred pounds for expenses. Happy is the lot of any politician who can grasp for empire with so little cost.

Leaving Williamsburg in December, Clark headed for Pittsburgh to recruit. He had limited success. He could not disclose the true target of his mission, and Pennsylvanians had small interest in the defense of Kentucky. Nevertheless, he signed up some 150 riflemen and started down the Ohio, taking in tow twenty families of settlers who were determined to farm Kentucky despite the hazards. He set up headquarters at the falls of the Ohio, choosing a sand spit in the middle of the river just above the rapids, hoping that the insular location would deter desertion. It did not. When he could no longer delay telling his men the true goal of the expedition, fifty waded ashore and headed for home.

A wilderness army was a type unto itself. Raising one was comparatively easy, for it was not difficult to persuade men that their homes were in danger. And, because every Westerner possessed a hunting shirt, powder horn, and rifle, equipping such an army was no problem. Training was lax, but there was little formality in wilderness fighting; individual enterprise was often more important than rigid discipline. Like the partisan bands of South Carolina, the Western armies functioned as guerrilla units. Given a likely target and natural-born leadership, they were all but unbeatable. The ranks had to be believers, however; skeptics were better off at home. Thus, discouraging as the desertions were, Clark was probably stronger as a result. Any commander would prefer a company of tigers to a regiment of grumbling civilians. "The more I reflected on my weakness," Clark wrote later, "the more I was pleased with the Enterprise."

On June 26, 1778, Clark started down the Ohio River with 178 men. As his boat bounced down the rapids, an eclipse suddenly darkened the sun. Ever on the lookout for a morale booster, Clark instantly proclaimed it a good omen. And so it seemed. The tiny force made the four-hundred-mile run to the mouth of the Tennessee River without mishap or discovery by Indians. At the river juncture they encountered a boatload of hunters who had been in Kaskaskia only a week before. They reported that the village was unwary and guarded only by French militia. The hunters predicted, however, that the French would probably fight because they regarded the Virginians as dangerous barbarians. Clark, ever the optimist, saw advantage even in that. "No part of their information pleased me more," he later recorded, "than that the inhabitants viewed us as more savage than their Neighbors the Indians." In the lonely wilderness fear was a weapon of incalculable value.

The weather was insufferably hot (Washington fought the sweaty battle of Monmouth while Clark was sweeping down the Ohio rapids), but otherwise their luck held. At the junction of the Ohio and Tennessee rivers a messenger caught up with them carrying news of the French alliance signed by Benjamin Franklin earlier in the year. Clark was delighted. The treaty was certain to confuse the French residents of Kaskaskia, whose attachment to the British was tenuous at best. Clark could now pose as either barbarian or ally — or both at once. It was an ace in an otherwise bleak hand.

Leaving his boats at the ruins of Fort Massac, an old French outpost at the mouth of the Tennessee, Clark plunged into the wilderness. To continue by river was to invite discovery, especially on the much-traveled Mississippi. Hiking single file, Indian fashion, pausing occasionally to feed on berries, the company made the 125 miles across southern Illinois in six days. On the night of July 4 they swooped silently upon the town. The surprise was complete. The French commandant was asleep in his bed when Clark and two of his scouts tapped him on the shoulder to inform him that he was a prisoner. The commandant's wife, putting up the town's only resistance, ordered the invaders out of her bedroom. The Virginians acceded, though at some cost to their reputation for barbarity.

The bit of gallantry was costly in other ways, as well. Left to herself until morning, the woman managed to burn her husband's official papers, thus depriving Clark of crucial intelligence concerning the intentions of British commanders in Detroit.

Clark posted guards around the edges of the town to keep anyone from escaping and conducted a house-to-house search for weapons. The French, aware of the sack and pillage that traditionally accompanied conquest, huddled fearfully in their homes. Clark played the role of wilderness Atilla. He stood beside the fort, towering almost to its ramparts, red hair and beard flaming in the sun, and barked orders to scampering minions.

When the village priest came to him to beg for clemency, Clark suddenly melted. He informed the astonished cleric that the inhabitants' property would be protected and their religion respected. The Americans had come as saviors, not enemies. He then dropped the news of the French alliance. Fear yielded to relief and then to rejoicing. The population readily subscribed to the loyalty oath that Clark requested; several French militia units offered their services.

Cahokia, the French settlement across the Mississippi from St. Louis, yielded as painlessly. Spanish authorities in St. Louis, who had lived in daily fear of British attack, also welcomed the American presence. Learning from them that there was no British garrison in Vincennes, Clark sent Captain Leonard Helm with a platoon to occupy that outpost on the Wabash. Taking along the Kaskaskia priest as intermediary, Helm occupied Vincennes without incident. The Indians were still a question mark, but the British power south of Detroit had been eliminated. A company of heroes had seized an empire.

Winter March to Vincennes

At Detroit, Henry Hamilton, the Scottish-born lieutenant governor of Canada, had plans of his own that summer. Satisfied that his Indian allies could keep Kentucky under guard, he planned to send his regular troops against Pittsburgh. Seizure of the forks of the Ohio would give Britain a stranglehold on the entire West and a commanding position at the peace table.

When he received the news of Clark's exploit, Hamilton simply changed targets. He would attack Vincennes instead of Pittsburgh. His army was ready; on October 7, 1778, he set out. Counting British regulars, Tory militia, and an assortment of Indians, his force numbered about 250.

Hamilton's route led across Lake Erie, thence due west up the Maumee River to its source (the later site of Fort Wayne). A six-mile portage brought him to the Wabash River, the water highway to Vincennes. Hamilton hoped to make the trip in three weeks, but low water slowed his march;

then an early winter coated the rivers with ice. Not until mid-December did Hamilton's hungry and frostbitten army struggle its way into Vincennes. In part because of the bad weather, however, he took Captain Helm and the Vincennes garrison by surprise. The French militia cheerfully switched sides again, and the Wabash Valley was once more in British hands.

Since Hamilton and his men had no stomach for another campaign, he delayed his attack on Kaskaskia until spring; he did not expect any trouble from Clark, who was also imprisoned by winter. Sending most of his regulars back to Detroit and discharging his Indians, Hamilton settled in, making himself as comfortable as possible in a woodland outpost. For companionship he sought out the only English-speaking gentleman available, his captive Captain Helm. He could not have found a more genial one anywhere, for Leonard Helm was one of that colorful species of mankind, a Virginian recast into a Kentuckian. Trim women, unmarked cards, thoroughbred horses, and well-aged bourbon were his pantheon. Helm was especially known for his apple toddy, a blend of whiskey, sugar water, spices, and whole apples, heated by a hot fireplace iron, a concoction guaranteed proof against any winter. Although Scots have firm convictions of their own on the subject of whisky, Hamilton proved adaptable. Captor and captive whiled away the winter with cards and toddy and a warm fire.

Clark received news of the fall of Vincennes from a trader who had been captured and released by Hamilton. The trader also informed him of the strength of the British garrison (a mere sixty soldiers) and Hamilton's plans for a spring offensive. Clark realized that he must act instantly. In the spring Hamilton would bring in fresh troops from Detroit and muster a thousand Indians. Against such a force Illinois had no chance, and even Kentucky was in peril.

Since his own force was no larger than Hamilton's, Clark had to appeal to the Kaskaskia militia for help. That required a bit of psychology, as the French were dubious about winter marches. Clark explained his technique in a letter to George Mason:

> I conducted myself as though I was sure of taking Mr. Hamilton, instructed my officers to observe the same Rule. In a day or two the Country seemed to believe it, many anxious to retrieve their Characters turned out, the Ladies also began to be spirited and interested themselves in the Expedition, which had great Effect on the Young men. . . . We set out on a Forlorn hope indeed. . . . I cannot account for it but I still had inward assurance of success.

Clark received the intelligence on Vincennes on January 29. When he launched his counterattack on February 5, his force numbered about 170, half American and half French. The terrain he had to cross — hardwood forests and thick bluestem prairie broken by marshy wetlands — was forbidding even in the summer. Heavy winter rains, which filled marshes and turned creeks into torrents, made it all but impossible. There was not even a trail to follow, since normal traffic went by river. And at the end of the line the swollen Wabash surrounded Vincennes like a gigantic moat.

The icy rains continued as the column wound its way across the mushy landscape. At night they built scaffolds for their baggage and gunpowder, while the men slept in the mud. Without pack animals to carry supplies, they had to live off the land, a difficult task since most of the resident fauna had sensibly bedded down for the winter. A stray raccoon or a fox treed by the high water were made into soups for a hundred. Clark kept up morale by turning hardship into a frolic. Each company took turns cooking whatever was available and then provided the evening entertainment (something on the order of Indian war dances, Clark later recalled).

The worst was yet to come. As they approached the Wabash, the pockets of dry land became rarer, the water in between grew deeper. When at last they came out on the river, a few miles below Vincennes, they beheld an inland sea, with only the tops of submerged trees visible on the far side. As Clark later told Mason: "This would have been enough to have stopped any set of men that was not in the same temper that we was."

He promptly set his men to building canoes and rafts. With numerous trips the army ferried itself across the channel. Luckily no enemy appeared at that perilous moment. Hamilton had scouts and hunters in the woods, but none of them encountered the American force. One British patrol did spot their campfires but decided that they were Indians on the hunt.

On the east bank of the Wabash was a series of small hillocks separated by more water. They had only a few canoes; to continue the ferry service would take all winter. Most of the men would have to wade. Clark led the way, plunging into the icy morass. To keep up morale, he struck up songs, cracked jokes, and told stories. The water came up to his armpits, then to his neck. At six feet, four inches tall, Clark made it through and even kept his powder dry. Some of his French followers had to be towed along, sputtering and cursing. After an interminable day of this, they bivouacked (February 22) on a bit of dry ground within earshot of the morning and evening guns of Vincennes.

They shivered through the night without fires, and at dawn Clark made a short speech, promising that they would soon be at an "End to their Fatigue." In translation this meant the only thing they had left to do was defeat an enemy with superior numbers, safely protected by a fort, and armed with cannon and dry powder. Not completely trusting his rhetorical powers, Clark set up a rear guard with orders to shoot stragglers and plunged once again into the water. In late afternoon they floundered ashore again, this time on a small knoll a few hundred yards from the village. They captured a French villager, who was hunting ducks in the area. He told Clark that the village and its garrison were still in wintry somnolence.

The fort lay in the middle of the village. To surprise the garrison, Clark decided, he would have to bring the French inhabitants into the secret. From somewhere he produced a piece of dry paper (itself one of the minor miracles of this expedition) and wrote out a "placart" for the duck hunter to carry into the village. Telling the French that he had come from Kentucky (knowing the terrain, they would never have believed Kaskaskia), he ordered them to stay in their houses or risk being treated as enemies. Then, after waiting a suitable time for the word to spread, he paraded his men around and around the hillock (which was hidden by houses from the fort), giving the French the impression that he commanded an army of thousands.

As usual, the psychological warfare worked. The French retired silently to their houses. They even managed to inform Captain Helm without alerting his card partner. The garrison went about its evening routine. When darkness fell, Clark's men slipped through the village and stationed themselves at the peepholes of the fort. That maneuver turned the stockade into a prison. Its walls protected the attackers! Kentucky rifles were trained on the blockhouse inside the fort.

The opening shot hit the top of the blockhouse chimney. Since Captain Helm's toddy was known to be warming on the hearth, some sharpshooting joker may have been trying to add to the ingredients. The British soldiers, suddenly alert, dashed out to man their cannon, only to be cut down by devastating fire from their own stockade. Amidst the pandemonium an indignant howl was heard from within the blockhouse (firmly attested to by a generation of Kentucky storytellers): "You have ruined my toddy!"

At nine the next morning Clark called a halt to the shooting and demanded the fort's surrender, accompanying his call with the usual warning that he could not guarantee the conduct of his men if they had to take the place by storm. This was not altogether an idle threat since Hamilton — nicknamed "the hair-buyer" in Kentucky — was widely believed to be the man behind the Indian wars. Hamilton nevertheless refused, and the firing resumed.

It appeared, for the moment, to be a stalemate. Clark held the outer walls, but he could not penetrate the blockhouse without artillery. Nor did he have time for a siege, since Hamilton's Indian allies might show up at any time. In fact, at that critical juncture a band of Indians did appear. It could have been disaster, but Clark, with his impeccable sense of timing, turned it into a psychological coup.

It was an Indian war party, just returned from a raid into Kentucky, so engrossed with its own success that it failed to spot the Virginians. Eager to show their scalps and prisoners to the British, the Indians dashed into town whooping and firing their rifles. Clark sent out a welcoming committee that greeted the warriors in like fashion, with arm waves and war whoops. "The Poor Devils never discovered their mistake until it was too late," Clark later recorded. Five of the Indians were shot dead and seven captured. Clark arranged the captives in a circle in full view of the fort (after freeing two who turned out to be white) and ordered them brained with tomahawks.

Still spattered with blood (it is uncertain whether Clark performed the deed himself or simply stood close by), Clark walked into the fort for a parley with Hamilton. The British commander, though scarcely able to conceal his agitation over the American's gruesome appearance, remained adamant; but he was also unwilling to break off the talks. Threats and counterthreats ensued; the afternoon slipped by in a war of nerves. At last Clark sensed that his man was ripe. Relaxing his demand for unconditional surrender, he offered to let the British march out of the fort under arms. Hamilton grasped at the straw, and the next morning, February 25, 1779, the Illinois Regiment formally took possession of the fort. Vincennes was again in American hands. The "hair-buyer" was sent all the way to Virginia as a prisoner of war. The capture of Vincennes had been the highpoint of Hamilton's career, just as its recapture was the highpoint of Clark's. Thereafter, the lifeline of both men ran steadily downhill. It was a mercy that neither could read the future.

The Fate of a Warrior

Spring, which comes early to southern Indiana, was already at hand, and the indefatigable Clark began planning his next move. A quick thrust at Detroit, he decided, might well succeed. The garrison there had been depleted by Hamilton's excursion to Vincennes. Remote and leaderless, it, too, might be susceptible to Clark's peculiar brand of warfare. Clark had the artillery (provided by the enemy); he needed only a few more men. At his request Kentucky mustered a regiment of riflemen; but, instead of marching to Vincennes, the commander of the Kentuckians became sidetracked in a raid on Shawnee villages. During the summer the British reinforced their garrison at Detroit. The opportunity was gone.

By the fall of 1779 the British had regained the initiative. The Indians, awed into a momentary neutrality by Clark's victories, returned to the warpath. Kaskaskia and Vincennes remained in American hands, but they were no more than beleaguered outposts. And by early 1780 Kentucky was bracing itself for the most furious onslaught of the war. A man less given to optimism than Clark was might well have wondered whether his heroic march had accomplished anything. Historians, at any rate, have occasionally expressed their doubts. They point out that the British claim to the Northwest was extinguished, not by Clark, but by Benjamin Franklin and his cohorts at the peace table. The Indians, moreover, retained both legal title and physical control for many years after the Revolution.

Clark's victory has significance, nonetheless, when we consider what might have happened had he stayed home. For more than a year Hamilton had been preparing his Indian allies for a major offensive. His own march to Vincennes (though hastened by Clark's presence) was but the spearhead of the attack. By the spring of 1779 five expeditions of Indians, involving more than a dozen different nations, were enroute to join him. In the face of such numbers Kaskaskia was sure to fall, and so, probably, was Kentucky. Hamilton carried with him artillery enough to splinter any wilderness stockade. Had Hamilton succeeded in his plans, the peace commissioners in Paris would have had nothing to negotiate. Benjamin Franklin would have been drawing his line along the Appalachians, not the Mississippi.

Clark's capture of Hamilton disrupted British plans and confused the Indians. It also boosted Western morale and unleashed a new flood of migrants down the Ohio. The British offensive was delayed only a year, as it turned out, but when it came, it found Kentuckians slightly more numerous and vastly more confident. And for that they had George Rogers Clark to thank.

Thank him they did, by promoting him to brigadier general and putting him in charge of Kentucky's defense. He had his hands full, for the British were ready to put their multipronged offensive into gear. The first blow fell on St. Louis — the Spanish, having entered the war, were now fair game. Clark was not obliged to defend St. Louis, especially since Spain had haughtily refused an alliance with the United States, but he rushed to aid anyway. He quickly lifted the siege and returned to Kentucky, while a mop-up detail chased the British back to Lake Michigan.

While he was gone, a stronger British army came down the Miami River and thrust into central Kentucky. On June 20 it drew up before Ruddle's Station on the Licking River, a tiny stockade sheltering three hundred terrified settlers. After only two shots from British cannon, the station surrendered — the first Kentucky fort to surrender in the war. The British then lost control of their Indian allies, who proceeded to butcher about half of the helpless prisoners. The expedition then marched on to Martin's Station, which surrendered before the British could even unlimber their cannon. This time the prisoners were protected, but at the cost of Indian morale. When word reached the expedition that Clark was back in Kentucky raising an army, the Indians fled for home. The British had to abandon the invasion and return to Detroit.

Clark was indeed back, and the Indian atrocities brought him an instant army of volunteers. In early August he crossed the Ohio River with a thousand men (including Daniel Boone and every other prominent Kentuckian) to retaliate against the hated Shawnee. So rapid was his advance that he caught the Indians by surprise, and after a brief but bloody skirmish he captured the Shawnee villages Chillicothe and Piqua. Both were burned to the ground along with the surrounding cornfields.

The wonder is that with so large a force Clark did not push on to Detroit. If he considered the possibility, he was no doubt deterred by the problem of supply. He had no baggage train, and a force that large cannot live off the land. Indeed, he ran out of food even while he was burning the Indians' corn and had to make a hasty retreat to Kentucky.

In December 1780 Clark journeyed east to Richmond to secure authorization for an attack on Detroit. Governor Jefferson was much interested, but in the midst of their discussions a British amphibious force, commanded by Benedict Arnold, appeared in the Chesapeake. Arnold's raids kept Virginia in turmoil for months; then in April 1781 Cornwallis appeared. Any thought of a Western offensive vanished.

Besides embarrassing Governor Jefferson (and ultimately causing his resignation), Benedict Arnold's campaign damaged Clark personally. In 1781 Arnold descended on Richmond to destroy government stores and munitions. Among the items put to the torch were a number of government papers, including the financial vouchers for Clark's Illinois campaigns. Clark was already in financial difficulties as a result of his public service; Arnold's action unwittingly helped condemn him to a lifetime of poverty.

Virginia had never had enough funds to carry out its imperial ambitions, despite the promises to Clark made by governor and council. Even if it had possessed gold, there was no way to transfer it to Kentucky; thus, from the beginning Clark was expected to operate on credit. The intermediary was a New Orleans merchant named Oliver Pollock. Clark was to supply and pay his army by drawing drafts on Pollock (like cashing checks on a bank account). Pollock was to be reimbursed by both the state and Congress. The two governments planned to send Pollock flour, which he could sell in New Orleans for Spanish gold.

Though sound enough, the scheme failed. War disrupted contacts with New Orleans, and the wheat fly ravaged Virginia's cereal crop. Pollock never got his flour nor any of the other commodities he asked for. For a while Pollock kept open Clark's supply line, using his own funds as well as money secretly given him by the Spanish. When Pollock dried up, Clark borrowed from Kaskaskia and St. Louis merchants, pledging as security his own land in Kentucky. He obtained enough to finish the Vincennes campaign, but it ruined him forever.

Soldiers are rarely good bookkeepers, and wilderness campaigns do not lend themselves to meticulous records. Clark's finances, in short, were a tangled mess. To add to the confusion, his officers financed their own units with drafts for which he was responsible. When these were sent to Virginia, the government refused to honor them on grounds that they lacked Clark's signature. These were among the papers waiting to be authenticated that Benedict Arnold burned. The tangle was now hopeless.

At the end of the war Virginia offered her Western army a tract of 150,000 acres in the territory north of the Ohio. Clark's men knew the area intimately, but they had never looked at it from the point of view of farming. They located their tract at the falls of the Ohio, across the river from Louisville. It was a poor choice. Though having some of the finest scenery in Indiana, the Virginia Military District (as it was called) was far too hilly for farming. Clark's own portion — a substantial slice because of his rank — was attached by Western merchants as security for his debts. Making the best of things, Clark settled in Louisville and became a surveyor for the military district.

The settlements on the north bank of the Ohio reopened the Indian war. The Revolution pretty well settled the ownership of Kentucky, but the Indians, especially the Shawnee, were determined to hold the Ohio River boundary. The Shawnees were further outraged when Congress, following the nefarious colonial practice, persuaded Delawares and Wyandottes to cede Shawnee lands in southern Ohio. By 1786 no settler north of the Ohio was safe, and there were periodic Shawnee forays into Kentucky. Virginia authorized a retaliatory expedition, and Clark was persuaded to command it. It was an utter disaster. He got just past Vincennes when half the army, fearing a shortage of supplies, mutinied and headed for home. Clark had no choice but to call off the campaign.

Rumors of his drinking began about this time. Corn liquor was part of life in early Kentucky, and those with a particular fondness for the bottle, such as Leonard Helm, were viewed with amused tolerance. Clark was vintage Kentuckian, but there was no mention of his drinking in earlier campaigns. The rumors started suddenly in the mid-1780s; from the beginning they were malicious and may have been politically inspired. By 1786 a Kentucky secession movement was in full swing. Some wished only for separation from Virginia; a few plotted separation from the Union and an independent Western republic. Among the latter was James Wilkinson, a Louisville merchant who had contacts in Spanish New Orleans. Wilkinson considered Clark a mortal enemy, in part because he symbolized the West's tie with the East. In his efforts to discredit the war hero, Wilkinson may well have helped spread the rumors of drunkenness. It would have been in character.

However the rumors began, they were well founded in fact before long. It is scarcely surprising. The loss of leadership (driven home by mutiny), the frustration of accounts, and the disappointment in lands would have driven many a lesser being to staring at his own visage in a cup of brew. Humiliations tumbled one upon another. The accounts sent in at the end of the war — after Arnold's raid — became lost. In 1787, Congress, having been given the Northwest, offered to reimburse Virginia for its expenses in conquering the country. When Governor Edmund Randolph asked Clark for his accounts and vouchers, Clark replied that they had all been sent to the state auditor's office. The governor could not find them, and Congress never paid. (They were finally discovered — twenty thousand items in all — in the attic of the Virginia state Capitol in 1913.) In 1791 the Virginia assembly landed the final blow when it turned down his claim of $20,500 for wartime pay and expenses.

The following year he contacted French agents with an offer to conquer

Spanish Louisiana. It was a curious gesture, for the world was then at peace. Spain was no friend to the United States, but neither was it an enemy. Whether Clark thirsted for new glory or simply wished to recoup his fortune will never be known. The outbreak of European war early in 1793, however, gave currency to Clark's proposal. Edmond Genet, French emissary to the United States, approving the idea, offered Clark a French commission as "major general of the Independent and Revolutionary Legion of the Mississippi." Clark borrowed money and began signing Kentucky militia, but the dismissal of Genet and President Washington's open disapproval brought the scheme to an end. The French Republic ended up owing Clark $4,680 — another debt never paid.

In 1803 he moved across the Ohio River to Clarksville, where he built a small house on the only parcel of land that he could call his own. His brothers took title to his other property, including a family inheritance, to keep it out of the hands of bill collectors. He never married. His only companions were a few books (history and geography were his favorites), some frayed memories, and the bottle. Thus he idled the time through long lonely years. In 1812 a stroke left him partially paralyzed, and six years later, February 13, 1818, another stroke finished him.

It was a life that held one fleeting moment of glory and unending years of sadness. By the time that he was twenty-five, he had seized an empire and was a national hero. By the time he was thirty, his life was nearly over. Was it the fate of the warrior? Not all of America's soldiers have been so badly treated. But those whose reputations endured, who were treated with affection as well as honor — Washington, Andrew Jackson, or Dwight Eisenhower — were revered for their civil qualities, for their ability to lay aside the sword and build in peace. Clark was a warrior, and the pure warrior has, except in military emergencies, always seemed out of place in the American republic. Americans can make war, but they do not enjoy it for long. George Rogers Clark simply outlived his moment.

SUGGESTIONS FOR FURTHER READING

John Bakeless, who has written biographies of a number of heroes of the Revolution, has the most detailed and colorful account of Clark: *Background to Glory: The Life of George Rogers Clark* (1957). Lowell H. Harrison, *George Rogers Clark and the War in the West* (1976), is more recent, somewhat more scholarly in tone, and less detailed. Dale Van Every alternates between Clark's adventures and those of the Mohawk Chief Joseph Brant in *A Company of Heroes, the American Frontier, 1775–1783* (1962). This volume is the second in a splendidly written trilogy on the early frontier.

14

James Wilkinson, Imperial Schemer

The American frontiersman is almost always cast in heroic mold. He is our original folk hero — hardy, independent, self-reliant, and bold. Like the virgin land that was his home, the Westerner

of American mythology was simple and uncorrupted, straightforward and resolute. Ever on the move, the pioneer was a being in the process of becoming, a symbol of promise, of growth and development, like the promise of the western Eden itself.

Life is often larger than myth. And the true story of the men and women of the West is far richer than any fanciful distillation. The West had its heroes, of course, among them Daniel Boone and George Rogers Clark. Yet it also had its share of promoters and schemers — perhaps more than its share, for a primitive land, where laws and customs were still unfixed, brought out the worst in human nature, as well as the best.

James Wilkinson (1757–1825). *Not everyone can be judged by his appearance, but Wilkinson's face certainly reflected his character. Bland in its features, a bit puffy from rich food and good wine, there was little in it to inspire men to action. Yet, it is a benevolent face with no hint of intrigue. Perhaps this quality enabled him to survive three official inquiries and two court martials.*

General James Wilkinson was more devious than most Westerners, more wooden of conscience, more given to self-promotion. Yet his story, a mixture of comedy and pathos, heroism and villainy, is a useful touch of Western reality.

Marylander on the Make

Like many Westerners of the time, James Wilkinson grew up in the East. He was born in Maryland in 1757, the son of a prosperous planter-merchant. His youthful environment was similar to that of Washington. He learned the rudiments of mathematics and Latin from a Scottish tutor; his ample leisure time was devoted to riding and hunting. Where Washington learned the surveyor's art as a youth, Wilkinson was apprenticed to a physician to learn the mysteries of medicine. There the similarity between the two ended. The plantation environment produced in Washington a man of well-mannered gentility, but one with the homespun virtue and devotion to duty of a Yankee Puritan. In Wilkinson it shaped a man of genial temperament whose chief devotions were attractive women and pedigreed horses. He got ahead in life by scheming, rather than diligence, and knew little of money except how to spend it.

At the age of seventeen Wilkinson went off to Philadelphia to study medicine. The Pennsylvania Hospital and the city's corps of physicians, many of them trained in Edinburgh, Scotland, had already earned the city a reputation as a medical center. Wilkinson glided smoothly through Philadelphia's social whirl, ingratiated himself with the prominent Biddle family, and absorbed a smattering of medical information.

Returning to Maryland just as the Revolution broke out, Wilkinson promptly joined a volunteer company that was headed for Boston. He signed on as a rifleman, though the army was desperately short of surgeons. (Perhaps the war was a welcome opportunity to escape a profession for which he had no calling.) In the fall of 1775 General Washington assigned the Maryland and Virginia riflemen to accompany Benedict Arnold on his expedition to capture Quebec. The expedition trekked across the Maine wilderness to take Quebec by surprise, joining another army that came north by way of Montreal. The bold enterprise came within an eyelash of capturing the whole of Canada, only to fail in a New Year's assault on the citadel of Quebec. General Richard Montgomery was killed, Arnold was wounded, and Daniel Morgan, commanding the riflemen, was captured. Wilkinson fought well, earning the praise of his commanders; he emerged from the campaign a major in rank.

During the summer of 1776, while Arnold's ragged army retreated southward toward Lake Champlain, Wilkinson served as aide-de-camp to General Arthur St. Clair, commanding at Ticonderoga, the fort that guarded the lake. In the fall, after a bout with typhoid fever, he started south to attach himself to the staff of General Charles Lee. A former officer in the British army, Lee was one of the few commanders in Washington's army with professional experience. After the disastrous New York campaign, Washington's critics looked to Lee as a possible replacement. Lee encouraged the view, announcing plans to retake New Jersey after Washington fled across the Delaware River. When Washington stationed his army across the river from Trenton and begged Lee to join him, Lee refused, undertaking instead a leisurely move into northern New Jersey. Convinced, apparently, that Lee's was a rising star, Wilkinson went in search of him. After an all-night ride from New York, Wilkinson found Lee comfortably ensconced in a New Jersey tavern. Just as the two sat down to breakfast, a British patrol appeared and surrounded the house. Wilkinson somehow escaped, but Lee was captured.

Wilkinson then sought out General Horatio Gates, another commander with a gift for political intrigue. Gates, like Lee, found himself with an independent command when the British advance scattered the American army. And, like Lee, he found a bundle of excuses for not joining Washington on the banks of the Delaware. When Washington, in desperation, told Gates of his intent to attack Trenton, Gates sent Wilkinson to tell the commander that he was ill. Wilkinson arrived on Christmas morning, just as Washington's army was making its crossing.

Gates, meanwhile, went in search of the Continental Congress, which had fled to Baltimore. A Virginian, he was a friend of Richard Henry Lee and, through him, of Samuel Adams. Gates quickly developed a following among Washington's critics, both in Congress and in the military; but, after Washington's victory at Trenton, he had to bide his time. So did Wilkinson.

The summer of 1777 found Wilkinson back at Ticonderoga as aide-de-camp to General St. Clair. A new British army, commanded by General John Burgoyne, started south from Canada that summer; by early July it was nearing Ticonderoga. The Americans had blocked the lake with a chain of logs and built breastworks on the Vermont shore across from the fort. Mountains protected their flanks; the British would have to make a frontal assault. As the British force crept through the woods, Wilkinson spied a redcoat wandering across an opening and ordered a sniper to shoot him. The shot sparked a fusilade of cannon and musket fire all down the American line. When the smoke cleared, the British had departed, leaving one man, Wilkinson's victim, lying on the field. He was found to be dead drunk, but otherwise unharmed.

Alerted to the American defenses, Burgoyne changed tactics. He had artillery pieces dragged to the top of a nearby hill. Since this emplacement gave Burgoyne command of the fort, St. Clair promptly surrendered. Not wanting to be burdened with prisoners, Burgoyne let the American defenders return home. The British then prepared to move south along the

Hudson River. By joining forces with the British army in New York City, they would cut the colonies in two.

The disaster at Ticonderoga prompted a change in American command, and in August 1777 Congress named Gates to head the northern army. In a gratuitous slap at Washington, Congress made Gates directly responsible to it. Wilkinson slipped through the shuffle, emerging as aide-de-camp to Gates. In that role he witnessed the showdown at Freeman's Farm, September 19 and October 7, as Gates's army twice stopped Burgoyne's thrusts. Most observers gave Benedict Arnold credit for the victories, but Gates, as commander, received the accolades. He sent Wilkinson to Congress with the news, suggesting in the same letter that Congress reward his emissary with promotion to brigadier general (in Europe it was customary to reward the bearer of good tidings — one of Martha Washington's ancestors was made governor of the Leeward Islands for that timely service to Queen Anne).

From Albany to York, Pennsylvania, where Congress had set up shop while the British occupied Philadelphia, was 285 miles. An ordinary traveler could cover it in six days, an express rider in three. It took Wilkinson eleven. A "convulsive colic" delayed his departure. Then he paused for two days in New York talking to Governor George Clinton and two days in Easton, Maryland, with his fiancée, Ann Biddle. Stopping again in Reading, Pennsylvania, he attended a party of military officers, drank too much, and began talking of plots to replace Washington. When he finally arrived in York, one ill-humored congressman suggested that a pair of spurs and a whip might be a more suitable reward than a generalship, but he got his promotion anyway.

The surrender of Burgoyne, the first important American victory in the war, made Gates a national hero. It also brought the muttered criticism of Washington into the open. At the suggestion of Samuel Adams and other congressmen fearful of the military, Congress in the fall of 1777 created a Board of War. Made up partly of officers and partly of civilians, the board was to superintend the army and to ensure congressional control. President of the board was General Horatio Gates; its secretary was Wilkinson. In this role Gates was technically Washington's superior. But before he and Wilkinson could exercise their advantage, they were dragged into the dust by the "Conway Cabal." When it was all over, Gates was politically isolated, Wilkinson was a civilian, and Washington's job was secure.

The imbroglio started with Wilkinson's liquor-loosened tongue. At the Reading drinking party, Wilkinson had apparently hinted that Gates might someday replace Washington. To bolster his point, Wilkinson cited a letter to Gates from General Thomas Conway denouncing Washington as a "weak General" with "bad Counsellors." An Irishman who had served in the British army, Conway was one of many foreigners granted military commissions by Silas Deane. When Washington refused to give him a command because it meant promoting him over the heads of others, Conway befriended Gates. As Wilkinson told the story, it sounded like an insidious intrigue among Gates, Conway, and unnamed members of Congress to unseat Washington.

That, at least, was the conclusion of one friend of Washington's, who was present at the party. He sent a warning to the commander in chief, together with the quote from the Conway letter; Washington, already troubled with a vicious winter at Valley Forge, angrily demanded an explanation from Gates. Alarmed at the leak, Gates asked Wilkinson who had invaded his personal files. Wilkinson pointed to another of Gates's aides.

Gates then concluded, incorrectly, that the spy was Alexander Hamilton, whom Washington had sent into Gates's camp in search of extra troops. Conveying his suspicions to Washington, Gates rashly suggested that Washington should surrender his young aide. Washington simply replied that his source was, in fact, Gates's own aide Wilkinson. Twisting the knife, Washington added that he had been on the point of warning Gates about the intrigues of General Conway, but he seemed to have been mistaken.

Realizing that he had betrayed himself, Gates turned on Wilkinson. Insisting that he was innocent, Wilkinson challenged his superior to meet him in the street behind the Anglican church in Albany. They would settle the matter with dueling pistols. Gates accepted but at the last minute asked for a meeting. As they walked along on Albany Street, so Wilkinson recorded in his memoirs (long after Gates's death), Gates broke down into tears and Wilkinson pronounced his honor satisfied.

Having alienated both Washington and Gates, Wilkinson faced a military future that was uncertain, at best. He accordingly resigned his commission and returned to Philadelphia to marry Ann Biddle. His military past continued to shadow him, however. When the army undertook to court-martial General St. Clair for his hasty surrender of Ticonderoga, Wilkinson was naturally summoned as a witness. His testimony conflicted with that of General Gates, and a bitter controversy ensued, resulting in another challenge to duel.

This time the combatants actually met, together with designated seconds, physicians, and other paraphernalia appropriate to the field of honor. In the exchange Wilkinson fired and missed, while Gates's pistol flashed harmlessly in the pan. They agreed to a second exchange, in which Gates, his honor satisfied, fired his shot in the air. Wilkinson aimed and missed again. That seemed to call for a third exchange. Gates's pistol misfired again, and again Wilkinson missed. At that point the seconds mercifully intervened, and both sides retired.

Wilkinson's marriage to Ann Biddle gained him entry into Philadelphia's ruling circle. When the British evacuated the city in the summer of 1778, they left behind a curious mixture of joy and guilt. Philadelphia's social elite, traditionally hospitable, had entertained the British as well, even while Washington's ragged army starved at Valley Forge. Some Philadelphians openly sided with the British. The experience seemed to weaken the city's moral fiber: corruption and speculation raged under the veneer of a sophisticated round of dances and parties.

Benedict Arnold, rendered unfit for field command by the loss of a leg at Saratoga, was put in charge of Philadelphia. Swept into the city's social maelstrom, he married the daughter of a prominent Loyalist, overspent his income, and profiteered on army contracts. When the profiteering was discovered, Washington — who admired Arnold's splendid battle record and felt that he deserved another chance — reassigned him to command of West Point. It was a gesture that Washington would later come to regret.

The investigation of Arnold's war contracts exposed further corruption in the army's clothier general office. When the officer in charge resigned, Wilkinson saw his opportunity. The Biddles pulled political strings, and in July 1779 Congress recommissioned Wilkinson as clothier general (quartermaster) of the army.

A capable man, despite his penchant for intrigue, Wilkinson at first worked hard in his new office. But the problems of supplying an entire army, when the nation had few facilities for manufacturing clothing, shoes, blankets, or tents, soon overwhelmed him. Nor had he the patience for the mundane details of army supply. Supply channels became clogged, and equipment piled in warehouses while Wilkinson strutted in military regalia through the usual round of dinners and balls.

The winters of 1779–80 and 1780–81 were the most ferocious of the war. Washington's army shivered and cursed at its hideaway in Morristown, New Jersey, its miseries made worse by a shortage of clothing and shoes. Washington bombarded Wilkinson with pleas for help and complained angrily to Congress. After the Pennsylvania and New Jersey troops mutinied in the spring of 1781, Wilkinson resigned his office and returned to civilian life. He remained there until a new war called him to arms.

The "Spanish Conspiracy"

At the end of the war Wilkinson decided to try his fortune in the West. Moving to Louisville, Kentucky, he opened a general store. Supplied with goods from Philadelphia and Pittsburgh, he retailed hardware, cloth, salt, liquor, and medicines while doubling as village physician and pharmacist.

Kentucky was a promising land at the end of the war. The Bluegrass Region around Lexington and Boonesborough was marvelously fertile and, because of Indian burnings, relatively treeless. Topsoil three feet deep threw up rich crops of corn, hemp, and tobacco. The Wilderness Road leading back to Virginia was good only for horse traffic, but the Ohio and its many broad tributaries — the Big Sandy, Kentucky, Green, and Cumberland rivers — created a network of transport arteries. All drained into the Mississippi and from there into the Gulf of Mexico at New Orleans. Farmers who floated their produce down to the mouth of the Mississippi could return overland by way of the Natchez Trace through Nashville, Tennessee. Encouraged by a liberal land policy (as Virginia sought to finance the war by selling Western lands), pioneers flooded into Kentucky from Pennsylvania and Virginia in the last years of the war. Wilkinson's new home, Louisville, at the falls of the Ohio, was one of the first Western "boom towns."

The one shadow in Kentucky's bright future was Spain's control of New Orleans and the Gulf Coast, territory that Spain had acquired from Britain in the peace settlement of 1783. In possession of New Orleans and the Gulf Coast, Spain had a stranglehold on the American West. Every river of the West, from the Chattahoochee of Georgia to the Mississippi, emptied into the Gulf of Mexico. And Western settlers were dependent on the rivers, for it was not commercially feasible to transport their heavy farm products across the mountains to Eastern markets. They were at the mercy of Spain.

Authorities in Madrid were too fearful to be generous. Their grip on the New World had been loosening for centuries. They had frittered away millions in precious metals taken from the mines of Mexico and Peru; by the 1780s they could not even afford to station an army or navy to defend their treasure trove. And they feared the Americans, a boisterous, bellicose people full of subversive republican ideas. New Orleans and the Gulf Coast had little intrinsic value to the Spanish, but they did serve as a useful buffer between greedy Americans and the riches of Mexico. In 1784, therefore, Spain closed the lower Mississippi to American traffic and refused to let Americans use the port facilities at New Orleans. To keep Americans preoccupied with troubles of their own, the governor of Spanish Louisiana sent arms to the southern Indians.

Spain's actions helped incite secessionist movements in both Kentucky and Tennessee. Kentucky pioneers, especially those from Pennsylvania, objected to Virginia's governance. Many had simply squatted on their lands without bothering to secure a Virginia title, and they resented the pretensions of Virginia land speculators. Others simply felt that their country would be better off governing itself. They could deepen rivers, build roads, and erect marketplaces without having to go all the way to Richmond to secure permission. Promoters in Tennessee, which was governed by North Carolina, felt the same way. Western leaders also realized that, once they severed the Eastern connection, they would be free to make their own bargain with Spain. Some even contemplated an independent republic in the West.

From 1784 to 1787 a dozen secessionist conventions were held in the West; constitutions were drawn and governments proclaimed. Tennesseans even established an independent state of Franklin, which lasted for two years before collapsing from internal dissension. Kentuckians were less successful because Virginia authorities were slipperier. The Virginia assembly agreed to the separation of Kentucky, provided it was admitted to the Union as a state. That turned the problem over to the Continental Congress, where it became entangled in sectional jealousies. New Englanders, afraid that the influence of their region might be diminished with the addition of new states, vetoed Kentucky. There the matter rested until the federal government was established.

In 1787, while the secessionist movement was at its height, James Wilkinson decided to visit New Orleans. The port had been closed for three years, and Kentucky was slowly strangling. He carried a boatload of merchandise in the event he got through, and to smooth the way he carried gifts for the military commanders at St. Louis and Natchez. As insurance, he carried information, word of a possible American attack on Florida (which then extended all the way from the present state of Florida to New Orleans). There is no evidence that such an attack was actually planned, but with Kentuckians one never knew.

No military commander in the field could afford to hold up an emissary with information for the governor, and Wilkinson slipped easily through to New Orleans. There he met Esteban Miró, governor of Florida and Louisiana. Asked to put his proposal in writing, Wilkinson drafted a plan for counteracting the American threat to Florida. Kentucky and Tennessee were disaffected with American rule, he explained, and a few key leaders might be induced to promote Spain's interests. It they did not place the West altogether in alliance with Spain, they would at least deter aggression. The inducement? Well, suggested Wilkinson, trade privileges were a possibility. To give a few merchants access to New Orleans would not expose the Spanish empire to barbarian hordes, and it would win Spain some important friends.

Miró was intrigued by the idea, especially since, as director of the king's warehouse, he would profit personally from an increase in custom. To his superiors in Madrid he could explain the crack in the imperial door as a conduit for intelligence. He asked only a firm commitment from Wilkinson — an oath of allegiance to the crown of Spain. Wilkinson took the oath, though without disavowing his allegiance to the United States. In return Miró granted him a tobacco monopoly: Wilkinson would be the only shipper for one of Kentucky's principal crops. Tobacco, which he could purchase in Louisville for two dollars a hundredweight, he could sell at the king's warehouse in New Orleans for nine dollars. It was pay enough for any spy.

Having made his bargain, Wilkinson returned home. In the fall of 1788 he stood for a seat in the Kentucky assembly to promote the cause of independence. To demonstrate the value of an independent course — with friendly relations with Spain — he sent several boatloads of tobacco to

New Orleans, netting about twenty thousand dollars (the dollar, or piece of eight, was a Spanish gold coin).

Then Governor Miró's greed, which exceeded even that of Wilkinson, undermined both Wilkinson's position and his argument. In the spring of 1789 Miró opened New Orleans to all shippers, provided that they paid a 15 percent duty on all goods. Tobacco flowed downriver to New Orleans, more even than the Spanish could handle. The price plummeted, and Wilkinson, who had borrowed money to finance a huge consignment, faced ruin. Just then the Spanish government in Madrid came to his rescue. Impressed with the information he had provided, it authorized Governor Miró to pay him seven thousand dollars for past services and a future pension of two thousand dollars a year. The bags of gold coin came overland by pack mule. Wilkinson explained to friends that they were the profits from the tobacco trade. Those who had made no profit in the trade were left to wonder.

The gold silenced his shrillest creditors, but Wilkinson was still short of money because of land speculation. In consort with other speculators, he had purchased a tract on the Kentucky River, laid out streets for a town, sold lots, opened a general store — and called it Frankfort. The town would eventually prosper — especially after the Kentucky legislature was persuaded to place the state capital there — but it started slowly; in the meantime Wilkinson faced a new band of creditors.

He considered turning once again to his old friend Miró, but that source held little promise. The Spanish conspiracy, as Westerners had come to call it, was dead. In 1790 the federal Congress erected Tennessee into a territory, with a promise of eventual statehood, and the following year it admitted Kentucky into the Union. Wilkinson continued to earn his pension by sending Miró lengthy reports on Western attitudes, but he knew that there was little more to be earned in that quarter.

So, to improve his income, he returned to the army. He had never dropped the title of general, even in civilian life, and military pomp appealed to him. Besides, there was opportunity at hand, for the Ohio country had become a giant battleground.

The Road to Fallen Timbers

Few Indians lived in Kentucky, but all the Ohio tribes regarded it as their hunting grounds. Nor had any Indians ceded Kentucky to the whites, except the Iroquois, who did not own it. Wyandottes, Shawnees, and Miamis resented white intrusion, and they kept Kentucky in a state of siege through the early years of the Revolution. Even after the war, raiding parties periodically attacked boats on the Ohio River. The Richmond government seemed powerless to stop them, and the Continental Congress lacked an army.

In 1790 President Washington, armed with new military powers under the Constitution, sent General Josiah Harmar with several regiments into the West. As Harmar advanced into Ohio, the Indians vanished into the woods. When Harmar divided his army into search parties, they ambushed it piecemeal. Harmar finally straggled back to Kentucky, having lost 180 men.

In the wake of the disaster Kentucky formed a force of its own. Wilkinson accepted a commission as colonel of militia and was made second in command. In the spring of 1791, the Kentucky troop crossed the Ohio River, ambushed a hunting party, burned a village, and returned claiming a victory. Wilkinson then organized a force of his own and conducted another marauding raid into Ohio.

That summer Washington sent another federal army into the West, commanded this time by General Arthur St. Clair. Wilkinson did not accompany this expedition. And it was lucky for him, because St. Clair suffered a crushing defeat at the hands of the Miamis, losing nearly half his army. Wilkinson was not idle, however; he was busy pulling wires in New York. In October 1791 the War Department, spurred on by a letter of recommendation from Secretary of the Treasury Alexander Hamilton, granted Wilkinson a commission as lieutenant colonel in the regular army and gave him command of Fort Washington on the Ohio (Cincinnati).

In view of Wilkinson's known connection with the Spanish conspiracy, this appointment is quite astonishing. Perhaps the government's intent was to co-opt him by offering him rewards of his own. At least one of his enemies approved the appointment because it would "place him under control, in the midst of faithful officers, whose vigilance will render him harmless, if not honest." President Washington seemed to share this view. To Hamilton he wrote that commissioning Wilkinson would "feed his ambition, soothe his vanity, and by arresting discontent produce a good effect." So tenuous was the government's hold on the West in that age of primitive communications that presidents sometimes felt it necessary to humor ambitious schemers, even when they considered them dangerous. Fifteen years later President Jefferson would handle Wilkinson in the same way.

In 1792 Washington named a new commander in the West, General Anthony Wayne, and authorized a new army. Setting up headquarters in Pittsburgh, Wayne began the slow task of building a disciplined fighting force. It took him more than a year. Wilkinson, now risen to brigadier general, cooperated in the task, though he had wanted the Western command himself. He improved discipline in his own ranks and stored supplies at Fort Washington for the thrust into Ohio.

In the summer of 1793 Wayne moved his legion downriver to Fort Washington and began constructing a road north into Ohio. During the autumn he built Fort Greenville near the headwaters of the Miami River

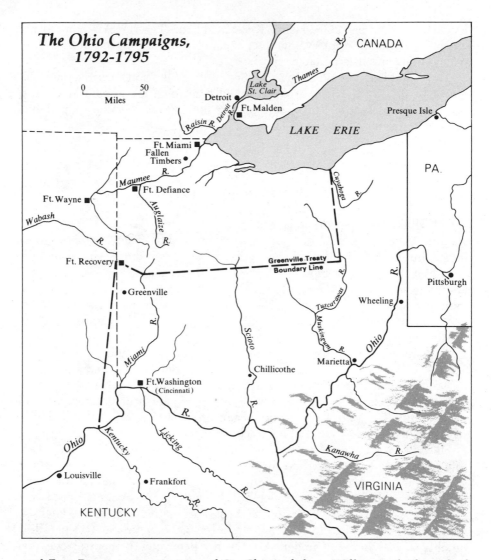

The Ohio Campaigns, 1792-1795

and Fort Recovery on the site of St. Clair's defeat. Wilkinson had worked well with Wayne at a distance, but in proximity the two leaders clashed. Clearly bored by Wilkinson's verbose reports, Wayne regarded his subordinate as a parade-ground general. Wilkinson, in turn, bombarded the War Department with complaints of Wayne's incompetence. Though he contemplated resigning his commission, he dismissed the idea, knowing that it would jeopardize his Spanish pension. Thus, he was present on the final march in the summer of 1794 and fought well enough at the battle of Fallen Timbers to earn Wayne's commendation.

The following year, while Wayne extracted the Treaty of Greenville from the Ohio tribes, Wilkinson spent in Philadelphia pulling political wires. His complaints did raise some doubts about Wayne in the War

Department, but Secretary Henry Knox held firm. The rumor among army officers was that he kept Wayne in command so that he would not have to read Wilkinson's interminable reports.

Then, suddenly in 1796, Wayne died, and Wilkinson was the ranking officer in the West. The War Department confirmed the appointment; his star was at its zenith. Spain, recognizing his increased value, upped his pension to twenty thousand dollars.

In Command of the West

James Wilkinson in 1798 was a man in his prime. He verged on over-weight, to be sure, and his nose was a bit ruddy from years of good living; but he still had the old charm, impressing even those who disagreed with him. His uniform boasted all the trimmings; his horse was well bred and immaculately groomed. He was an easy spender of both his own money and the government's. His tavern bills streamed into the War Department, but envious clerks could only grumble and harass him by holding up payments.

The army had no other complaints. He worked hard and traveled constantly, overseeing a command that extended from Detroit and Cleveland to Natchez and Mobile. He suffered a major crisis in the year 1798 when the secret agents who had been conveying his Spanish gold threatened to expose him. The War Department began an investigation, but it led no-where; Wilkinson had covered his tracks too well.

He remained on good terms with Spanish authorities in Florida, even though the old conspiracy had long since died. Tennessee became a state in 1796, and Pinckney's Treaty, signed the previous year, settled the Flor-ida boundary at the 31st parallel. In the agreement Spain surrendered claims to Alabama and Mississippi and ceased sending arms to the Creeks. It meant that Spain had to yield certain outposts north of the 31st parallel, notably at Natchez, but under Wilkinson's benevolently neutral eye the transfer went smoothly. Peace on the southwest frontier nevertheless re-duced his utility to Spain; his pension payments dwindled.

By 1798, too, Wilkinson could see the coming political changes in the nation's capital. He opened secret contacts with the Jeffersonians so that, when the turnover came in 1800, he was retained in office. His job became more difficult under the Republican administration, for army morale suf-fered when Congress cut the service to a mere three thousand men. Border peace, moreover, meant that the army was confined to the tedium of gar-rison duty. Wilkinson maintained discipline and even attempted reform. In 1801 he ordered short hair throughout the Western army. For ages soldiers had worn their hair long, tied in a queue. (Officers tied the queue with ribbon; enlisted men used a leather thong.) Wilkinson considered the queue expensive, because it required powder, and unclean. Whether he knew it or not, he was also in the vanguard of hairstyle, for the French Revolution did away with the aristocratic wig and ushered in the age of short hair. The army grumbled, but Wilkinson got his way, although he had to court-martial one hardheaded colonel.

Then in 1803 President Jefferson purchased Louisiana from France. And that presented a new array of opportunities for the restless army and its ambitious commander.

The Louisiana Purchase

The region west of the Mississippi, given the name Louisiana by the French, was transferred from France to Spain at the end of the French and Indian War (1763). When Spain obtained Florida and the Gulf coast from Britain at the end of the Revolution, it had the American Southwest nearly surrounded. During the 1780s and 1790s, as we have seen, it used this position to good advantage. By Pinckney's Treaty (1795), Spain agreed to open New Orleans to American traffic for a period of three years, but then in 1802 the port was closed again. In the meantime Spain returned Louisiana to France, whether as a loan or outright gift was unclear. In any case, it was part of the general understanding by which Spain had become an ally of France in the European war. Napoleon, who came to power in France in 1799, was eager to re-create the old French empire in the New World.

France and Spain tried to keep the retrocession secret, even to the point of keeping Spanish officials in New Orleans. Learning of it anyway, Jefferson told his minister to France, Robert R. Livingston, to buy New Orleans, if possible, but at least to secure access to the port. When Spain closed New Orleans in 1802, Jefferson sent an additional emissary to Paris, James Monroe, armed with a threat that the United States would ally itself with Great Britain if Napoleon refused an agreement.

Napoleon was willing to talk. His dream of a New World empire collapsed in 1802 when a French army in the West Indies was decimated by yellow fever. Unprotected New Orleans was at the mercy of the British navy; Napoleon, ever short of funds, decided to sell it. He offered Monroe and Livingston, not just the port but all of Louisiana from the Mississippi to the Rocky Mountains, for fifteen million dollars. Monroe and Livingston leapt at the bargain, and Jefferson agreed. It was not clear how much of the Gulf coast east of New Orleans was included in the deal, but the administration decided to claim as much as possible. The controversy over West Florida kept the United States and Spain at loggerheads for years thereafter. A diplomatic imbroglio such as this offered a fertile field for intrigue — especially for someone in the employ of both nations.

The Louisiana Purchase caused other problems as well. The Creole population of New Orleans was not at all happy with the American takeover. Of French or Spanish ancestry, Roman Catholic in religion, and used to Latin customs and laws, the Creoles looked with apprehension at the sprawling, Nordic, Protestant giant that now demanded their allegiance. Whispers of secession, perhaps a union with Spanish Mexico, swept through the drawing rooms and counting houses of the old French Quarter. A "Mexican Association" was formed, with what ultimate design no one really knew.

Into this whirlpool of intrigue dropped the American army commander of the West, General James Wilkinson. And with him a man of equal guile and grander dreams, Aaron Burr.

Wilkinson and the Burr Conspiracy

After Congress approved the treaty of purchase, Jefferson sent General Wilkinson to New Orleans to supervise the changeover from Spanish to American rule. Encountering the Spanish governor of West Florida, he took the occasion to ask for a renewal of his pension, which was then twenty thousand dollars in arrears. The governor, after consulting Madrid, agreed. In return, Wilkinson was to keep the Spanish informed of any threat to Florida or Mexico. Wilkinson then departed for the East to seek appointment as governor of the new American territory.

After brief stops in Washington and Philadelphia in the spring of 1804, Wilkinson moved on to New York. He arrived in the midst of a furious election campaign, at the center of which was Aaron Burr. Burr had been vice president to Jefferson since 1801, but early in 1804 the Republican party dropped him from the ticket, choosing George Clinton of New York as Jefferson's running mate for the presidential election of 1804. Excluded from national party councils, Burr ran for the governorship of New York in the spring of 1804, and he made an open bid for Federalist support. His old enemy, Alexander Hamilton, blocked that, and Burr lost the election. His political career seemed at an end.

Shortly after the election, Wilkinson asked Burr for a private meeting. The two had first met on the Quebec expedition of 1775, and apparently they had had occasional contacts over the years. At Burr's magnificent Richmond Hill estate they discussed the future of the Southwest and Wilkinson's prospects for winning the governorship. Some weeks later, after killing Hamilton in a duel, Burr fled to Philadelphia and stayed at the home of Charles Biddle, a cousin of Wilkinson's wife. There the conspirators met again. Burr, under indictment in New York and politically dead, was no doubt prepared to try anything. From Philadelphia the pair moved on to Washington, where Burr had a few more months to serve as vice president. The winter of 1804–5 the conspirators spent trying to secure Wilkinson's nomination as governor of Louisiana.

For administrative purposes Congress divided the Louisiana Purchase, erecting the southernmost part into the territory of Orleans (later admitted as the state of Louisiana). The remainder (extending from present-day Arkansas to Montana) was styled the district of Louisiana. Ignoring Wilkinson's importunities, Jefferson appointed a trustworthy Virginian, W.C.C. Claiborne, governor of the Orleans territory; but he did make Wilkinson the military administrator of the district of Louisiana. Wilkinson thus became the supreme civil and military authority for all the vast empire west of the Mississippi. Writing to his brother-in-law in Philadelphia, he boasted that he was "on the high road to Mexico."

After departing the vice presidency in March 1805, Burr went to the British minister in Washington with a request for aid in a scheme to separate the West. The minister agreed to communicate the request to London, and Burr then set out for a tour of the West himself. He talked to politicians in Ohio and Kentucky and met again with Wilkinson at Fort Massac, where the Tennessee joins the Ohio. Wilkinson gave him a letter of introduction to leaders of the Mexican Association in New Orleans. From New Orleans, Burr returned overland to Nashville, where he interviewed Tennessee leaders, among them Andrew Jackson. We know little of what was said in these conversations, but Burr probably talked mostly of an attack on Spanish territory. If he discussed Western secession, it was in strict secrecy. Secession and an attack on·Mexico, however, were not incompatible. Burr may well have dreamed of ruling an empire that extended from the Appalachians to the halls of Montezuma.

On his return to Washington, Burr hurried to the home of the British minister, only to learn that British help would not be forthcoming. Britain had her hands full fighting Napoleon; she had no wish to make an enemy of the United States. Without British help, Burr was foredoomed to failure, but a sudden flare-up in Spanish-American relations gave him new hope.

The United States and Spain had quarreled over West Florida since 1803, the U.S. maintaining that it was part of the Louisiana Purchase, Spain denying that it was ever France's to sell. In the fall of 1805 Napoleon entered the fray. Always happy to sell Spanish real estate when he was short of funds, Napoleon offered to help the United States buy West Florida from Spain, with the understanding that part of the purchase money would be paid to France. Accepting the offer, Jefferson asked Congress for an initial appropriation of two million dollars. To increase the pressure on Spain, he ordered Wilkinson to occupy disputed territory between Louisiana and Texas.

The diplomatic crisis revived the flagging conspiracy, for it gave Burr and Wilkinson a perfect cover. Whatever they did, they could claim to be furthering the President's warlike policy. Burr headed west again in the summer of 1806 and established a base of operations at Blennerhassett's

Island in the Ohio River. Harman Blennerhassett was an Irish immigrant with imperial dreams of his own, and Burr found him a willing agent. From his New Orleans acquaintances Burr had obtained title to a tract of land in Texas. He persuaded Blennerhassett to buy into the operation and to find settlers to go there. Whether Blennerhassett was aware of Burr's other plans, or of his connection with Wilkinson, is uncertain. Nor is it certain what Burr then had in mind. Was he still scheming to divide the Union? Or did he intend to attack Florida or Mexico? Or was peaceful settlement in Texas his only aim? We shall never know for certain. But it is likely that Burr's plans were open-ended — he would go as far as opportunity presented. And much of that opportunity depended on Wilkinson.

In July 1806 Burr wrote Wilkinson a coded letter, telling him that he had obtained funds and had put their plan into operation. He expected to move downriver with a sizable force in November. He also added, untruthfully, that a British naval squadron was proceeding to New Orleans to help. Leaving Blennerhassett to gather men and supplies on his island, Burr toured Kentucky and Tennessee seeking recruits. In Nashville he even persuaded General Andrew Jackson, commander of the Tennessee militia, to construct some boats for his expedition.

Wilkinson, stationed on the Texas frontier, did not receive Burr's coded letter until September. He quickly saw through Burr's lie and realized that there was no hope from the British; without them the conspiracy was likely to fail. Yet he did not know how much Western support Burr could command. Given the weakness of federal authority, almost any uprising had a chance of success. Wilkinson pondered his problem for some days and then resolved it in characteristic fashion — he joined both sides.

In October, Wilkinson wrote President Jefferson to warn him of a conspiracy to attack Mexico. For some time Jefferson had been aware of brewing trouble; he had even sent an agent into the West to shadow Burr. But he did nothing further until he received Wilkinson's letter. That forced him to act. On November 1, 1806, Jefferson issued a proclamation ordering the army to arrest anyone found conspiring to attack Spanish territory. Jefferson did not name names, for Wilkinson had not supplied him with any. If Jefferson suspected that Wilkinson was involved, he kept silent. Wilkinson was the key to the West. By showing faith in him, Jefferson may have hoped to secure his loyalty.

On November 12 Wilkinson wrote Jefferson again to sound the alarm, enclosing this time portions of Burr's coded letter. He had delayed long enough so that he would not interfere with Burr's timetable, should the conspiracy actually succeed; yet he had covered his tracks should it fail. At the same time he wrote the governor of Florida to warn him of the conspiracy, claiming that he had spent $111,000 of his own money to prevent it. He then sent an agent to Mexico City to collect the reimbursement. (It never came.)

Hearing no further news from Burr, at the end of November Wilkinson raced to New Orleans, where he seized control of the government. Declaring martial law, he jailed all of Burr's associates, for Wilkinson knew well who they were. Held in jail without benefit of counsel, they were also effectively silenced. All fronts secured, he lay in wait for Burr.

Burr, meantime, had troubles of his own. Alerted by Jefferson's secret agent, the governor of Ohio had ordered a raid on Blennerhassett's Island. The Irishman had escaped with only part of his supplies and a few boats. Burr himself underwent a grand jury investigation in Kentucky, only to be released for lack of evidence. He joined Blennerhassett at the mouth of the Cumberland River; together they proceeded down the Mississippi. Stopping in Natchez early in January 1807, Burr saw a local newspaper with Jefferson's proclamation splashed across the page. Next to it were portions of his July letter to Wilkinson. He knew that he had been betrayed.

Burr then offered himself up to the authorities of the Mississippi territory; but still another grand jury failed to find any evidence of wrongdoing. Set free, he proceeded overland toward West Florida. At the border above Mobile, he was recognized by an alert army officer, arrested, and shipped east for trial.

Wilkinson's decision to betray Burr was not a difficult one. Once he reached New Orleans, he must have realized that Burr had little support. The pathetic boatload of men coming down the Mississippi could do nothing — unless Wilkinson brought the Western army to Burr's side. And there was no assurance he could accomplish that. Far easier, and probably more rewarding, was to pose as savior of the Union. Having secured New Orleans and arrested Burr's accomplices, Wilkinson departed for the East. He was, after all, the government's star witness.

After gathering reports from their agents in the West, Jefferson and his attorney general decided to prosecute Burr for treason. The locus of the conspiracy was Blennerhassett's Island, which was part of Virginia; hence the trial took place before the federal circuit court in Richmond, Chief Justice John Marshall presiding (justices of the Supreme Court at that time also served on the federal circuit courts).

Always hospitable, Richmond did its best to entertain the visiting dignitaries. There was a round of dinners and balls, and Wilkinson, resplendent in his military uniform, glided into the social whirl. Burr, who won release from jail pending the trial, was the center of attention everywhere. Richmond Federalists, realizing that he was an embarrassment to the Jefferson administration, were attentive to his every wish. And Justice Marshall, himself a Federalist and a resident of Richmond, joined the festivities, though eyebrows arched briefly when he and Burr appeared, by chance, at the same party.

When the grand jury began its hearings in May 1807, Wilkinson's world began to crumble. Burr's attorneys forced him into some damaging admissions. He had to admit, for instance, that he had omitted important parts of the coded Burr letter that he had sent to Jefferson, and he confessed that the code itself was devised as early as 1794. The grand jury ended by indicting Burr, Blennerhassett, and two of Burr's couriers, but it also came within two votes of indicting Wilkinson as well.

Burr's trial, which opened in August, focused on the events on Blennerhassett's Island. Wilkinson, mercifully, knew little of that; hence the government's chief witnesses were local farmers and Ohio officials. Because of Burr's long absence from the island, the government did not have two witnesses who actually saw him there at the same time (the Constitution requires two witnesses to the same "overt act" of treason). John Marshall thus threw out much of the testimony, and the government dropped the case. Burr still faced a misdemeanor charge for conspiring to attack Mexico (as well as charges in New York and New Jersey for the Hamilton affair), but the government let him escape to Europe. Further trials would only embarrass the administration and its star witness.

Troubled Years

Burr's acquittal by no means ended Wilkinson's troubles. The foreman of the grand jury, John Randolph of Roanoke, a Republican at odds with the president and a member of Congress, set out to expose him. At Randolph's instigation Congress appointed a committee to investigate its Western commander. Wilkinson's enemies in New Orleans told it of their suspicions concerning the Spanish pension and supplied details of the Burr conspiracy. Wilkinson retaliated by challenging Randolph to a duel, but the congressman blandly ignored him, even when Wilkinson posted him publicly as a coward. Wilkinson then demanded an army court-martial, got it, and once again was acquitted for lack of evidence.

After two years in Washington defending his reputation, Wilkinson returned to the West in 1809. Amid worsening relations with Great Britain, President Madison ordered him to improve the defenses of New Orleans. He promptly marched his men into the bayou swamps of southern Louisiana, where half of them died of fever. When young Captain Winfield Scott exposed the blunder, Wilkinson had him court-martialed. His limitations as a military commander, concealed for years by luck and bravado, were beginning to show.

Another congressional investigation in 1810 unearthed new evidence of the Spanish pension and led to another court-martial. The army this time had evidence of the gold shipments to him while the Spanish were in control of New Orleans. He was able to produce records of tobacco sales, however, and once again he was acquitted. Thus, when war with Britain broke out in 1812, he was still titled general of the army and was the ranking commander in the West.

The War Department fortunately kept him in New Orleans through the first year of the war. As a result, the disasters in the Northwest — General Hull's surrender of Detroit and the Indians' capture of the Lake Michigan forts — were not his responsibility. But in 1813 the department transferred him to upper New York, where he became part of General Henry Dearborn's command. Wilkinson was not at all happy with the transfer. He was unaccustomed to cold weather, and the New York wilderness was a perilous theater of war (as Burgoyne might well have testified). His command was based at Sackett's Harbor on the northeastern corner of Lake Ontario.

Because of General Dearborn's preoccupation with the Niagara front in the summer of 1813, the Secretary of War took charge of Wilkinson's theater. Since most of the British-Canadian army was mustered along the Niagara River, the secretary suggested that Wilkinson attack along the St. Lawrence toward Montreal. Wilkinson, whose army had been badly mauled in a spring raid on York (Toronto), was slow getting started. In the midst of the preparations he was stricken with fever, and his physician's prescription of opium only added to his troubles. Excessively expansive and deeply depressed by turns, he spent the summer bombarding the War Department with grandiose plans alternated with requests for permission to surrender should he encounter difficulties. Ordered at last to march or suffer court-martial, he got under way in late October. On the first leg of the journey his army lost one-third of its rations because Wilkinson forgot to order somebody to look after them.

On November 11, 1813, the advance guard of Wilkinson's army (some twenty-five hundred men) encountered a British-Canadian force at Chrysler's Farm on an island in the St. Lawrence River. The Americans were decisively defeated, whereupon Wilkinson abandoned the campaign. He retired up the St. John's River toward Lake Champlain and went into winter quarters. He occupied the snowbound months with long reports to the War Department on ways to conquer Canada.

In March 1814 the Secretary of War relieved him of command. Wilkinson promptly demanded a court-martial, expecting it to exonerate him of wrongdoing. The trial, scheduled for August but interrupted by the British capture of Washington, D.C., finally took place in the spring of 1815. Once again he was acquitted. But by then the war had ended, and Congress was slashing the army to peacetime proportions. Since only two generals were needed for such a force, Wilkinson was discharged.

He spent two years writing his memoirs, which were published in three volumes in 1817. Tedious in style and marred with inaccuracies, the *Memoirs* nevertheless present in elaborate detail the many events with which Wilkinson was associated. Having met his obligations to posterity, Wilkinson tried cotton planting in Louisiana but failed. He was never able to focus on the minute detail required for business success.

The year 1820 found him in Texas, abetting Mexico's bid for independence from Spain. Through his old military contacts he helped procure arms for the revolutionaries, and he helped write the first constitution for Texas-Coahuila (one of the states in the Mexican federation). The year 1822 saw him in Mexico City writing President James Monroe with an offer to serve as ambassador to the new republic south of the border. Befriending young Stephen F. Austin, he helped him obtain the grant that brought the first American settlers into Texas. Wilkinson himself obtained a similar grant in 1825. He might have become revered as one of the fathers of Texas had he not died of a fever later that year. To be deprived by death of the last opportunity for fortune was sad, but somehow fitting.

His was a life of failure, on the whole, mingled with chicanery and double-dealing. Yet he had the grand vision of the empire builder, a vision shared by the promoters who mastered the continent after his death. Men of his leathery conscience would, in a later day, turn crystalline streams into industrial sewers and bulldoze prairies into shopping centers. Perhaps he was more typical of the builders of the West than were the Clarks and Frémonts, whom history has chosen for fame.

SUGGESTIONS FOR FURTHER READING

Wilkinson presents a problem for biographers, for a friendly treatment of the man requires considerable explanation of his devious behavior. There are some more recent accounts, but the most objective biography probably is still James R. Jacobs, *Tarnished Warrior, Major General James Wilkinson* (1938). Thomas Perkins Abernethy devotes a great deal of space to Wilkinson's activities in *The South in the New Nation, 1789–1819* (1961), and Abernethy's *The Burr Conspiracy* (1954) is the definitive treatment of that incident. Those mystified by the convolutions of Kentucky politics should consult Patricia Watlington, *The Partisan Spirit: Kentucky Politics, 1779–1792* (1972).

15

Tecumseh:
Indian Statesman

Empire building is a zero-sum game. For every imperial victory there is a loss, some sorrowful being who is deprived of land, of life, or both. The losers are the more to be pitied because they

are so soon forgotten. Historians, being the troubadours of mankind, prefer to chronicle success. How many remember the story of the Persians under Alexander the Great, the Etruscans under Rome, the Saxons after the Norman Conquest, the Slavs under the Hapsburgs, or the Incas under Spanish rule? The North American natives, living in more recent times, have left a brighter memory, yet they too were victims of the rising American empire. Some, like Chief Joseph of the Nez Percé, were heroic, even in defeat. Others had imperial visions as grand as any transplanted European. Among these was the Shawnee leader Tecumseh, who dreamt of a vast Indian confederacy extending from

Tecumseh (1768–1813). *Tecumseh, who considered portraiture a white man's craft, never allowed himself to be painted. In 1808, Pierre Le Dru, a French trader at Vincennes, did a pencil sketch of him from memory. To this about fifty years later were added a cap and the uniform of a British brigadier general. He was thus as misrepresented in death as he had been misunderstood in life.*

the Great Lakes to the Gulf of Mexico. For more than a decade he held the white frontier at bay, only to succumb at last to the imperial tide. He deserves a place in history alongside other martyrs to empire — Hannibal of Carthage, Boedicea of the Britons, Montezuma the Aztec, and Kossuth the Magyar.

A Shawnee Boyhood

It is fitting that Tecumseh was a Shawnee. The Shawnee were wanderers who had never found a true homeland, but as a result of their migrations they had friends and blood relatives in many parts of the land. The dream of an Indian confederacy with land open to all, as free as air and water, came naturally to a Shawnee.

The Shawnee spoke an Algonkian tongue, a language similar to that of many tribes in the northeastern woodlands. Their first home was probably present-day Pennsylvania, but one branch of the tribe moved south to settle along the Tallapoosa River of Alabama. The neighbors, and some-time enemies, of this branch were the Iroquoisan-speaking Cherokees and the Creeks, who belonged to the Muskogean language group. Tecumseh's father was a Shawnee; his mother was a Creek.

After the French and Indian War the southern Shawnee moved north into Ohio, apparently at the invitation of the Wyandottes, who wanted help in resisting white encroachment. They settled at Old Piqua in the fertile valley of the Scioto River. There Tecumseh was born in 1768, the fifth child of eight, which was an unusually large family among Indians.

Tecumseh's name remains a mystery. Some say the original spelling was Tecumthe, meaning "to cross someone's path," or metaphorically "springing panther." White men changed the spelling to Tecumseh and said that it meant "shooting star," though in fact that word has no meaning in Shawnee. But that is the spelling recorded in the history books. It may be the least of the wrongs that the white man has done him.

Our knowledge of Indian village life comes principally from the accounts of white captives. Because of a low birth rate and frequent wars, Indian tribes were often short-handed. They welcomed captives, both men and women, often taking them into the tribe. Because they were well treated, captives usually found a means of escape. Daniel Boone, captured in Kentucky, spent three months at Old Piqua in 1778 before escaping to warn Boonesborough of an impending raid. Captives' memoirs were the first form of "wild West" literature.

The Shawnees had a formal school for boys where elders taught the traditions of the tribe, its remembered history, and lessons in oratory. Because the Indians lacked a written language, spoken communication was developed into a fine art. Young boys also received lessons in handicraft, hunting, fishing, and the art of survival in the wilderness. If the worth of a school is to be judged by its products, the Old Piqua school was a good one. Tecumseh could recite from memory the terms of every treaty signed by whites and Indians — and when it was broken. An army physician who heard him on one occasion could compare him only with the great Henry Clay.

Because physical prowess was the key to wilderness survival, sports were an important part of a young Indian's upbringing. Football was the favorite game of the Shawnees, and a demanding one it was. It was played on a field five or six acres in size with apparently no limit on the number of players. Both men and women participated. Men were allowed only to kick the ball; women could carry it or throw it. More than one captive commented on the lightning speed of women ballcarriers. The object, apparently, was to get the ball between the goalposts, set six feet apart at each end of the field. Tecumseh, according to tribal legend, was a star.

He knew tragedy and grief early in life. When he was only seven, his father was killed while hunting in the woods. A pair of white hunters had asked him to carry a deer they had killed; and when he refused, they shot him. This sort of racial bias, which placed Indians in the same category as wild animals, was the worst evil of the American frontier. Even had the white murderers been tracked and caught, no jury would have convicted them. Tecumseh ever after hated whites and everything about them — their dress, customs, manners, speech, and so-called "civilization." His hatred would carry a heavy price.

Fallen Timbers: The Indian View

While still in his teens Tecumseh accompanied war parties that attacked boats coming down the Ohio River. When George Rogers Clark marched into Ohio in 1786, Tecumseh moved north to a Miami village on the Auglaize River. Little Turtle of the Miamis was then the recognized leader of the Ohio tribes, and Tecumseh offered him his services. In 1791 he led the scouting party that kept watch on St. Clair's invasion force, and he helped spring the Indian trap. The ambush of St. Clair, resulting in the loss of seven hundred men, was the worst military defeat in the history of the frontier.

In 1792 Tecumseh journeyed to the South. His mother had returned to her Creek people after his father died, and one of his brothers lived among the Cherokees. Besides giving him valuable contacts, the visit certainly widened his intellectual horizon. The idea of an Indian confederacy began to germinate within him.

The year 1793 was occupied with prolonged negotiations between the emissaries of General Anthony Wayne and the Ohio tribes. When the talks ceased, the Indians issued a formal declaration of war against the United States. The protocol may have been the idea of their British allies. British agents, working out of Fort Malden on the Canadian side of the Detroit River, provided encouragement and supplies to the northwestern Indians. The supplies were particularly important. Because an Indian army lived off the land, it could not remain in the field very long. British logistics improved their staying power.

In the fall of 1793, while Wayne pushed north into Ohio constructing forts, British soldiers crossed into the Miami country and built a fort on the Maumee River. Its name, Fort Defiance, was certainly apt, for it was clearly on American territory. Britain and the United States were on the verge of war anyway that winter, as a result of British ship seizures in the Atlantic. If war should come, the governor general of Canada told the Indians, the border would be drawn by warriors. The Indians naturally assumed that the governor would back them with British arms.

Little Turtle, softened by age, yielded leadership that year to a Shawnee chief, Blue Jacket. Tecumseh became his chief scout. Blue Jacket was a fighter but unfortunately one given to rash moves. General Wayne's construction of Fort Recovery on the site of St. Clair's defeat was more than he could bear. When the fighting season arrived in the summer of 1794, Blue Jacket laid siege to the fort. It was a bad mistake, for Indian armies had neither the discipline nor the equipment for a siege. The tiny cannon given them by the British failed to penetrate the log walls. The fort held out for nearly a month, until Wayne came to its rescue. With sagging morale, the Indian force retired north to the Auglaize, and some of Blue Jacket's allies returned home. The morale of Wayne's army surged, meanwhile, especially when it discovered British-made shot in the walls of the fort. It was proof for what Westerners had long suspected: that the British were behind the Indian uprising. Angry Kentuckians by the hundreds streamed into Wayne's camp.

From Fort Recovery, Wayne resumed his march into northwestern Ohio. Blue Jacket made his stand along the banks of the Maumee River in a spot where a windstorm had leveled the forest. He was but a few miles from the British outpost. A few British soldiers disguised as Indians entered Blue Jacket's ranks, but that was the only support he got. Knowing of the Indian habit of fasting before a battle, Wayne delayed his attack for two days. Then a disciplined volley followed by a bayonet charge drove the Indians from their cover. The Indians retreated to the British outpost only to find it firmly barred against them. To Tecumseh it was the ultimate perfidy: no white could be trusted, not even an ally.

In the summer of 1795 General Wayne summoned delegates from all the northwestern tribes to a conference at Greenville. With a mixture of bribery and threat, laced with generous amounts of whiskey, he extracted a treaty from them involving the cession of nearly all of present-day Ohio. The Greenville Treaty also established a boundary between white and

Indian territory, running from the southwestern corner of Lake Erie to a point just above the falls of the Ohio River. Most Indians considered the Greenville line to be permanent, but those familiar with the history of such treaties knew better. Tecumseh, in fact, refused even to consent to the agreement. He was the only Indian leader to do so.

Attorney for the Defense

Tecumseh at age twenty-eight was a magnificent specimen of manhood. He stood five feet ten inches tall, about average for a Shawnee, but his erect carriage gave an impression of greater height. We have only written descriptions of him, for he never allowed himself to be painted. Portraiture, he felt, was a white man's craft. His face was the first thing that caught the visitor's attention. He had heavy eyebrows, penetrating eyes, and glistening teeth. Almost alone among the men of his time, white or red, Tecumseh did not smoke or chew tobacco. Nor did he drink hard liquor. He dressed plainly in a suit of buckskin, for white men's garments were as alien to him as their language was. He also scorned Indian adornment, except for a single white eagle feather on ceremonial occasions.

He married that year, 1796. He chose, curiously enough, a half-breed for a bride. She had one child by him and was then pushed out of his life. What happened to her no one knows. Tecumseh never remarried, but he did fall in love. Again it was a curious choice — Rebecca Galloway, the daughter of a white trader. She taught him English and acquainted him with the history and literature of the Atlantic community. He enjoyed English writers, especially Shakespeare and Milton, but the Bible mystified him. The story of the crucifixion was especially confusing, for he could not understand why whites would kill a man that they considered divine — or why they would make a religion out of such a dishonorable story. Even their church, it seemed, was founded on perfidy.

He did offer marriage to Rebecca Galloway (the Shawnees permitted polygamy). She was agreeable but insisted that he adopt white ways of living, including Christianity. That he could not do, and the romance ended.

By then Tecumseh had acquired a considerable reputation as a warrior, and his refusal to accede to the Greenville Treaty spread his fame. Moving to Greenville, he defiantly built a house astride the treaty line. Other intransigents came to join him. After a couple of years Greenville became too crowded for him, so he moved his base to the White River in central Indiana. His band of followers continued to grow. Indian leadership was not a matter of birthright, or even election; it was something to be earned, through general recognition. The requisites were courage, physical strength, oratorical powers, and — when white pressures intensified — a defiant spirit.

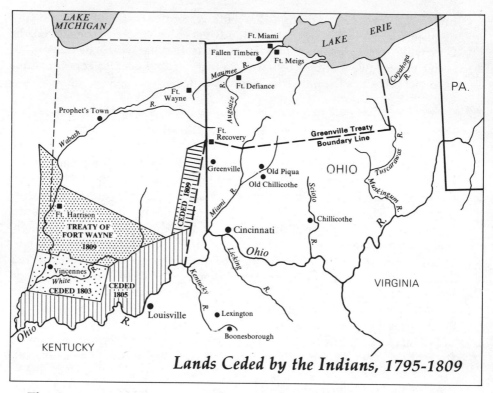

Lands Ceded by the Indians, 1795-1809

The Greenville settlement brought a decade of peace to the frontier. The Indians were defeated, discouraged, and without allies. By Jay's Treaty the British agreed to evacuate their forts south of the Great Lakes. In 1796 they handed over to the American military such key points as Michilimackinac, which guarded the straits between Lake Huron and Lake Michigan, and Detroit, which lay between Lake Huron and Lake Erie. Wayne also won at Greenville permission to establish forts in the Indian country. Fort Wayne on the Maumee River and Dearborn at the foot of Lake Michigan kept the Indians geographically divided and under surveillance. British agents at Malden remained active, but Indian leaders avoided them after their experience at Fallen Timbers.

Tecumseh spent those years pleading Indian grievances before state and territorial officials. Ohio became a territory in 1800, with the rest of the Northwest designated the Indiana territory, and in 1803 Ohio achieved statehood. The governor of the Indiana territory, William Henry Harrison, originally of Virginia, was an aggressive land buyer. In 1803 he secured from the Indians a tract in the vicinity of Vincennes on the lower Wabash River, which he made his capital. Two years later he acquired the land along the Ohio River, from the Wabash to the Greenville line. Tecumseh opposed these land sales, but to no avail.

He was more successful in defending Indians wrongfully accused of crimes. Indians were at the mercy of Western courts because they were not allowed to testify against whites. Even government officials commonly took advantage of them. When the Sauk and Fox tribe learned that one of its own was being held in a St. Louis jail, it sent a delegation to recover him. Government officials held the entire delegation hostage until they signed a treaty ceding several million acres of Illinois land. Tecumseh could not always prevent such outrages, but he traveled widely and spoke often. A sample case involved the 1806 slaying of a white man in Ohio. Witnesses laid the blame on a member of the Pottawatomie tribe, but they could not identify the individual. Ohio authorities called up the state militia and surrounded the Pottawatomie camp. The Indians were told to yield the guilty one or to suffer retribution against the whole tribe. The chiefs were nonplussed, for they had no more evidence than the officials had. They asked for a council with white authorities, and Tecumseh spoke in their behalf. Tecumseh rehearsed every treaty signed by the Ohio tribes, pointing out that none called for such unusual judicial proceedings. Taking the offensive, he spent three hours detailing white crimes against Indians. The charges against the Pottawatomie were dropped.

Tecumseh and the Prophet

The concept of Indian unity took shape during these years of travel and pleading. It seemed the only way to halt the advancing frontier and to secure Indian rights. Logical as the idea was, it was difficult to persuade tribes accustomed to minding their own affairs and suspicious of their neighbors. A bond was needed, some sort of mystical cement that would hold a union together. The cement appeared by chance; and, with the irony that often attended Indian-white relations, it originated among the whites. A great religious revival swept the Kentucky settlements in 1800, and echoes of it reverberated through the West for years thereafter. Among those who listened and learned was Tecumseh's younger brother, the Prophet.

Laulewasika was a ne'er-do-well and a drunk. His name, which translated as "loud mouth," reflected the general opinion of those who knew him. Then, some time around the year 1805, Laulewasika had an emotion-shattering revelation, something akin to the Christian conversion experience. He swore off alcohol and took to the circuit, preaching with the oratorical bombast familiar among the Western evangelists. His converts multiplied. They called him the Prophet.

The Prophet's creed was a powerful one, an amalgam of evangelical promises and Tecumseh's ethical code. The Indians were promised a form of salvation, even a millennium, in a victory over the advancing frontier and the eventual return of whites to Europe. The red man, said the Prophet, was a superior being; his troubles were the result of white corruption. To achieve his victory, he had to throw off white habits, abstain from alcohol, and return to Indian customs and modes of dress. Then victory over corrupt and degenerate whites was assured — the land would be theirs.

The Prophet ordered his followers to construct a meetinghouse in Greenville as a center for the faithful. It was a magnificent structure for such a place, 150 feet long and 34 feet wide, and symbolized the strength of the growing creed. It worried Governor William Henry Harrison, who considered the Prophet a dangerous agitator. In the spring of 1806 the Indiana governor sent runners into the woods with a special message designed to cast doubt on the Prophet's powers. "If he really is a prophet," said Harrison, "ask him to cause the sun to stand still, the moon to alter its course, the rivers to cease to flow, or the dead to rise from their graves. If he does these things, you may then believe he has been sent from God."

The governor should have known better. The woodland Indians lived in a world of mysteries. Spirits roamed the woods, soughed in the wind, barked in the thunder, and disguised themselves as animals. For an enterprising prophet a miracle was no particular problem. Laulewasika sent his own runners into the woods, inviting the tribes to his Greenville church to witness a marvelous happening. He would personally cause the sun to die.

The appointed day was June 16, 1806. The faithful and the curious by the hundreds descended on Greenville, and the Prophet staged the ceremony with masterful precision. At a few minutes before noon he began his incantations and then raised his hands to wipe away the sun. The great red ball disappeared and the world grew dark. Amid gasps of astonishment mingled with horror, the Prophet resumed his incantations. Then he beckoned the sun to new life, and suddenly all was light. The miracle was done.

Harrison later grumbled that the British had given the Prophet advance word of the eclipse, but that seems unlikely. Neither Tecumseh nor his brother had any contact with the British after the fiasco at Fallen Timbers. Nor did they need British intelligence. The eclipse was widely anticipated. Harvard College had set up a telescope at Springfield, Illinois, to observe it, and the federal government had one at Burlington, Iowa. Any well-connected Indian could have gotten the word.

News of the miracle spread swiftly across the West, spawning a host of minor miracles. Giant squash, bumper crops of corn, deer that wandered into camp for slaughter foretold the approach of the red millennium. On the shores of distant Lake Superior the ferocious Ojibwa built a log tabernacle to the Prophet and cast their old medicine pouches into the water. Some said that there was less fighting among the Western tribes, less drunkenness among those in contact with whites.

In every tribe the Prophet had some loyal converts, quite often the younger and bolder warriors. Sometimes those who scoffed at the Prophet, especially those who had accepted the white man's religion, mysteriously disappeared. Old chieftains, who counseled peace and moderation, lost their influence; young and strident voices took their places.

Seeing all this, Tecumseh used it to advantage. The mystic revival was a good foundation on which to build Indian unity. The puritanical ethos preserved Indian energies for the long struggle. Yet his aim was peace, not war.

Vision of Empire

Exactly what Tecumseh planned was never clear. He preached a doctrine of tribal unity but took no steps toward a political confederation. He talked of hatred for whites but never advocated war. It is conceivable that these were ultimate aims, that with a single mighty Indian nation behind him he might have taken the offensive. Yet he was also realistic enough to know that it was too late to recover the continent. He would have gladly settled for the Ohio River as a permanent boundary, though even that was unrealistic after Fallen Timbers. As a result, Tecumseh posted only limited diplomatic aims, hoping that a modest denominator would have the most common appeal. He asked for neither confederation nor war; he asked only that the tribes agree among themselves that there would be no more land sales.

Land sales were problem enough for any reformer. The Constitution gave the federal government control of all Indian relations, and the government recognized the Indian title to the West. At the outset of Washington's presidency, Secretary of War Henry Knox outlined federal policy. "The Indians, being the prior occupants, possess the right of soil," he told the president. "It cannot be taken from them unless by their free consent or by right of conquest in case of a just war." The sentiment was fair enough, though what exactly might constitute a "just war" was terribly unclear. But in practice there were serious difficulties. What, after all, was "free consent"? Did that involve a vote by the entire tribe, or was the consent of a few chiefs sufficient? Too often, government officials simply bribed minor chiefs with whiskey and trinkets to cede the lands of the whole. Then, when the tribe resisted, it became a "just war."

To some extent the European notions of contract, ownership, and alienation were foreign to the Indians. Few of them understood the permanence of a bargain or the meaning of possession. Few realized, for instance, that they could no longer hunt on lands that had been sold. Tribal boundaries, moreover, were ill defined and frequently overlapping. A cession by one tribe might easily be protested by another. In some instances tribes sold lands for which they had no claim at all. The cession of Kentucky by the Iroquois, who lived in New York, was a classic example.

Even when the nature of the contract was clear and the boundaries well defined, there was still a question of price. The Indians, who lived essentially on barter, had little conception of money. And no one was sure what value to set on unimproved wilderness. One index might be the price that the government placed on the land for sale to farmers — two dollars an acre was the minimum at auction before 1820; $1.25 thereafter. But the government paid the Indians far less than that. By 1820 the government had bought some 190 million acres east of the Mississippi, paying the Indians about $2.5 million dollars for it. Even if it were sold at only the minimum of $1.25 an acre, the profit was enough to pay the entire national debt resulting from both the Revolution and the War of 1812.

A just resolution of this sort of conflict was probably not possible. Given white biases, moreover, certain alternative policies were simply not politically feasible for the government — leaving large chunks of Eastern land in the hands of Indians, for instance. Even so, there was a moral ambivalence among even the most honorable of white Americans. President Jefferson advocated teaching the Indians to farm and assimilating them into white society, an idea far in advance of its time; yet he also suggested selling the Indians more goods than they could afford so they would have to yield their lands in payment. And when Governor Harrison boasted of using whiskey to obtain land cessions, Jefferson said nothing.

Tecumseh opposed not just crooked deals, but all deals. Land, he argued, was there for the use of all; it could no more be converted to private possession than air or water could. That argument had some pitfalls of its own, since even Tecumseh conceded a family's right to the bounty of its cornfield. Tribes, moreover, had claims of possession. When he and the Prophet established a new headquarters in the spring of 1808 at the junction of the Tippecanoe River and the Wabash, the Miamis objected. The Pottawatomies had granted Tecumseh the site, but the Miamis claimed it as theirs. Tecumseh replied that Indian land was held in common, and nothing further was said. Perhaps no one wanted to cross the Prophet.

In the fall of 1808 Tecumseh left his brother in charge of the new town and headed west. He ventured into Illinois for talks with the Sauk and Fox, then north to the Wisconsin River to see the Winnebagoes and Menominees. On his return to the Wabash, the Wyandottes of northwestern Ohio pledged allegiance to him. It was a league for mutual defense, prepared to fight, if necessary, to prevent further land cessions. Tecumseh's one failure that winter was the refusal of the Iroquois to join him. That once proud tribe had had enough of warfare.

Tippecanoe

Tecumseh's alliance did slow the pace of land sales. After the Sauk and Fox cession of 1804, there were no further deals of note, despite Governor Harrison's best efforts. In the interval, however, the governor came under intense pressure from land-hungry whites. President Jefferson also encour-

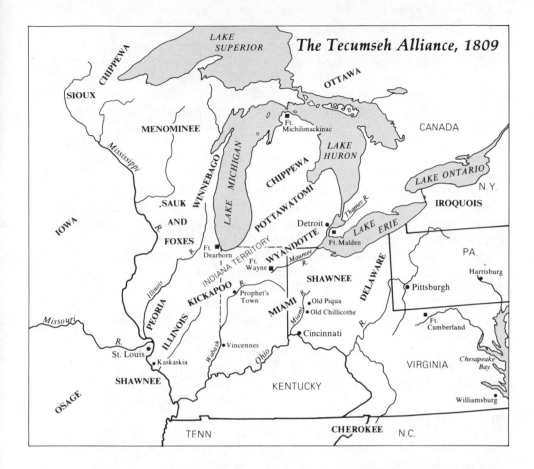

The Tecumseh Alliance, 1809

aged him to seek further revision of the Greenville line. In the summer of 1809 Harrison summoned an enormous council at Fort Wayne. Every important chief and sachem in the Ohio Valley was invited, except for Tecumseh and the Prophet. Nor was a Shawnee invited, an insulting reminder that they had no land to sell. Harrison demanded the cession of the central third of Indiana, including the lower Wabash Valley. The tribal leaders were reluctant. It took several barrels of rum and whiskey to bring them to terms, Harrison confessed to the president. By the treaty the Ohio tribes gave up their claims to three million acres in return for ten thousand dollars, payment to be spread over several years.

Tecumseh's reaction was predictable. Parading into Vincennes with an entourage of three hundred warriors in battle paint, he informed the governor that the chiefs who signed the Treaty of Fort Wayne would all be executed and that, if the governor sought to occupy the ceded lands, there would be war. The chiefs fled in terror; many were never heard from again. The governor stayed his greedy frontiersmen. For two years there was a stalemate.

In the interval Tecumseh searched for allies. He paid a visit to Fort Malden to expand the British connection. British agents had supplied the Prophet's Town with some food and blankets, but only enough guns and ammunition for hunting. They could do no more because the ministry in London had no wish to provoke the United States. The prime minister, his hands full with Napoleon, also feared that an Indian war would bring the destruction of the Ohio tribes and endanger Canada.

Rebuffed by the British, Tecumseh in the summer of 1811 journeyed south in search of allies. He stopped first at Vincennes to assure Governor Harrison of his peaceful intentions; then his flotilla swept down the Wabash and the Mississippi. Traveling across Alabama and Mississippi, from clan to clan in the giant Creek confederacy, he held a running debate with Creek leaders. He made some converts, chiefly among the younger warriors, and passed out bundles of red painted sticks among them. When war was declared, he told them, they were to throw away a stick a day until the bundles were gone — and then attack. It was an ingenious way to coordinate a wilderness uprising.

Tecumseh had less success among the Cherokee, who had not taken the field in anger since the French and Indian war. Adopting one of the Prophet's tactics (and feeling perhaps that he could not lose), Tecumseh told the Cherokees they would know when he reached home because he would stamp his foot and the earth would shake. Actually, he had no way of anticipating the great earthquake that struck the eastern United States in December 1811. That one was pure luck. The Cherokees were doubtless impressed with his powers, but they remained at peace.

On his return Tecumseh stopped among the Osage Indians of Missouri, where his mother and some of his brothers and sisters had gone to live. Then he headed for home, arriving on the banks of Tippecanoe Creek in March 1812. He found the Prophet's Town in ashes. Harrison had struck in his absence.

Harrison, in fact, began planning his raid shortly after Tecumseh passed through Vincennes. He called up the Indiana militia and borrowed a regiment from Kentucky. October was late in the season to start a military campaign, but the governor was eager to be done with it before Tecumseh returned. With an army numbering close to nine hundred men, he marched northward along the Wabash. By early November he was camped near the Prophet's Town and inviting attack.

The Prophet was under Tecumseh's strict orders not to fight, especially without summoning allies. But Harrison's challenge was something that the Prophet could not avoid. To abandon his personal shrine without a fight would have cast doubt on his powers and cost him support. He spent the night of November 5, 1811, whipping his followers into a religious frenzy with chants and dancing. He convinced them that they were immune to bullets, and then he attacked at dawn.

Harrison, surprisingly, was not well prepared. The Indians were in the middle of his camp before the alarm sounded, and only his superior numbers saved him (he outnumbered the Prophet two to one). After two hours of bloody combat, he drove off the Indian attack. With no sense of victory, Harrison dug in, awaiting another attack. It never came. Instead the Prophet unaccountably abandoned his town and vanished into the woods. After waiting behind its breastworks for two days, Harrison's army moved into the empty village and burned it to the ground. Then he headed for home trumpeting victory.

War in the West

In the Prophet's Town Harrison's men discovered crates of British-made weapons. The Indians had not even unwrapped and assembled them. It was good evidence that the Prophet was not much of a threat to anyone, but it was also evidence of British interference. When the word flashed across the West, a cry of outrage erupted. Politicians called for war, even the cession of Canada. In Washington, D.C., a newly elected Congress assembled on the day after the battle. Among the newcomers were war-hungry Westerners, led by thirty-year-old Henry Clay of Kentucky. Elected speaker of the House of Representatives, Clay loaded the key committees with war hawks and launched the Congress on the road to war. President Madison, long distressed by Great Britain's high-handed treatment of American ships and seamen, openly cooperated. In June 1812, the nation declared war. Many considered it a second war for independence.

Tecumseh understandably felt otherwise. The victim of American agression, he had no choice but to ally with the British. His runners brought in warriors from all over the West, more than a thousand strong, and Tecumseh led them to Fort Malden. A sketch of him done many years later placed him in the uniform of a British officer. There is no evidence, however, that he actually accepted a military commission while at Fort Malden or that his warriors were absorbed into the British army. For Tecumseh, it was an alliance among equal nations.

Tecumseh's warriors fanned into the woods to capture the forts along the lakes before they could fully prepare themselves. The only sizable American force in the Northwest was an army of twenty-five hundred at Detroit, commanded by General William Hull. Even so, it was more than a match for the British-Canadian force of four hundred at Malden. In July 1812 Hull crossed the Detroit River and issued a proclamation asking the Canadians to join the American side or seek safety at home. Canadian morale quivered; several hundred deserters came into Hull's camp. Then Hull received the shattering news that the Indians had captured Fort Michilimackinac guarding the straits between Lake Huron and Lake Michigan. The fall of that strategic point, he had long since predicted, would unleash a horde of Indians from the far Northwest. Hull recrossed the river to Detroit.

In early August, General Isaac Brock arrived at Malden with reinforcements from the Niagara front. Bold and imaginative, Brock had taken advantage of confusion in the American command in New York to race to the rescue of western Canada. His men doubled the British-Canadian force at Malden to seven hundred, still far short of Hull's number. But Tecumseh's warriors more than made up the difference.

The Englishman and the Shawnee were two of a kind. "A more sagacious or more gallant warrior does not exist," Brock wrote to the British prime minister, noting that Tecumseh had battled the American government for years without British help. Tecumseh, in turn, admired the general's courage. When Brock outlined a plan for advancing against Detroit, even though he was outnumbered, Tecumseh took out a roll of birch bark and with his knife drew a map of the country around the fort.

In Detroit, Hull grew increasingly nervous. On August 4 a detachment sent to guard a supply column coming up from Ohio was ambushed at the Raisin River and slaughtered by the Indians. Alone and surrounded, he peered anxiously at the hostile forest.

Brock knew how to play on Hull's fears. Crossing the river with his combined force, Brock on August 15 sent a message demanding the surrender of Detroit. He added: "It is far from my intention to join in a war of extermination, but you must be aware that the numerous body of Indians who have attached themselves to my troops, will be beyond control the moment the contest commences." Hull surrendered the next day, yielding the fort without firing a shot.

The fall of Detroit rolled the frontier back to Fort Wayne and Vincennes. Tecumseh's followers made themselves masters of everything to the West. Shortly before he surrendered, Hull had ordered the garrison of Fort Dearborn, at the foot of Lake Michigan, to abandon its post and proceed east to safety. The commander was reluctant but felt obliged to follow orders. On August 15 his party, which included women and children, was ambushed by Pottawatomies. Half were killed, the rest taken prisoner. In September the governor of Kentucky sent an army into the Illinois country to seek vengeance. When the Indians set fire to the prairie, the Kentuckians fled in panic.

Tecumseh ruled the Northwest for a year, but he was not without troubles. In October the gifted Brock was killed in battle on the Niagara front. He was replaced by Henry Proctor, a supercilious man scornful of Indians and a mediocre strategist. On the American side of Lake Erie, President Madison placed William Henry Harrison in command. Harrison promptly organized an expedition against Detroit, but he bogged down in the Maumee marshes that oozed with autumn rains.

In January 1813, with the marshes frozen, an army of fifteen hundred under General James Winchester started toward Detroit. Proctor's British-Canadian force, bolstered with hundreds of Indians, ambushed it at the

Raisin River and forced its surrender. Tecumseh was not present, for he was among the Wabash villages seeking recruits. Proctor lost control of his force, and the Indians began massacring the wounded and the prisoners. The tragedy gave the West a new rallying cry: "Remember the River Raisin."

The disaster forced Harrison to call off his winter campaign, but he did manage to build a stronghold on the Maumee, Fort Meigs, from which he could launch a summer offensive. In May, Proctor and Tecumseh attacked the fort, bombarding it with fire-heated shot for four days. Harrison held out, but a relief force of Kentuckians, coming to his rescue, was ambushed and captured. Again the Indians fell upon the prisoners, even killing one British soldier who stood in their way, while Proctor stood helplessly by. Tecumseh moved quickly to restore order, and then turned his fury on the British commander. "Begone!" The word spat from his lips. "You are not fit for command. Go and put on petticoats."

Proctor lifted the siege and returned to Canada. But a few weeks later, feeling that he had to do something or lose his Indian allies altogether, he returned to Ohio. This time he attacked a smaller fort on the Sandusky River. The American defenders possessed a single cannon, Old Betsey, which they loaded with scrap iron and nails. It mowed down the advancing British while the Indians ran for cover. Once more Proctor and Tecumseh returned to Canada, their army's morale sagging.

Both sides knew from the beginning that the key to the Northwest was naval control of Lake Erie. By using the lake, Harrison could bypass the Indians and keep his supply line secure. Both sides spent the summer of 1813 building ships; the two fleets met in September at Put-in Bay, off Sandusky, Ohio. The Americans, commanded by Oliver Hazard Perry, won the battle, and promptly shuttled Harrison's army across the lake.

When Harrison landed at Malden with an army of forty-five hundred men, Proctor was ready to abandon western Canada. Summoning a council of war, he proposed a retreat to Niagara. Tecumseh denounced the move as cowardly, and his warriors gestured menacingly. Proctor shifted uneasily. Would they prefer, he asked, to move northward to the Thames River and there make a life-or-death stand? *Yes* was the response. And so it was ordered.

The Thames was a small stream that flowed into Lake St. Clair, opposite Detroit. Proctor moved "by easy marches," as he described it in his report, to a place some fifty miles upriver. He probably planned to make a stand at Moraviantown, which offered a good defensive position. But so slowly did he move that Harrison's army was soon on his heels. On October 5 Proctor drew his army up in a wooded area along the river. Protecting one flank was a swamp; on the other was the river.

The two armies were about equal. Harrison had left garrisons behind at Detroit and Malden. His army had shrunk to about twenty-five hundred. Proctor possessed around four hundred British regulars, a handful of Canadians, and perhaps a thousand Indians. But he also had the advantage of a defensive position with a narrow front. He might have turned the Thames into a Thermopylae, but Proctor was no Spartan. When the battle opened, he was in his carriage far to the rear, ready to flee should anything go awry.

Harrison, on the other hand, was more imaginative than usual. Instead of ordering an infantry assault through the woods, he sent his cavalry — a mounted regiment led by Colonel (and former war hawk congressman) Richard M. Johnson of Kentucky. It was a move, Harrison admitted, that "was not sanctioned by anything I had seen or heard of, but I was fully convinced that it would succeed. The American backwoodsmen ride better in the woods than any other people. . . . I was persuaded, too, that the enemy would be quite unprepared for the shock, and that they could not resist it." He was right. The British infantry was caught wholly offguard when Johnson's men came splashing through the swamp on their flank. They reeled in confusion and ran. That part of the battle was over in ten minutes.

Johnson had split his mounted force, sending only half against the British. The rest he led himself along the river against the Indians. Tecumseh's men, dug in among the trees, waited until the cavalry was within a few paces and riddled it with gunfire. His charge broken, Johnson ordered his men off their horses and into hand-to-hand combat. The Indians fought well until Tecumseh fell and the flight of the British brought a new enemy on their flank. Then they fled into the woods, and the Battle of the Thames was over.

When the fighting stopped, a group of American soldiers found a gaudily dressed Indian body on the field; thinking it was Tecumseh, they stripped its skin off for souvenirs. They almost surely had the wrong man, for Tecumseh never wore gaudy clothing, especially in battle. Tecumseh, in all likelihood, was carried from the field by his friends and buried in the silent majesty of the wilderness.

The battle helped carry William Henry Harrison ("Old Tippecanoe") into the White House and Richard M. Johnson into the vice presidency, while Tecumseh's death ended forever the idea of an Indian confederacy. A few months later General Andrew Jackson slaughtered the Creek "Red Sticks," at the Battle of Horseshoe Bend. Organized Indian resistance east of the Mississippi was at an end.

Tecumseh lived on in legend, but the best estimate of the man may have come from his foremost enemy, William Henry Harrison. After Tecumseh's second visit to Vincennes in the summer of 1811, Harrison described Tecumseh as "one of those uncommon geniuses, which spring up occasionally to produce revolutions and overturn the established order of things. If it were not for the vicinity of the United States, he would perhaps be the founder of an Empire that would rival in glory that of Mexico or Peru."

SUGGESTIONS FOR FURTHER READING

Glenn Tucker is one of the best storytellers plying the historian's craft. His *Tecumseh, Vision of Glory* (1956) is knowledgeable yet immensely entertaining. The story of Tecumseh is placed alongside that of other Indian heroes in Alvin Josephy, *The Patriot Chiefs, a Chronicle of American Indian Leadership* (1961). Francis Jennings, *The Invasion of America: Indians, Colonialism, and the Cant of Conquest* (1975), focuses on colonial New England, but its angry tone makes it the sort of history that Tecumseh himself might have written. For the government's side of the story see Francis Paul Prucha, *American Indian Policy in the Formative Years* (1962).

16

Thomas Jefferson: A Summary View

President John F. Kennedy, who was fond of graceful gestures, once told a dinner company of scholars and artists that it was "the most extraordinary collection of talents . . . that has ever

been gathered together at the White House, with the possible exception of when Thomas Jefferson dined alone."

Diplomat, political theorist, architect, musician, builder, inventor, empire builder, politician, Jefferson was truly the American Leonardo, the last Renaissance man. So varied were his talents, so diverse his activities that he touched the lives of many in his generation. In an age of versatiles, his may have been the most multifaceted personality of them all. He was as comfortable in the company of a George Rogers Clark as with an Abigail Adams or a Benjamin Franklin. His biography is a fitting summary of the Revolutionary generation.

Thomas Jefferson (1743–1826). *Gilbert Stuart did this study in 1805, just as Jefferson was entering the second term of his presidency. The triumphs of his first term were behind him; the disasters of his second term were yet to come. Stuart caught a placid moment in a great and stormy life.*

The Enlightened Virginian

He was born April 13, 1743, at Shadwell, a crude farmhouse along the banks of the Rivanna River in what was soon to become Albemarle County. This was Virginia's western Piedmont, a mere twenty miles from the Blue Ridge and still a trackless wilderness at Jefferson's birth. His father, Peter Jefferson, of Scots descent, was one of the first settlers in that part of Virginia. Like Augustine Washington, he was a self-made planter who married into one of Virginia's foremost families, in this case the Randolphs.

Peter Jefferson possessed an estate of a thousand acres when his son was born, but it was no more than average. Some of his neighbors had garnered princely domains amounting to tens of thousands of acres. Having led the way onto the Virginia frontier, the wealthy had implanted the gentlemanly ideal on its society. Jefferson was raised in this genteel atmosphere; indeed, he spent much of his early life at the Randolph plantation of Tuckahoe on the James River. Though of ungainly frame and somewhat homely appearance, he bore all his life the dignity, manners, and tastes of a gentleman.

Yet he always associated himself with the West and the frontier, for Albemarle County was the homeland of pioneers. Peter Jefferson himself explored the southwestern mountains and surveyed the boundary line that separated Virginia from North Carolina. Together with Joshua Fry, a mathematics professor from the College of William and Mary, Peter Jefferson drew up the first accurate map of Virginia (1755). Another Albemarle associate, Dr. Thomas Walker, was the first white man to penetrate the mountains and to view the Bluegrass Region of Kentucky. The young Jefferson thrived on the romance of exploration. Among his youthful associates were Meriwether Lewis and George Rogers Clark. It was a community of empire builders.

Like Washington, who grew up in a similar environment, Jefferson lost his father at an early age. Peter Jefferson died in 1757, leaving an estate of seventy-five hundred acres. His will provided for his widow and six daughters, but most of the estate went to the eldest son, Thomas. Peter Jefferson had risen into the front rank of gentry; he was a member of the county court and the House of Burgesses. Though his death was premature, he had marked a path that his son might follow with relative ease. For the moment, however, the estate was in the hands of trustees until Thomas attained his majority. In the interim he decided to go to college. The decision altered his life.

Williamsburg was something new for the farmer's son from the frontier. Though small in size (150 houses), it was a seat of empire that attracted an annual pilgrimage of politicos and landed grandees. The Capitol stood at one end of mile-long Duke of Gloucester Street; the College of William and Mary at the other. The two symbolized the twin forces that would tug at Jefferson all his life — the quiet pursuit of knowledge and truth combating the raucous expediency of politics and fame.

When Jefferson arrived in 1760, the college was just recovering from a political crisis brought on by its connection with the Church of England. It had been founded, like its northern counterparts Harvard and Yale, as a seminary for clergy, but the scions of Virginia who populated its halls had long since given it a secular turn. The instructors were nearly all ministers, however, and the church still collected taxes in its behalf. Public assessments, in fact, were one source of the college's trouble. To ease its critics, the college had hired a lay professor of mathematics, Dr. William Small of Scotland. It was to this man that Jefferson gravitated. Small, he later confessed, "fixed the destinies of my life."

Because of the chance dismissal of another teacher, Small was in charge of nearly all the liberal arts — mathematics, natural history, logic, rhetoric, ethics, and fine arts. He distilled for Jefferson the heady mixture of science, philosophy, and history known as the Enlightenment. The discoveries of the English physicist Sir Isaac Newton revealed a rational universe governed by natural laws. In the universe that Newton portrayed, everything had a place, an explanation; there was no room for mystery, no need for miracles. Scholars of the Enlightenment carried Newtonian rationalism far beyond the realm of physics. They applied it to religion, to government and law, even to the fine arts. Wrote the poet Alexander Pope: "God said, 'Let Newton be,' and all was light." And Jefferson absorbed it all.

After two years at the college, Jefferson took up the study of law. He never claimed to love the law, as he did science and the arts; but it was a promising profession, one that left him time to manage his landed estate and held open the possibility of public service. Professor Small introduced him to George Wythe, already considered, at age thirty-five, the most learned man in the profession. More than a practicing attorney, Wythe was a scholar immersed in ancient history and languages. From him Jefferson studied the law as part of the whole human experience.

There was no prescribed course of legal studies. Case books did not exist; the student read the commentaries of learned jurists. When the student considered himself ready, he went before the justices of the general court for examination. If they admitted him, he could open a law practice. Patrick Henry won admission to the bar after only six weeks of preparation, though the judges made him promise to read more. Jefferson labored at his books for five years; in the process he learned as much of political theory and government as he did of law.

The chief law book available to Americans was the multivolume *Institutes* by the seventeenth-century English jurist, Sir Edward Coke. Chief Justice of the King's Bench until dismissed by James I, Coke was the first to contest the theory of rule by divine right, the notion that the king's power was absolute. Dredging up the half-forgotten Magna Carta and other medieval limitations on the king, Coke argued that the law was supreme, that even the king and his agents had to work through the due process of judicial procedures. It was the opening salvo in the grand battle between king and country that dominated the seventeenth century. The *Institutes* kept the revolutionary tradition alive. "We were all Whigs then," Jefferson later said of the generation of lawyers nurtured on Coke.

The Emerging Radical

In 1767 Jefferson was admitted to the general court and began the practice of law. Though he never had his heart in the profession, he was a successful attorney; his work load increased annually to around five hundred cases by 1773. In spare moments he looked after the plantations inherited from his father. He even purchased additional lands and slaves.

The law widened his circle of acquaintances and led him, by easy stages, into politics. He would never have confessed a liking for the political stage — it was too rough, noisy, and cruel — but he took to it naturally. All his education and training had centered upon statecraft. He entered the House of Burgesses in 1769 and quickly attached himself to the group of radicals led by Patrick Henry and Richard Henry Lee.

In that year, too, he began constructing Monticello. The "little mountain" was part of his father's original tract in Albemarle. Its summit commanded a magnificent view of the Blue Ridge to the West, the rolling Piedmont to the east, and the rough crossroads that was slowly expanding into the village of Charlottesville. Jefferson had the summit of the mountain cleared and leveled in 1768; the following year he began digging the foundations and constructing brick kilns. He tried to import an architect from England; when that failed, he undertook the design himself. His father had given him some instruction in drawing to scale, and he had English architectural handbooks for texts. From one of these he selected a Palladian model for his initial plan. The Adamesque style that Bulfinch adopted had not yet come into vogue. Jefferson probably would have rejected it anyway as too ponderous. He had little to say for the James River plantations (such as William Byrd's Westover), which has been inspired by earlier English architects.

Not content with English interpretations of Palladio, he went to the works of the Italian master himself. The plan for Monticello that finally emerged is reminiscent of Palladio's Villa Rotunda but with significant changes. He retained the classical porticoes, while confining them to front and rear, but he reduced their scale and substituted simpler Ionic and Doric columns. He disguised the overall height (three stories) by incorporating the third story with the dome and half submerging the first floor. The resulting effect is one of unpretentious artistry, the hospitably engaging home of a Virginia squire.

It took a dozen years to complete the house and many more to finish its surroundings. The outbuildings, which Jefferson placed under ground level so as not to detract from the mansion, were not finished until the 1790s. In a sense he never really finished Monticello, for he tinkered with it to the end of his life. Design, invention, the building process itself is what interested him, not the finished product.

In 1770 Jefferson established bachelor quarters in one of Monticello's outlying pavilions ultimately intended as a library. Two years later he married and brought his bride to this structure, called thereafter the "Honeymoon Lodge." Like Washington, he chose a recently widowed heiress: Martha Wayles Skelton was the eldest daughter of John Wayles, a lawyer who had accumulated a fortune in land and slaves. Wayles's death in 1773 doubled Jefferson's estate, to a total of about ten thousand acres and 180 slaves. Jefferson also inherited Wayles's sizable debts to British merchants, the payment of which caused him no end of headaches. He sold lands in order to discharge the obligations, but the Revolution intervened; and the purchasers, who had bought on time payments, paid him in worthless Virginia paper money. When the war ended, he had to sell other property to discharge the debts. It was many years before he was fully free.

Jefferson abandoned his law practice in 1774 to devote full time to the management of his plantations. By then, too, he was immersing himself in revolutionary politics. Parliament's brutal response to the Boston Tea Party united the colonies as never before. When the Virginia assembly met in the spring of 1774, the radical clique — Patrick Henry, the Lee brothers, and Jefferson — "cooked up a resolution" (that was Jefferson's phrase) appointing June 1 as a day of fasting and prayer in support of Boston. When the assembly approved the motion, the governor instantly dissolved it. Instead of heading home, the Burgesses reconvened at the Raleigh Tavern, two blocks from the Capitol, and suggested that the colonies form a Continental Congress to make a united appeal to king and Parliament. The Burgesses also called for a specially elected convention to meet in Williamsburg in August to organize a boycott of British goods and to elect delegates to the Congress.

Jefferson was elected to the convention but, falling sick on the road, never reached Williamsburg. As a result, he was not included in the delegation sent to Philadelphia. He had, in the meantime, drafted some instructions for the congressional delegates. From his sickbed he sent copies of the essay to convention leaders. The convention, which sent to Philadelphia a delegation carefully balanced between radicals and conservatives, decided that Jefferson's instructions were too bold, but it did order the essay printed. Under the title *A Summary View of the Right of British America* the piece was read throughout the colonies and established Jefferson's reputation as both a writer and a radical.

A Summary View abandoned the distinction between internal and external legislation that had been current since the time of the Stamp Act. Jefferson argued that Parliament had no right whatsoever to legislate for the American colonies. He rested his case on the familiar Whig thesis that the colonists had left the mother country deliberately in order to form a society of their own. Parliament had ignored them at the beginning and had no claim over them now. Americans had submitted to Parliament's regulations in the past, said Jefferson, because its violations of American rights were rare and sporadic. But the chain of aggressions, from the Revenue Act of 1764 to the destruction of the Massachusetts government, revealed, he felt, "a deliberate, systematical plan of reducing us to slavery."

Jefferson himself admitted that his argument was in advance of its time. Taken to its logical conclusion, it meant a declaration of political independence. It was another two years before a majority of his countrymen came to his view; when they did, his pen was again ready for service.

Self-Evident Truths

Jefferson was among the Virginians sent to the Second Continental Congress, which opened in May 1775. His reputation having preceded him, Congress quickly assigned him to draw up a "Declaration of the Causes and Necessity for Taking Up Arms." John Adams especially liked his writing, as much for its "felicity of expression" as for its spirited tone. In succeeding months he drafted a number of manifestoes for Congress, though he seldom spoke in debate, leaving that to Virginia's silver-tongued duet, Patrick Henry and Richard Henry Lee.

When Lee introduced his resolution for independence in May 1776, Congress appointed a committee of five to draft a declaration, placing Jefferson at the head. At the insistence of Franklin and John Adams, two of the other members, Jefferson penned the draft of the Declaration. Franklin and Adams suggested a few changes, Jefferson rewrote it, and the committee presented it to Congress on June 28. Richard Henry Lee's resolution passed on July 2, and two days later Congress approved the Declaration of Independence.

The purpose of the Declaration was to inform the world why Americans felt it necessary to rebel. But Jefferson was not content with that. He wanted to put forth an ideological foundation for the new republic. He did it with a syllogism characteristic of an age that deified reason. His premise was "self-evident," as obvious to any rational being as the sum of two and two: "that all men are created equal." Being equal, he continued, all are endowed with certain "unalienable rights," among which are the right to "life, liberty, and the pursuit of happiness." This immortal phrase was a variation on the triad of rights prescribed by John Locke: life, liberty, and property. Coming from a society of poor-white tenant farmers and black slaves, Jefferson was not at all sure that everyone had a right to property; and he felt that property, or wealth, was too narrow in any case. By "pursuit of happiness" he meant the right to live as one saw fit, provided that a person did not infringe upon the rights of others.

Then came the next step in the syllogism: "to secure these rights governments are instituted among men." Not for pomp nor pride, not to enhance the glory of the king or create an empire, but simply to protect rights by maintaining law and order — that was the function of government. And to ensure that it performed this task, it derived its "just powers from the consent of the governed." There, of course, was the key — majority rule, democracy.

Jefferson did more than paraphrase Locke and other British Whigs — he turned their governmental theory upside down. In the Lockean thesis the dynamics of government were in the relationship between king and Parliament. The people were a passive factor; they had rights but no power. Jefferson instead located the constituent power in the people. It was they who created the government; governors and legislators were simply their agents. Thus, when government destroyed rights instead of protecting them, "it is the right of the people to alter or to abolish it, and to institute new government." The remainder of the Declaration was a lengthy list of the king's usurpations, constituting a legal indictment that justified his overthrow.

Jefferson later claimed that he had not intended to enunciate any new principle or theory of government in the Declaration, but simply "to place before mankind the common sense of the subject." He was too modest, for the foundation on which he rested government was both novel for its time and radical in its implications. With logic as pure as Jefferson's own, the concept of human equality could be extended far beyond the society of white property owners for whom he wrote. It could be extended to the powerless poor, to the enslaved Blacks, and to females. The redemption of Jefferson's promise has been the central theme of American history.

The Revolution Within

Jefferson eagerly sought an opportunity to put the philosophy of the Declaration into practice. The Virginia convention began drafting a state constitution in the spring of 1776. The document was approved a few days before Congress passed the resolution of independence. Unable to leave Philadelphia, Jefferson had to content himself with sending a draft for a constitution to Williamsburg by way of his old friend George Wythe. It arrived just as the Virginia convention was completing its labor, and weary delegates gave it only a glance. It was too radical for their tastes, in any case. The document they had drafted was a minor rewrite of Virginia's colonial charter. It retained property qualifications for voting and holding office, preserved the status of the church, and conferred disproportionate power on the long-settled East. To Virginia's squirarchy, independence was not a signal for social upheaval.

Jefferson thought otherwise. The writing of a constitution, he felt, presented a unique opportunity to rest a government upon justice and rationality. His drafts — and he undertook several, both in 1776 and in later years — differed markedly from the convention document. To begin with, Jefferson's government rested upon people, not places. Under the Virginia constitution, as under the colonial charter, each county sent two delegates to the lower house of assembly, regardless of its size or population. This enabled the smaller and more numerous eastern counties to control the legislature, even though the center of population had shifted westward. Jefferson would have installed a system of proportionate representation so that each voter would have equal weight.

Jefferson also proposed to expand the electorate to include nearly all white adult males. He agreed that a property qualification was desirable, so as to ensure that voters had a stake in the system; but he would have granted to every adult male who did not meet the qualification fifty acres of public land. Jefferson's constitution also contained a number of social reforms — separation of church and state, curbs on slavery, and revision of the law code. Had his draft been adopted by the Virginia convention, it would doubtless have stood, alongside the Pennsylvania constitution of 1776, as one of the great liberal expressions of the age.

Disappointed with the short treatment given his draft constitution, Jefferson decided to return home. From the floor of the assembly, which was the most powerful branch of Virginia's government, there was still much that could be done to make the war for independence a social revolution. When the assembly opened for its fall session, Jefferson was in his seat.

On October 12, 1776, the House of Delegates asked him to prepare two bills: one to abolish the law of entail, the other to revise the legal code. The first was comparatively easy. Jefferson considered entail one of the great bulwarks of aristocracy and its abolition a signal victory, but in fact entail was neither widely used nor popular, even among the wealthy. Entail was a restriction, or "tail," on property that limited the ways in which it could be sold or otherwise alienated. In England it was used to keep landed estates intact through the generations. In Virginia, where land was abundant, it was a nuisance that reduced the desirability, and hence the commercial value, of a tract of land. It was a feudal relic that Jefferson toppled with ease.

Revision of the law code was more difficult and far more time consuming. Jefferson's aim was to codify the laws passed by the colonial assembly, while retaining those features of the English common law that seemed desirable. He also wanted to streamline the law, ground it on rational principles, and simplify its wording. In the criminal code, for instance, Jefferson eliminated cruel and unusual punishments, such as branding and maiming; and he tried to cut the number of capital crimes to two: murder and treason. His coworker in the revision was Edmund Pendleton, a respected attorney of conservative views. Pendleton balked at some of the social reforms that Jefferson wanted to slip into the code revision (such as abolition of primogeniture, the practice of conferring an estate on the eldest son when a person died without a will, which Jefferson considered, like entail, a bulwark of aristocracy).

After three years of labor and numerous compromises Jefferson and Pendleton submitted their revisal to the assembly, only to see it torn to pieces. The assembly divided it into several bills, and some proposals it dropped altogether. Then it gathered dust while the assembly coped with military crises. At length, in 1785, after Jefferson departed for France, James Madison steered the various bills through the assembly. Though some of Jefferson's original aims were lost, the revised code was a model of rational revolution.

Jefferson's other target was the established Church of England. He had long since parted company with the Anglican church, accusing it of failing to provide moral or spiritual guidance. Its clergy were ignorant and lazy, given to the same sins, drinking, gaming, and horse racing that plagued the rest of Virginia society. Much of the church's difficulty, Jefferson felt, stemmed from the political connection; given tenure and status, it lost its missionary zeal. Nor did society profit by having an established creed, he felt. "It is error alone which needs the support of government. Truth can stand by itself."

So ineffectual was the Anglican establishment that a majority of church-going Virginians were dissenters, mostly Presbyterians, Baptists, Methodists, or Quakers. The congregations showered the assembly with petitions praying for the separation of church and state. In 1776 the assembly exempted dissenters from paying taxes to the Anglican church, but it left open the possibility that they might be taxed for the support of their own. Nor did it sever the official connection between church and state.

The result was a form of religious toleration, which, as Jefferson realized, was a far cry from total freedom of belief. Toleration implied an official creed, even though it permitted deviation from it. Jefferson felt that the government had no business committing itself to any belief; it must allow complete freedom of conscience, including the freedom to disbelieve.

He drafted a statute to that effect as part of his revision of the law code, but for tactical reasons he delayed introducing it until 1779. In that year the assembly repealed all taxes for the support of the church, and the following session it legitimatized marriage ceremonies performed by dissenting clergymen. Those measures spelled the end of the establishment;

Jefferson's statute would merely have made it official. Even so, the assembly could not bring itself to approve it. The preamble to Jefferson's bill, a ringing indictment of organized religion as it had worked through history, seemed too radical. Dissenting churches opposed the Anglican establishment, but they could not countenance an assault on religion itself. In 1786, after a misguided attempt by Patrick Henry to reinstitute a religious assessment split the church forces, Madison at last slipped Jefferson's bill through the assembly. Jefferson was in France at the time, but to the end of his life he regarded the Statute for Religious Freedom one of his major accomplishments.

Jefferson concocted other social changes during the Revolution, but they ran into the stone wall of Virginia conservatism. A public educational system was high on his list. He wanted a hierarchy of elementary and secondary schools leading to the College of William and Mary, which he would have converted from small Episcopal college to state university. The assembly, however, never gave the plan serious consideration. ·

Slavery, too, was one of his targets, though he could not quite bring himself to the principle of immediate emancipation. In 1778 he pushed through the assembly a bill prohibiting the further import of slaves into the state. He also prepared a plan for gradual emancipation under which children of slaves would attain freedom when they reached a certain age. His thought was to include the plan in the new law code, but it became lost in the lengthy contest over the revisal. In 1784, when Jefferson was a member of Congress, he included the antislavery clause in a plan for erecting territories in the Northwest. To his disappointment Congress eliminated the section, but three years later the Northwest Ordinance, which established territorial government north of the Ohio River, banned slavery from the area. Jefferson could properly claim credit for this vast extension of free soil.

Mission to France

Late in the war (1779–81) Jefferson served a tour as state governor. It was a difficult time, for the British were at the height of their southern offensive. General Cornwallis's troops slashed through the state, chasing both governor and legislature across the Blue Ridge, while a naval squadron under Benedict Arnold* ravaged the seacoast. Under such conditions no executive would have fared well, but Jefferson seemed to many unnecessarily weak. He had no military skills and no taste for dictatorial methods. Yet his regime was not a total disaster. The government he turned over to his successor (a general) was humiliated but functioning. And the surrender of Cornwallis

---

* Arnold, who was commander at West Point, had turned traitor in 1780, unsuccessfully trying to give the fort to the British.

at Yorktown just four months later redeemed him. At the end of the war the assembly sent him to the Continental Congress, and in 1784 Congress named him its minister to France, replacing Benjamin Franklin.

He remained in France for six years (1784–1790), and the experience certainly broadened his intellectual horizons. European scientific and political theories had long enticed him, and the rationalism of the *philosophes* was akin to his own. The French Revolution, which burst forth with the storming of the Paris Bastille in July 1789, made a profound impression on him. The revolutionaries at first sought only a constitutional monarchy modeled on Great Britain, rather than a republic, but Jefferson welcomed the change. To diplomatic friendship France was adding political kinship with America.

Inspired by the uprising, Jefferson searched for a universal principle of revolution. His conclusion was that the earth belongs to the living. "Each generation," he explained, "has the usufruct of the earth during the period of its continuance. When it ceases to exist, the usufruct passes on to the succeeding generation, free and unencumbered." His choice of "usufruct" to express the concept was a characteristic adaptation of ancient law to modern needs. Usufruct was the legal right (by the ward of a minor, for instance) to draw the profits from an estate without reducing its extent or value. Applied to land, Jefferson's concept would serve well the needs of modern conservationists, but he had in mind social and governmental institutions. Each generation, he felt, had a right to choose its own constitution and laws. It need not accept inherited institutions merely because they were old and venerated; it was free to pick and choose, even to experiment with, new ones.

Jefferson's concept was particularly important in light of the philosophical debate that the French Revolution provoked. The following year Britain's Edmund Burke criticized the Revolution for overthrowing established institutions. The past, Burke thought, was both keel and rudder to the present; without it society would drift aimlessly into anarchy. Change and reform were permissible, even desirable at times, but they had to be undertaken within the framework of established institutions, such as the monarchy and the church. (*Reflections on the Revolution in France*, 1790)

Burke's thesis became the foundation for British Conservatism, a tradition carried to the present by Benjamin Disraeli and Winston Churchill (and usually graced with a capital *C* to distinguish it from the "stand pat" American variety). Jefferson's proposition was quite the opposite. It was a form of liberal rationalism, derived in part from the French *philosophes*. Human institutions, ran the liberal argument, were to be judged not by their age but by rationality. That which could not be defended by reason (a monarchy, for instance, or an established church) ought to be swept away. Tom Paine would give this theory its classic statement in his *Rights of Man* (1791). Jefferson was one of its progenitors; it directed his politics ever after.

The European experience also reinforced Jefferson's pride of country. Critical of the pomp and waste that attended European royalty, he was quick to contrast it with the poverty of the countryside. "If anybody thinks that kings, nobles, or priests are good conservators of the public happiness," he wrote George Wythe, "send them here. It is the best school in the universe to cure them of that folly."

Jefferson was proud but not provincial. There was much in Europe that he felt might benefit America, and he made himself a sort of one-man clearing house for scientific information. In a single letter to Reverend James Madison, president of William and Mary College, he described a new Parisian fire engine, summarized the recent articles in French scientific journals, conveyed news of the discovery of a new planet, noted the latest balloon ascensions, described a newly invented screw propeller for boats (the French inventor put the propeller in the air; Jefferson thought it would work better in water), and diagramed a letter-copying machine. Everywhere he traveled he collected seeds and plant specimens for trial in Virginia. Long a critic of tobacco, Jefferson deluged his friends with more than seven hundred seed varieties — Italian rice, sugarcane, coffee, grasses, melons, cork oak, fig trees, grapes, broccoli, and cauliflower.

He was also a one-man chamber of commerce, especially in refuting European misconceptions about America. The commonest of these was that the American environment was debilitating. Knowing nothing of biological evolution or the migrations of early man, European scientists were at a loss to explain the primitiveness of the New World. Some blamed the American climate, pointing out that it was colder and more humid than Europe's. Thus American species were fewer, smaller, and weaker, and imported varieties invariably degenerated. Everything in America, wrote the French naturalist Buffon, tends to "shrink and diminish under a niggardly sky and an unprolific land, thinly peopled with wandering savages."

Jefferson, a lifelong observer of landscape and weather, was well equipped to respond. The only notation in his diary under the date July 4, 1776, for instance, was that he purchased a thermometer in Philadelphia. His *Notes on Virginia* (1785), written in response to the queries of an Italian friend, are one of the best regional descriptions of the age. He openly contested Buffon's hypothesis, citing the moose as one example of a sizable American species. Buffon retorted that moose was merely another name for the Scandinavian reindeer, whereupon Jefferson wrote to the governor of New Hampshire, asking him to shoot one, stuff it, and send it over. It arrived somewhat moth-eaten, but Jefferson had his victory when the moose received special mention in the 1788 edition of Buffon's *Histoire Naturelle*.

Jefferson's diplomatic mission can also be counted a success. In 1786 he negotiated a commercial treaty with France that incorporated "most favored nation" principle. This meant that no nation would receive better treatment in French ports than the United States did; concessions subsequently granted to a third party would automatically redound to the U.S. as well. It was a major step toward free trade, which would shortly become, if it was not already, the cardinal principle of American foreign policy.

His success abroad and the experience that it gave him made him the natural choice for secretary of state when Washington began organizing the federal regime. He accepted the post, packed his numerous books and papers, and departed for home in the spring of 1790.

The Gentle Partisan

Jefferson supported the Federal Constitution, but with reservations. He worried about the extensive powers given the president and the fact that he could be reelected every four years indefinitely. This, Jefferson feared, made the president little more than an elected monarch. He also thought that a Bill of Rights, guaranteeing the citizenry protection from misuse of power, would have been appropriate. Nor did Jefferson share the Federalists' fear that the nation was degenerating into anarchy in the 1780s. His casual view of Shays's Rebellion in Massachusetts was that "a little rebellion now and then is a good thing, and as necessary in the political world as storms in the physical." A worse danger, he felt, was that the people might become complacent about their liberties and indifferent to their government. "The tree of liberty must be refreshed from time to time with the blood of patriots and tyrants. It is its natural manure."

Jefferson worried more about tyranny than anarchy, and the past experience of republics was not reassuring. Most had succumbed to military rule, a Caesar or a Cromwell, and then to monarchy. He thus took up his duties in the new administration with a wary eye, and what he saw disturbed him. The president, anxious that the new government win respect, surrounded himself with formality and protocol. Jefferson thought it too reminiscent of European royalty.

Within weeks of his arrival he was drawn into a conflict between Madison, who sat for Virginia in the House of Representatives, and Secretary of the Treasury Alexander Hamilton. Hamilton's treasury policies openly benefited Northern merchants and moneylenders. By tying that powerful class to the government, Hamilton hoped to restore its credit and to ensure its permanence. Madison, a Southerner and a farmer, considered it an unholy alliance. So did Jefferson, especially after Congress chartered the Bank of the United States, a national corporation jointly owned and managed by the government and private business. Jefferson, who knew little of banking functions, feared that the government was creating an aristocracy of paper profiteers, who would subvert the republic as surely as any Caesar could.

In the spring of 1791 Jefferson unwittingly publicized his growing concern about the direction of the government. Tom Paine had written his

Rights of Man in answer to Burke's *Reflections* and sent a copy to America for publication. The recipient, a Virginian friend of Jefferson's, lent the pamphlet to Jefferson for perusal with the request that he forward it to a Philadelphia printer. Since Jefferson was unacquainted with the printer, he added an ice-breaking note expressing his approval of the essay. He was pleased, he wrote, "that something was at length to be publicly said against the political heresies which had of late sprung up among us, not doubting that our citizens would rally again round the standard of Common Sense." To his amazement the printer published the note at the head of the pamphlet, noting that it came from the secretary of state. Jefferson was acutely embarrassed because the "heresies" he had in mind were the writings of his old friend John Adams, whose defense of executive power seemed a defense of monarchy. "I tell the writer freely that he is a heretic," Jefferson admitted, "but certainly never meant to step into a public newspaper with that in my mouth."

The gaffe ended for a time the Adams-Jefferson friendship and exposed the rift in the administration to public view. It also established Jefferson, so far as the public was concerned, as the leader of the opposition, even though Madison had been the administration's chief antagonist in Congress. By the end of that year Jefferson and Madison were calling themselves Republicans (implying that their opponents were monarchists). Name identification was the first step toward the formation of a political party; what they needed next was grass-roots organization. That resulted from a diplomatic crisis, in which Jefferson was again the center.

In the early weeks of 1793 the French revolutionaries executed King Louis XVI, declared the government a republic, and declared war on the meddling monarchies that surrounded them. Though without desire to intervene, Jefferson sympathized with the French because he felt that theirs was the cause of republicanism generally. "The liberty of the whole earth [depends] on the issue of the contest," he exclaimed to a friend. If the British-led coalition of monarchies triumphed over France, the American republic might be next on their list.

Washington called a cabinet meeting to discuss American alternatives. Hamilton leaned toward the British, though he, too, had no desire to enter the war. Britain to him was a symbol of governmental stability, of law and order; it was also America's chief trading partner and source of income. After some furious infighting the cabinet agreed to respect the nation's obligations under the treaty signed by Benjamin Franklin in 1778 (notably to help defend the French West Indies), but otherwise it would remain neutral. Washington accordingly issued a proclamation warning American citizens not to join the fighting.

At that juncture a French emissary, Edmond Genet, arrived in America. Americans, appreciative of French aid during the Revolution, greeted him warmly, and Genet took the welcome as a sign of support. He began outfiting private warships ("privateers") to prey on British shipping. When

Jefferson warned him that this was a violation of American neutrality, Genet took to the newspapers to appeal to the American people. When Jefferson reported the emissary's antics to the French government, Genet was stripped of his commission (he remained in America as an immigrant).

The Genet affair embarrassed Jefferson, but it did help polarize public opinion. Republicans sympathized with the French cause; Federalists with the British. Both formed town and county committees; these in turn organized popular meetings and nominated candidates for office. The well-orchestrated uproar over the Jay Treaty with Britain in 1795 demonstrated how far local organization had proceeded by the end of Washington's term.

Jefferson was never a comfortable partisan. He was firm in his ideas and quick to voice his apprehensions, but he had no taste for controversy. The vitriolic attacks of Federalist newspapers wounded him, and he was disturbed by the tension within the administration. At the end of 1793 he resigned his cabinet post and retired to Monticello. He spent the next four years rebuilding his house and restoring his long-neglected fields. Then, in 1796, the Republicans induced him to head their presidential ticket. For the next decade and more he would again be at the center of political controversy.

A Creed for the Republic

The men who wrote the Constitution had not anticipated the appearance of political parties, nor did they envision a contest for the presidency. Under their plan, as outlined in the Constitution, the nation's best would gather in the electoral college and choose the wisest and most virtuous person available. So long as Washington was available, the system worked; but when he retired, there was no longer general agreement on either wisdom or virtue. The newly emerged parties stepped into the gap by providing nominating procedures, which at least narrowed the field. They averted chaos in doing so, but they also changed the system.

In 1796 the congressional leaders of each party summoned their followers into secret caucus to decide upon presidential candidates. Each caucus decided upon a ticket (the word had recently come into use): candidates who would run for president and vice president as a team. The Federalists' choice was John Adams and Thomas Pinckney of South Carolina; Republicans selected Jefferson and Aaron Burr of New York. The election was very close, giving Federalists only a slim majority in the electoral college. The ticket system, moreover, was still in the formative stage, and some electors were not committed to it. Thus, while Adams won the election and became president, Jefferson emerged in second place with vice presidency. It was to be an uncomfortable team.

To make matters worse, President Adams inherited a French crisis that brought partisan passions back to the boiling point. Assuming that the Jay Treaty amounted to an Anglo-American alliance, the French refused to accept an envoy sent by Washington and began seizing American ships. When Adams sent a three-man commission to settle differences, the French foreign minister demanded a personal bribe and an official loan. Americans were outraged at such high-handed treatment; Congress built up the army and navy. Formal war never came, but there was fighting on the seas whenever American and French ships met.

Republicans watched the military preparations in dismay, convinced that the president had fabricated the whole crisis; but there was little that they could do. As their French sympathies cost them public support, their ranks thinned. Federalists' errors, however, soon granted them a reprive.

After securing the nation against foreign invasion, the Federalists turned on their domestic enemies. They restricted the rights of aliens, supposing most of them to be Republicans, and gave the president power to deport any aliens that he considered dangerous. A Sedition Act made it a crime to criticize the president or the congress (leaving the vice president fair game). Federalist-dominated courts convicted and sent to jail a dozen Republican news publishers. Because the laws were so patently partisan, they violated Americans' sense of fair play. Federalist popularity began to wane.

Jefferson and Madison considered the Alien and Sedition laws unconstitutional, a violation of human rights. There was no point in appealing to the courts, for they were dominated by Federalists. So they turned to the states. At a secret meeting at Monticello in the summer of 1798, they decided to submit anonymous resolutions to the two legislatures where the Republicans still had majorities, Virginia and Kentucky. Madison penned the Virginia Resolutions; Jefferson wrote the ones sent to Kentucky.

The two sets of resolutions were similar, revealing some collaboration between the two friends. Like the Declaration of Independence, the Virginia and Kentucky Resolutions rested on a logical syllogism. The premise was the social contract. The Constitution, they argued, was a compact among the states. Thus, whenever the federal government exceeded its authority, as in the case of the Alien and Sedition laws, the states had the right to intervene. Jefferson claimed that the states had a right to "nullify" an unconstitutional federal law; Madison merely asserted their right to "interpose" themselves against federal tyranny. Either way the resolutions were a distillation of Jeffersonian thinking, a combination of Lockean Whiggery and liberal rationalism. They envisioned a government of limited powers — sharply limited when the rights of citizens were involved. The resolutions could function as both a creed for the republic and a platform for the Republican party.

A Pliable President

Tainted with the image of militarism, accused of foul play, and blamed for crushing the people with taxes, the Federalists never recovered their popularity. Within a few years the party disappeared in all but a few states. Even so, the election of 1800 was close, primarily because of sectional allegiance. New England stuck with Adams; the South was Jeffersonian. Pennsylvania split and canceled itself; to a large extent the election turned on New York. There a smooth Republican organization carried the state, and the election, for Jefferson and Burr. This time party discipline in the electoral college was too strong, for every Republican elector voted for Jefferson and Burr. As a result, they tied, and the contest had to be decided by the House of Representatives. Jefferson ultimately won, but Burr's failure to withdraw and the rumors that he was courting Federalist support cost him his career. Jefferson dumped him from the ticket in 1804, and that set in motion the chain of events that led to the Burr-Wilkinson conspiracy.

A permanent site for the nation's capital was laid out during Washington's presidency. The district, ten miles square, straddled the Potomac River on land granted by Virginia and Maryland. The government moved there in the last year of Adams's administration; there, on the steps of the half-finished Capitol, Jefferson took his oath of office, March 4, 1801.

His inaugural address was both a plan of action and a summary of the liberal faith. In foreign policy he promised "peace, commerce, and honest friendship with all nations; entangling alliances with none." That was the liberal formula outlined by the French physiocrats — free trade and interdependence among all nations, but no military alliances designed to exalt kings or exact tribute.

The address openly appealed for domestic unity and an end to party strife — "We are all Republicans, all Federalists," he said, reminding his listeners that they were all Americans. But he also promised a new political order. In contrast to Federalists' support of established religion in New England and a muzzled press elsewhere, Jefferson endorsed "freedom of religion, freedom of press, freedom of person." The nation was fundamentally sound, stable, and prosperous, he stated. All it needed was "a wise and frugal government, which shall restrain men from injuring one another, shall leave them otherwise free to regulate their own pursuits of industry and improvement, and shall not take from the mouth of labor the bread it has earned." He had first enunciated the principle in the Declaration of Independence: the function of government was to maintain order, protect rights, and otherwise leave its citizens alone, each to pursue happiness as he pleased.

The task of lightening the burden of government was left to Jefferson's secretary of the treasury, Albert Gallatin. Swiss by birth, Gallatin had represented Pennsylvania in Congress in the 1790s. He was widely regarded

as the one Republican who could meet Hamilton on his own ground —
finance. In 1795 he had inspired creation of the House ways and means
committee to strengthen Congress's role in fiscal policy. As treasury secretary, Gallatin cut the army to three thousand men and put the navy in
dry-dock. These savings enabled him to eliminate all taxes except customs
duties and to pay off the debt rapidly. Of an estimated annual revenue of
nine million dollars, Gallatin planned to devote only two million to the
expenses of government; the remainder would go to debt retirement. As
it happened, domestic prosperity and a mushrooming foreign trade brought
even bigger surpluses than he anticipated (luckily for him, perhaps, because in ordinary times his deflationary policies would have dampened the
economy). As early as 1806 he reported to the president that the national
debt was nearly paid off.

Though often accused by his enemies of being fanatical and visionary,
Jefferson in power was a practical politician, capable of compromising his
principles for the sake of efficiency. He sold the government's holdings in
the Bank of the United States but otherwise left Hamilton's institution
untouched. When Gallatin reported in 1806 that the national debt was
nearly eliminated and that the treasury faced a surplus, Jefferson directed
him to draft a plan for federal improvement projects. The surplus never
materialized because of the embargo; and the only project undertaken was
the National Road, which ran from Washington, D.C., along the Potomac
and across the mountains into Ohio. Even so, Jefferson's scheme for using
federal funds for development was hardly in line with the philosophy of
states' rights that he enunciated as recently as 1798. In power, practicality
came before principle.

The Louisiana Purchase followed the same pattern. Jefferson was delighted with the acquisition, calling it "an empire for liberty," but he did
worry some about the constitutionality of the treaty. Did the president have
the power, he wondered, to buy or to conquer foreign territory? Gallatin
resolved his doubts by pointing out that there were no limits on the president's treaty-making power. With the Senate's consent he could enter into
any sort of agreement that he wished. Neither man appeared to see the
larger principle involved. By acquiring an empire of its own, the federal
government established a sovereignty of its own. If it had ever been a
mere creature of the states, as Jefferson theorized in 1798, it was no longer.
States' rights would remain a rallying cry for political minorities, but as a
political philosophy it was dead.

Jefferson did not trouble himself with the philosophical implications
of his policies because he was immersed in the routine of administration. He
was concerned that the government function smoothly, and for the most
part it did. Although the nation expanded swiftly in population and wealth
during his eight years in office, the bureaucracy held even. There were
ninety-six officeholders in the nation's capital when Jefferson took office, and
ninety-four when he retired. He met regularly with congressional leaders

to make his wishes known, and he had the satisfaction of seeing most of his proposals enacted into law. No other president prior to the Civil War got on so well with Congress.

Jefferson's pragmatism did create a few enemies. John Randolph of Roanoke, floor leader in the House of Representatives during Jefferson's first term, resented pressure from the executive; and, as an ideologue of 1798, he objected to Jefferson's desertion of states' rights. Yet Randolph quickly found himself in political isolation, as the overwhelming majority of the party remained loyal to the president.

Not all of Jefferson's achievements in office were apparent to his contemporaries, however. The reduction of taxes and the purchase of Louisiana were popular, and he won reelection in 1804 by a handsome margin. But the policies of his last years, particularly the embargo, quickly reversed the flow of opinion. He left office in 1809 under heavier criticism than he had suffered at any time in his life.

The embargo was the result of renewed British provocations on the high seas. In 1805, after a decade of relative harmony in Anglo-American relations, Britain resumed her interference with American trade in the West Indies, and British ship captains stepped up the impressment of American seamen. Jefferson tried some limited forms of commercial retaliation; when that failed to work, he asked Congress for a total cessation of American trade. The purpose of the embargo, enacted in December 1807, was two-fold: to pressure both Britain and France into recognizing America's neutral rights of trade, and to give the nation time to prepare for war in the event that negotiations failed.

The embargo brought the country to a standstill because most of its commerce went by water. Jefferson had to prohibit even the coastal trade to keep ships from slipping off to the West Indies or Europe. The South, because of its heavy dependence on foreign markets, suffered the most, but the loudest outcry came from Federalist New England. Sending an army of customs inspectors into the Northeast to stop illicit trade, the government gave them broad powers of search and seizure. These powers, conferred by the Embargo Enforcement Act, violated some of the guarantees of the Bill of Rights, but Jefferson was not unduly troubled. He considered the republic itself at stake. In such a crisis he could not be bothered with constitutional niceties.

This was not the reaction of a philosopher. Unfortunately, it was not even good politics. Privation and discontent mounted while the administration dallied, neither declaring war not seeming to prepare for it. The embargo did put some pressure on the British; but, because of the communications lag, the effect came too late to help Jefferson. In early 1809 Congress repealed the embargo, the repeal to take effect on March 3, Jefferson's last day in office. Although Madison was elected his successor, the Federalists made substantial gains in Congress. It was an inglorious end to a successful presidency.

The American Leonardo

All his life Jefferson had looked forward to retirement from politics, for a return to the peace and repose of Monticello. In remarkably good health for a man of sixty-seven, he quickly fell into a pleasant routine. Mornings were devoted to writing letters, afternoons he rode his fields and visited friends, and evenings were spent reading. He enjoyed conversing with his neighbors about farm methods and seed qualities, even politics, if they wished, for he was at last "free to say and do what I please, without being responsible to any mortal."

A few shadows clouded his days. He left the presidency deeply in debt, having outspent his income by some ten to twelve thousand dollars. Jefferson blamed the deficit on the tendency of Americans to make "a general tavern" of the president's house. In his house Jefferson had pointedly abandoned the formality of his Federalist predecessors, setting a tone of genial simplicity. Dinner guests were invited in alphabetical rotation, and they seated themselves pell-mell, without regard to rank or station. Newcomers to the city, whether foreign dignitaries or simple tourists, never hesitated to knock on his door. But the open presidency had its drawbacks; visitors consumed enormous amounts of time and money.

Monticello and Jefferson's outlying farms were in sad disrepair after years of neglect, and the value of his lands was declining. Virginia lost ground steadily during Jefferson's last years. Its economy, so heavily dependent on foreign trade, was severely disrupted by embargo and war; and, when the war ended, the Hessian fly ravaged its wheat crop. Jefferson was never able to clear himself from debt, and he added to his troubles by endorsing the notes of a financially precarious friend, Wilson Cary Nicholas. When Jefferson died, almost his entire estate went to paying his own debts and those of Nicholas.

The great project of his waning years was the University of Virginia. A state university had intrigued him ever since the Revolution, when he sought to place the College of William and Mary at the apex of a statewide educational system. While president he advocated the founding of a national university as part of his scheme for spending Gallatin's treasury surplus. He reverted to the idea again in retirement, but the Virginia assembly remained obdurate, even though by then state universities had been established in the Carolinas and Georgia. The plan finally won approval in 1817, with the backing of Governor Wilson Cary Nicholas and a cadre of "Monticello men" in the assembly.

Jefferson by then was ready with the design. Instead of a single college hall, where students and faculty lived and worked in noisy confusion, he distributed the physical plant around a rectangle eight hundred feet long. At intervals along each side he placed two-story pavilions, which were both residence and classroom for professors. Joining the pavilions was a single-story range of dormitories for students, the whole bound together

University of Virginia, West Lawn (1856 lithograph).

by a Doric colonnade. Various orders, Doric, Ionic, and Corinthian, adorned the pavilions, serving both to instruct and to improve the artistic tastes of students.

Jefferson's curriculum was as revolutionary as his physical plant. He desired a complete break from the colonial tradition, which combined dead languages with theology. Benjamin Franklin's College of Philadelphia (since renamed the University of Pennsylvania) had experimented with curriculum reform, but the institution had not flourished. In 1818 Jefferson thought better of Harvard, where theological training had fallen into the hands of religious rationalists, than of Pennsylvania.

Jefferson placed in his curriculum such modern fields as physics, chemistry, geography, and mineralogy. He made modern languages a separate branch of learning, distinct from the ancients; and he included professional schools, such as law and medicine. Nowhere in the curriculum was there a place for religion, except as it might be taught by the professor of ideology (a field that included philosophy and fine arts). Most revolutionary of all was Jefferson's introduction of electives. No course of study was prescribed, since all subjects were equally useful. Students were to pick and choose as they wished. Nor were students divided by classes or levels. Each proceeded at his own pace until the requisite credits were attained.

Although the university opened its doors in 1819, Jefferson by no means considered his job done. He devoted a substantial part of his final years interviewing prospective teachers and prescribing books. He was insistent that the Revolutionary Whig tradition be instilled in the young, so as to preserve the integrity of the republic. His prescriptions were not the product of dogmatic or illiberal attitudes (he had always been intolerant of Tories and religious fanatics); they resulted instead from a lack of confidence in the young. It is a common failing among the aged.

"The little of the powers of life which remains to me I consecrate to our university," he wrote in October 1825. Eight months later, on the fiftieth anniversary of the Declaration of Independence, he was dead. By his last will he freed five slaves who had been closest to him. The debts that encumbered his estate, he felt, prevented him from freeing the rest. He was buried on the side of his "little mountain," his tombstone recording the achievements by which he most wanted to be remembered:

> *Here was buried*
> *Thomas Jefferson,*
> *Author of the Declaration of American Independence,*
> *Of the Statute of Virginia for Religious Freedom,*
> *And Father of the University of Virginia.*

Jefferson's importance today may well be summarized in another phrase, which he penned many years before his death, during the Federalist sedition mania of 1799–1800. "I have sworn upon the altar of God eternal hostility to any form of tyranny over the mind of man." That could also serve as the epitaph for the Revolutionary generation.

SUGGESTIONS FOR FURTHER READING

The most thorough, painstaking account of Jefferson's life is by Dumas Malone, *Jefferson and His Time* (5 vols. to date, 1948–1974). Although Malone's study is, at this writing, still incomplete, it does extend through Jefferson's presidency. The best one-volume biography is Merrill D. Peterson, *Thomas Jefferson and the New Nation* (1970). Peterson's account, though splendidly written, is somewhat lengthy. The reader interested in a faster pace might try Adrienne Koch, *Jefferson and Madison, The Great Collaboration* (1950, reprinted 1964). Daniel Boorstin discusses the intellectual milieu of the late eighteenth century in *The Lost World of Thomas Jefferson* (1948). The best of the recent appraisals of Jefferson's presidential leadership is Noble E. Cunningham, Jr., *The Process of Government Under Jefferson* (1978).

Index

Adam, Robert, 122–23, 125

Adams, Abigail: early life, 74–75; marriage, 75; political beliefs, 76; and women's rights, 76–77; life during the Revolution, 78–80; in Europe, 1780s, 80–82; wife of Vice President, 82–84; First Lady, 84–85; view of Washington, D. C., 85; last years, 85–86; and phonetic spelling, 105; and Thomas Jefferson, 80–81, 84–85

Adams, John: marriage, 75; and Boston Massacre, 28; and Continental Congress, 30–35; and women's rights, 76–77; and peace negotiations, 15–17; minister to Britain, 80–82; Vice President, 82–84; President, 84–85, 245–47; on American literature, 100–01; and Charles Willson Peale, 113; and Benjamin Rush, 147

Adams, John Quincy, 85

Adams, Samuel: early life, 21; enters politics, 21–22; and Sugar Act, 24; and Stamp Act, 24–26; and Boston Massacre, 27–28; and Hutchinson letters, 11, 29; and Boston Tea Party, 29–30; and First Continental Congress, 30–33; and Battle of Lexington, 33; and Second Continental Congress, 34–35; and French alliance, 14, 34; and Massachusetts Constitution of 1780, 34–35; last years, 35

Albany Plan of Union, 10

Alien Acts, 246

American Fur Company, 170–71

American Revolution: and democracy, 19–20; as a guerilla war, 57–58; and American society, 73–74, 151–53; battles of, 44–48, 60–70

American Spelling Book, 101–02

Annapolis (Md.), 111

Annapolis Convention, 51

Architecture: in colonial America, 122; Jefferson and, 124–25, 234–35; *see also* Bulfinch, Charles

Arnold, Benedict, 189, 194, 196, 198, 240

Astor, John Jacob; as a businessman, 166, 173; immigrant, 167; enters fur trade, 168; and China trade, 168–69; forms American Fur Company, 170–71; land speculation of, 172

Astoria, 171

Attucks, Crispus, 28

Awkright, Richard, 163

Backus, Isaac: religious conversion, 131–32; itinerant evangelist, 133; accepts adult baptism, 133; and church organization, 135; and religious freedom, 135–36

Backus, Susanna (Mason), 133

Bank of the United States, 53

Baptist Church: in Virginia, 38; origins of, 133–34; institutionalization of, 134–35

Barnum, P. T., 115, 118

Beaumarchais, Pierre Augustine Caron de, 13–14

Bernard, Gov. Francis, 27

Biddle, Charles, 206

Blennerhassett, Harmann, 208–10

Blue Jacket, 216

Boerhaave, Dr. Hermann, 143–44

Boone, Daniel, 178, 188, 214

Bordley, John Beale, 112

Boston, Caucus, 22, 25

Boston Massacre, 28

Boston Tea Party, 29–30

Breed's Hill, battle of, 34

British debts, 17

Brock, General Isaac, 226

Brown, Charles Brockden, 99, 103

Brown, Mather, 121

Bulfinch, Charles: first professional architect, 121–22; early life, 123–24; designs Massachusetts State House, 124–25; designs private homes, 125–26; Lancaster meetinghouse, 126–27; capitol architect, 127–28

Burgoyne, Gen. John, 195–96

Burke, Edmund, 241

Burr, Aaron: as Vice President, 245, 247;
  conspiracy of, 206–10
Business, in colonial America, 161–62
Byrd, William, 122, 139

Cahokia, 183
Calvin, John, 130
Camden, battle of, 48, 62–64
Cherokee Indians, 59
China trade, 168–69
Chrysler's Farm, battle of, 211
Church of England, in Virginia, 38, 239–40
Cincinnati, Society of, 49
Claiborne, W. C. C., 207
Clark, George Rogers: early life, 176–77;
  in Dunmore's War, 176–77; settles in Ken-
  tucky, 178–79; attack on Kaskaskia,
  181–82; attack on Vincennes, 183–87;
  last years of the Revolution, 187–88;
  tangled finances of, 189; Indian cam-
  paigns, 1780s, 189–90; intrigues with
  French, 191; last years, 191
Clay, Henry, 225
Clinton, George, 206
Clinton, Gen. Henry, 48, 60–61
Cobbett, William, 156
Cochin, Charles Nicholas, 3
Coercive Acts, 30
Coke, Sir Edward, 233–34
Congregational Church, and the Baptists,
  132ff.
Connecticut "Wits," 104
Constitution, U. S.: *see* Federal Conven-
  tion
Continental Congress (First), 30–33, 147
Continental Congress (Second), 34–35, 236
Conway Cabal, 46, 150, 196–97
Copley, John Singleton, 19, 109, 111–12
Cornwallis, Gen. Charles, 45, 48, 61–67
Cotton gin, 163–65
Cowpens, battle of, 65–66
Cullen, Dr. William, 143–44

Davies, Rev. Samuel, 142
Deane, Silas, 13–15
Dearborne, Gen. Henry, 211
Declaration of Independence, 236–37
Democracy: *see* American Revolution
Dennie, Joseph, 106–07
Detroit, 226–27
Dickinson College, 152–53
Dickinson, John, 12
Dinwiddie, Gov. Robert, 41
Diseases of the Mind, 157
Dunmore's War, 176–77
Dwight, Timothy, 104

Edes, Benjamin, 26
Education: Franklin on, 9; Rush on, 151–52;
  Jefferson on, 152, 240, 250–52

Edwards, Jonathan, 131
Ellsworth, Oliver, 103
Embargo, 249
Enlightenment, 233
Eutaw Springs, battle of, 69–70
Evangelical religion, and politics, 142

Fairfax family, 39–40
Fallen Timbers, battle of, 202–03, 215–16
Federal Convention, 51, 81–82
Federal style, in architecture, 124–25,
  127–28
Federalists: and Adams administration,
  85, 245–48; and American culture, 107
Fort Cumberland, 41
Fort Dearborne, 218
Fort Duquesne, 41
Fort Granby, 68
Fort Greenville, 202, 220
Fort Malden, 218, 224–25
Fort Massac, 182
Fort Michillimackinac, 218, 225
Fort Motte, 68
Fort Necessity, 41
Fort Ninety-Six, 69
Fort Ticonderoga, 194–96
Fort Watson, 67
Fort Wayne, treaty of, 223
Fothergill, Dr. John, 145
Franklin, Benjamin: and Gospel of Work,
  3–4; early life, 4–5; *Pennsylvania
  Gazette,* 5–6; *Almanac,* 6–7; scientist,
  7–8; Junto Club, 8–9; political career,
  9–11; colonial agent, 10–11; and Hutchin-
  son letters, 11, 29; and Pennsylvania
  constitution, 12; minister to France,
  13–15; peace negotiations, 15–17; last
  years, 18; and Charles Willson Peale,
  112; on American literature, 100, 105; on
  education, 9; on slavery, 18
Franklin, state of, 199–201
Freeman's farm, battle of, 196
Freneau, Philip, 99
French alliance, 34
French and Indian War, 10, 23, 41–42
French Revolution, 241, 244

Gadsden, Christopher, 59
Gage, Gen. Thomas, 27, 30, 33, 75
Gallatin, Albert, 247–48
Galloway, Joseph, 12, 31
Galloway, Rebecca, 217
Gates, Gen. Horatio: Battle of Camden, 48,
  62–64; Newburgh Addresses, 49; and
  Conway Cabel, 196–97; president of
  Board of War, 46, 195; and Saratoga
  campaign, 196
Genet, Edmond, 191
Georgetown (S. C.), 69
Germain, Lord George, 180

Gibbon, Edward, 15
Gist, Christopher, 40–41
Gospel of Work, 3–4
Great Awakening, 131
Greathouse Massacre, 176–77
Greene, Catherine, 162
Greene, Gen. Nathanael, 48, 65–70
Greenville, treaty of, 203, 216–18
Grenville, George, 24

Hamilton, Alexander, 52–54, 105, 197, 206, 244
Hamilton, Henry, 183–87
Hancock, John, 26, 29, 33, 113
Harmar, Gen. Josiah, 202
Harrison, Peter, 122
Harrison, William Henry, 218, 220–29
Harrod brothers (Ky.), 179
Hartford (Conn.), 103–04
Helm, Capt. Leonard, 183–86
Henderson, Richard, 178–79
Henry, Patrick: and coming of Revolution, 25, 234–35; in First Continental Congress, 31, 147, 236; and Mount Vernon convention, 51; opposes disestablishment, 240; and George Rogers Clark, 179–81
Hobkirk's Hill, battle of, 68
Hospital, Pennsylvania, 194
Howe, Gen. William, 45
Hull, Gen. William, 225–26
Hutchinson, Thomas: political position, 22; and Stamp Act, 25; letters intercepted, 11, 29; and Boston Massacre, 28–29; and Boston Tea Party, 29–30

Internal Revolution: *see* American Revolution
Iredell, James, 53

Jackson, Andrew, 207–08
Jay, John, 17, 53, 74
Jay Treaty, 54, 83, 218, 245
Jefferson, Martha (Wayles Skelton), 235
Jefferson, Peter, 232
Jefferson, Thomas: youth, 232; education at William and Mary, 232–33; in the House of Burgesses, 234–36; and Declaration of Independence, 236–37; and Virginia constitution, 237–38; role in the Revolution, 237–41; liberal philosophy of, 241, 246–47; *Notes on Virginia,* 242; in France, 241–43; Secretary of State, 243–45; and Republican Party, 243–46; Vice President, 245–47; President, 247–49; and architecture, 124–25, 234–35; and Burr conspiracy, 206–10; and education, 152, 240, 250–52; and Indians, 222–23; and language, 107; and Louisiana Purchase, 205; and religious freedom, 239–40; and Univer-

sity of Virginia, 250–52; and West Florida, 205; and Abigail Adams, 80–81, 84; and John Adams, 244; and Clark, 179; and Peale, 117, and Rush, 147; and Whitney, 166
Jews: in America, 88–89; and American Revolution, 93
Johnson, Richard M., 228
Johnson, Samuel, 105–06
Jones, Inigo, 122

Kaskaskia, 181–82
Kentucky: settlement of, 178–79; in Revolution, 179–89; secession movements in, 199–201
King's Mountain, battle of, 64
Knox, Henry, 44, 204, 221
Kosciusko, Gen. Thaddeus, 47

Layfayette, Marquis de, 47–48, 119
Lancaster meetinghouse (Mass.), 126–27
Latrobe, Benjamin H., 127
Le Dru, Pierre, 213
Lee, Arthur, 14–15
Lee, Gen. Charles, 60, 195
Lee, Gen. Henry, 54, 65–68
Lee, Richard Henry, 12, 31, 234–36
Leutze, Emmanuel, 114
Lexington, battle of, 33
Liberalism, Jeffersonian, 241
Lincoln, Gen. Benjamin, 60–61
Little Turtle, 215–16
Livingston, Robert R., 205
Locke, John, 237
Logan, Chief John, 177
Lopez, Aaron: Portuguese background, 88–89; emigration, 89–90; business interests of, 90–92; in the Revolution, 92–95; death, 96
Lopez, Dom Diego, 88
Lopez, Moses, 88–89
Louisiana Purchase, 205–06, 248
Loyalists, in South Carolina, 70–71

McGuffey Reader, 102
McIntyre, Samuel, 126
Mackintosh, Ebenezer, 25
Madison, James: and Washington, 50–53; and War of 1812, 210, 225; ally of Jefferson's, 239–40, 246
Maham, Hezekiah, 67
Marion, Francis: early life, 58–59; leadership qualities, 59–60, 62; in the Revolution, 61ff.; and Loyalists, 70–71; last years, 71
Marshall, John, 209–10
Mason, George, 184
Massachusetts: Circular Letter, 27; constitution of 1780, 34–35; State House, 124
Mather, Cotton, 100

Medicine: in colonial America, 139–40
142–43; in the 1780s, 152–55; in Phila-
delphia, 194; *see also* Rush, Benjamin
Methodist Church: in Virginia, 38; in the
West, 136
Mexican Association, 206–07
Miller, Phineas, 164–65
Miró, Gov. Esteban, 200–01
Model Treaty, 14
Monmouth, battle of, 48
Monroe, James, 205
Monticello, 234–35
Morgan, Gen. Dan, 65–66, 194
Morgan, Dr. John, 143–45
Morris, Robert, 13, 114
Morristown (N. J.), 198
Morse, Samuel F. B., 161
Moultrie, Gen. William, 59–60
Mount Vernon convention, 51

Napoleon, 205
National Road, 248
Newburgh Addresses, 49
Newport (R. I.), 87–88, 90
Newton, Sir Isaac, 233
Nicholas, Wilson Cary, 250
Northwest Company, 170–71

Ohio Company, 40
Otis, Harrison Gray, 126
Otis, James, Jr., 23, 25–26, 29
Otis, James, Sr., 22

Paine, Thomas: *Common Sense*, 1, 76,
147; and French alliance, 14; *Rights of
man*, 241, 243–44
Parker, Comm. Peter, 60
Peale, Charles Willson: cultural nationalist
110; early life, 110–11; residence in Eng-
land, 112; military service, 113–14; and
Pennsylvania politics, 114–15; and the
Philadelphia Museum, 115–16; family,
116; and Jefferson, 117; recovering the
mastodon, 117; last years, 118–19
Peale, Rembrandt, 117
Pendleton, Edmund, 239
Pennsylvania: constitution of 1776, 12;
Hospital, 194
Pennsylvania Gazette, 5–6
Perry, Oliver Hazard, 227
Philadelphia: College of, 9, 142, 152,
251; under British occupation, 197–98
Pickens, Gen. Andrew, 58
Pinckney, Thomas, 245
Pinckney's Treaty, 204–05
Piqua (Ohio), 214–15
Pitt, William, 112
Pollock, Oliver, 189
Poor Richard's Almanac, 6–7
Potomac Company, 50–51

Pottawatomie Indians, 219, 226
Presbyterian Church: in Virginia, 38;
"old lights" and "new lights," 142
Priestley, Joseph, 117
Princeton (College of New Jersey), 142
Proctor, Gen. Henry, 226-28
Prophet, The, 219–25

Quakers, and Pennsylvania politics, 9–10, 12

Raisin River Massacre, 227
Randolph, Edmund, 190
Randolph, John of Roanoke, 210, 249
Rawdon, Lord Francis, 66–69
Redman, Dr. John, 142–43
Religious freedom: in Massachusetts, 135–36;
in Rhode Island, 88; in Virginia, 239–40
Republican party, 244–46
Revenue Act of 1764, 24
Revere, Paul, 32–33
Revolution: *see* American Revolution,
French Revolution
Rittenhouse, David, 117
Rush, Benjamin: early life, 140–41; in Edin-
burgh, 141–44; medical practice of 1770s,
144–45; scientific essays of, 145; in
Revolutionary politics, 146-147; family of
147; and Conway Cabal, 150; and social
change, 151–52; and yellow fever epidem-
ic, 155–56; and controversy over bleeding,
156–57; last years of, 157; on care of in-
sane, 154, 157; on education, 151–53;
on slavery, 145–46
Rush, Julia (Stockton), 147

St. Clair, Gen. Arthur, 194–95, 202, 215
Saratoga campaign, 195–96
Scott, Winfield, 210
Sedition Act, 246
Sevier, John, 58, 64
Shawnee Indians, 214ff.
Shays's Rebellion, 35, 243
Shelby, Isaac, 58, 64
Shippen, Dr. William, 149–50
Shirley, Gov. William, 10, 22
Slave trade, 90–91
Slavery: and Benjamin Franklin, 18; and
Benjamin Rush, 145–46, 151
Small, Dr. William, 233
Smith, Sir Sydney, 99
Sons of Liberty: in Massachusetts, 25,
27–29; in South Carolina, 59
South Carolina: economy of, 58–59; in the
Revolution, 59ff.
Spanish Conspiracy, 198–201, 206
Stamp Act, 11
Steuben, Baron von, 47
Stuart, Col. Alexander, 69–70
Stuart, Gilbert, 55, 109, 117, 167, 231
Suffolk Resolves, 32